Letters of the Law

THE CULTURAL LIVES OF LAW

Edited by Austin Sarat

Letters of the Law

Race and the Fantasy of Colorblindness in American Law

SORA Y. HAN

STANFORD LAW BOOKS

An Imprint of Stanford University Press
Stanford, California

Stanford University Press
Stanford, California

Library of Congress Cataloging-in-Publication Data

Han, Sora Y., author.
Letters of the law : race and the fantasy of colorblindness in American law / Sora Y. Han.
pages cm. — (The cultural lives of law)
Includes bibliographical references and index.
ISBN 978-0-8047-8911-0 (cloth : alk. paper)
ISBN 978-1-5036-0279-3 (pbk. : alk. paper)
1. Race discrimination—Law and legislation—United States. 2. Post-racialism—United States. I. Title. II. Series: Cultural lives of law.
KF4755.H355 2015
342.7308'73—dc23

2014036168

ISBN 978-0-8047-9501-2 (electronic)

Printed in the United States of America on acid-free, archival-quality paper

Typeset by at Stanford University Press in 10/13 Minion

To Nara *and* Namu

Acknowledgments

This book owes its existence to two events that cast the horizon of my study. Those events were two conferences: "Critical Resistance: Beyond the Prison Industrial Complex," Berkeley, CA, in 1998; and "The Color of Violence: Incite! Women of Color against Violence," Santa Cruz, CA, in 2000. Such collective forms of thought and movement have animated and sustained this book's writing.

Angela Y. Davis, Gina Dent, and Devon Carbado guided the first iteration of this book as my dissertation committee. Each, in the practice of teaching and mentoring, bestowed the greatest gift a student could receive: the unfettered pursuit of questions as a way of being in this world. Angela Y. Davis, in particular, as my advisor, was and is incomparable in this respect. Ruth Wilson Gilmore, Kimberlé Crenshaw, Cheryl Harris, David Marriott, Teresa de Lauretis, Donna Haraway, Jennifer Gonzalez, David Hoy, and Herman Gray also gifted me with this freedom. All errors and flaws in this book are my own, but if this book resonates at all, it will be because of what I learned from them while at UCLA School of Law and the Department of History of Consciousness at UC Santa Cruz.

Much of this book's writing was made possible by a fellowship from Columbia Law School's Center for Law and Culture, and the University of California President's Postdoctoral Fellowship, which I took to Berkeley Law School's Center for the Study of Law and Society. I thank Kendall Thomas, Elizabeth Povinelli, Katherine Franke, Gary Okihiro, Robin D. G. Kelley, Leti Volpp, Angela Harris, and Jonathan Simon for their hospitality, encouragement, and support. I am especially grateful to Leti Volpp.

I also received substantial resources to continue working on this book while at UC Irvine, in my department, Criminology, Law and Society. Simon Cole, Mona Lynch, Susan Coutin, Carroll Seron, Valerie Jenness, and Elliott Currie have been especially generous colleagues and mentors. It has been a pleasure to work with graduate students across campus, including Jasmine Montgomery, Afiya Browne, James Bliss, Christopher Chamberlain, Jacob Kang-Brown, Akhila Ananth, Kate Henne, and Megan McCabe, who provided assistance at various stages of writing. A special thanks goes to Jasmine Montgomery for support across teaching, writing, and organizing; and James Bliss and Christopher Chamberlain for such careful and engaged preparation of the book manuscript. The Elsevier Foundation New Scholars Grant supported my work on the book after the arrival of my two children. And the Hellman Foundation and the University of California Center for New Racial Studies provided generous resources at the final hour to complete the manuscript.

For the past five years, the Anti-Colonial Machine—David Lloyd, Fred Moten, Nasser Hussain, Colin Dayan, Dylan Rodriguez, Atef Said, Denise Ferreira da Silva, Stefano Harney, and J. Kameron Carter—gave me something to belong to, and reinvigorated my work on this book and beyond. Our conversations are present in and between the lines on every page. I give special thanks to David Lloyd for his felicitous invitation.

Much gratitude and appreciation must go to Michelle Lipinski, Kate Wahl, and Austin Sarat at Stanford University Press. Because of their patience and foresight, the process of transforming many drafts into book form was an affirming experience in a most fundamental way. I also must thank Courtney Berger, at Duke University Press, for her patience and understanding early on and over the years. This book was immeasurably improved with reviews from both presses. I especially thank the anonymous reviewer from Stanford University Press for such a careful and critical reading. Two reviewers, Colin Dayan and Fred Moten, made themselves known to me, and responding not only to their readings, but also writing as part of our ongoing conversations, was a happy challenge.

Roshy Kheshti read the entire manuscript, multiple times, through years of revision and life changes, and amplified what mattered most. Jared Sexton, Andrea Smith, Dylan Rodriguez, Rashad Shabazz, Nicole Santos, Sirida Srisombati, Cassandra Shaylor, Anita Starosta, Sara Clarke Kaplan, Zakiyyah Jackson, and the late Adam Henry have been supportive friends and colleagues. For their invitations and editorial support on portions of this book that have appeared in prior published form, I am grateful to Renee Heberle, Patricia Clough, Craig

Willse, Eunice Cho, Kelly Hannah-Moffat, Mona Lynch, and Anne Richardson Oakes. Anitra Grisales provided essential editorial assistance at every stage.

Finally, this book would not have been possible without the love and support of my family. Walter and Stella Han imprinted in me the exhilaration of protest and a resonant conviction in all power to the people. Lamont Cardon embarked with me on a partnership that enriched my life beyond measure. And Nara and Namu remind me every day that there is always the chance to experience being together anew.

Contents

Letters of the Law

Introduction: Letters of the Law

Rights are to law what conscious
commitments are to the psyche.
—Patricia Williams, *The Alchemy of Race and Rights*

The Fantasy of Colorblindness

This book is a deconstruction of colorblindness as a founding fantasy of modern American law. It seeks to clarify how the fantasy of colorblindness is essential to maintaining a constitutional split between the social particularities of civil rights and the declaration of universal equality founding American democracy. By detailing the fantasy of colorblindness legal reform writes itself through, this book hopes to offer a new protocol of reading the relation between race and law.[1]

From the outset, then, I understand fantasy, according to Vicky Lebeau's conceptualization, as a "'real event' . . . a presence, or a pressure, within and on the real"[2] that is repeated across the American legal archive. As fantasy, colorblindness defies the telos of racial progress that legal discourse projects.[3] The fantasy of colorblindness both confounds and gives language to a national desire to make general assessments about the direction of legal reform and how political mobilizations of bodies, affects, and knowledges might either falsify or validate legal declarations of equality. Lisa Duggan might call the overdetermination of this desire on 1990s left political culture the "twilight of equality." And this political condition has been theoretically elaborated by Wendy Brown's critique of identity-based politics that mobilize legal rights in a progressive politics of *ressentiment*.[4]

But what if we were to take the law and its various objects, not as some political or cultural barometer of American democracy's successful or failed negotiations of social differences generally, but as the place where a certain psychical life is staged in the scene of American democracy's birth from New World slavery? This is the question posed by Patricia Williams's formulation in the epigraph above, and that drives this book's reading of the fantasy of colorblindness and the objects of legal language it leaves in its wake. The aim is a more intimate engagement with law as a governing psychic formation through a descent into the particular condensations of law's writing on racial inequality that I am calling the *fantasy of colorblindness.*

One of the most significant implications of beginning an analysis of race and law via a question about the fantasmatic nature of colorblindness is the possibility of approaching the plural temporalities of the judicial opinion. The judicial opinion's unique authority relies on a never-the-same set of citation and precedent, or a *recursive legal present* that reproduces authority through a textual arrangement in the present of past and future authorities. Past and future are written into a citational present in the service of founding, in each decision presented by the judicial opinion, a new (which is not to say different) manifestation of authority from and against the infinite variations of social circumstance raised by the claim of racial inequality. The fantasy of colorblindness, as an iterative form of psychical foreclosure imposed on the legal text works against this plural temporality, and holds out a more manageable diagnostic understanding of the history of legal reform, whether episodic, cyclical, or progressive.

My emphasis on this recursive legal present always available in the law, to a certain extent, is a rejoinder against critical studies of race and law that continue to periodize the legal history of civil rights reforms in order to argue whether a judicial decision, legislative enactment, or executive order is a sign of racial progress or retrenchment. This attachment to periodization, compulsively expressed today in declarations of the arrival of a "post–civil rights era," structures any number of contemporary debates about racial inequality and its various intersections with other forms of inequality. Indeed, this periodization reads like the academic cousin of the fantasy of colorblindness in modern American law. Just as the fantasy of colorblindness, as we will see in the following chapters, is symptomatic of modern American law's self-valorizing transcendence from slavery, the declaratory arrival of a post–civil rights moment today is symptomatic of critical theory's self-valorizing transcendence from enduring questions about race, democracy, and freedom posed by the black radical tradition.[5] My hope in this book is to find a way out of the deadlock this compulsory post–civil rights declaration imposes on complex matters of the law by returning to and dwelling with the words of the judicial opinion on civil rights and racial inequality. So many want to read through and beyond civil rights, which is to say, reduce law to policy, when in fact, the language of those cases exposes the dangerous myopia of such (non)reading.[6]

The more faithful tracing of the fantasy of colorblindness this book offers will reveal that this symbolic designation of a new period of legal reform is not borne out by legal history or empirical reality. More specifically, the legal devolution staged by the historical demarcation of a "post–civil rights era" assumes the past success (even if incomplete) of an established civil rights regime. However, if the fantasy of colorblindness is approached as a formal element of law's language, civil rights only ever appear as a recursive structure of reference to a fundamental problem slavery posed, and continues to pose, in the development of modern legal principles, such as freedom, citizenship, due process, equality, and civil rights. Precisely at stake here is the recognition that law's language *itself* refuses critical theory's tendency to use law to construct historical narratives and map political change. Major historical events shaping American modern law—namely, the First and Second Reconstructions, and relatedly, the Civil War and the modern Civil Rights Movement—are not merely misrecognized or erroneously recounted by the law, but are structuring doctrinal events that are always present in law. While the social and political histories of these events are not elaborated in this book, they are a necessary backdrop, and more important, as we will see, are always available in the law's citational world for return through the fantasy of colorblindness.

Revealing the fantasmatic production of the developmentalist telos of civil rights, however, is not meant to be a corrective gesture. Fantasy cannot be corrected, as if there are right and wrong fantasies. Fantasy, can, however, be inhabited differently. And this is what I hear as Williams's invitation to a different inhabitation in law by a different protocol of reading law. What I am after, following Williams, is a possible grammar of civil rights in which the memory of black freedom struggle *can* take flight, and as this book argues, *does* take flight both in the life of law's words and the law's most faithful critics. For while the fantasy of colorblindness produces the telos of racial progress as a kind of political hallucination, the actual words through which the fantasy of colorblindness materially takes place in the legal text reveals a past-present and future-present of a civil rights to come across the whole of the American legal archive. Racial equality is never given full presence (if it ever was or is possible, anyway), but its negative imprint takes place through various aporetic figurations of civil rights in legal discourse.

Williams's analogic association, that "rights are to law what conscious commitments are to the psyche," is less a prescription for how to proceed with a systematic application of psychoanalytic theory to the study of race and law, and more the broaching of a horizon. This horizon is a knowledge of race and law that is both before us and has yet to be thought, a knowledge that makes civil rights struggles both easier and harder to continue, a truth about why legal articulations of racial equality always elude various institutional reforms. At this horizon, law is the interior space of political life where emotions, desires, wishes, and thoughts intermingle with calculation, analytic logic, scientific rationality, and factual predicates usually in highly disciplined ways. *The Alchemy of Race and Rights* founds a genre of reading and writing law—what I would call "speculative law"—that both challenges and invites us to, as NourbeSe Philip puts it, "'Break and Enter' the text to release its anti-meaning."[7] Williams's words reach for some other way to go to that place where she suggests the law is.[8]

Yet, there is no royal road that would take us there. For modern American law, like the modern psyche, cannot shake itself of a history, from the ancients to the postmoderns, that concludes that law and reason have only ever had a paradoxical relationship.[9] The cultural assumption that this paradox can and should be resolved in a definitive written text and its standardized interpretation, one might say, is law's profession and is the source of law's violences, even as formal legal reasoning itself admits its excesses and failures. *Brown v. Board of Education* (1954) illuminates, as it continues to beguile legal scholars who continue to debate whether the ruling that segregation is unconstitutional is good law, just law, moral law, or not law at all but politics "by other means." I will discuss *Brown* in a moment, but for now, I wish to elevate it as the paradigmatic example of this stubborn paradox.

Fantasy, then, fills in the absence of this royal road between law and reason. More specifically, we have rights and conscious commitments, continuing to follow Williams. For Freud, the psyche designated the inner life of the modern subject—its drives, moral beliefs, and identifications. He would organize this interiority according to what he called in *The Interpretation of Dreams*, a "psychical apparatus" of unconscious desires and conscious thoughts. And his idea of dreamwork would designate how the labor of sleep might render unconscious desires knowable, against the logic of the psychical apparatus that divides sensory dream-wishes from psychical material and censors it from waking ideational life.[10]

Freud promised that the "picture" of the psyche's doubled and reversing movements between censorship and knowledge would "repay us for having constructed it."[11] Freud admitted, in fact, that we had seen this picture before. A footnote added to the 1914 publication of *The Interpretation of Dreams*, fifteen years after its first publication, served to remind us that "Hobbes writes in the *Leviathan*: 'In sum, our dreams are the reverse of our waking imaginations, the motion, when we are awake, beginning at one end, and when we dream at another.'"[12] Freud's reminder references a repayment owed to political life, to the *civitas* securing modernity, for Hobbes is writing here of an "us" that is a metaphor for thinking about the state as an artificial man, and rights its artificial gifts.[13]

While we don't have to take Freud's word on Hobbes, we nonetheless cannot ignore the significance of Freud's gesture to political thought. We might extend this gesture to Williams, who suggests a repayment on a similar trajectory, but of a radically different order of political life that is consonant with Derrida's understanding of Freud's idea of dreamwork as a "scene of writing." Derrida observes:

> Freud doubtless conceives of the dream as a displacement similar to an original form of writing which puts words on stage without becoming subservient to them; and he is thinking here, no doubt, of a model of writing irreducible to speech which would include, like hieroglyphics, pictographic, ideogrammatic and phonetic elements. But he makes of psychical writing so originary a production that writing such as we believe to be designated in the literal sense of the word—a script which is coded and visible "in the world"—would be only its metaphor.[14]

Williams's repayment is an approach to the legal text that, as an "original form of writing," has its own radical structural relation with politics that cannot be comprehensively understood through available theories of political realism or literary criticism. Thus, she writes with and against both schools of critical legal theory and stages the law's original form of writing as an "immense alchemical fire" by which the United States as a nation was constituted from "the kindling of several generations."[15] This scene of law's origin as a form of writing is not simply a counterimage to constitutional originalism. It is an argument about a certain primordial law of race and rights that haunts the constitution of American democracy. On this point, Williams's specific rendering of rights in this scene is crucial:

> "[T]he recursive insistence of those rights is also defined by black desire for them [rights]—desire fueled not by the sop of minor enforcement of major statutory schemes like the Civil Rights Act, but by knowledge of, and generations of existing in, a world without any meaningful boundaries—and "without boundary" for blacks has meant not untrammeled vistas of possibility but the crushing weight of total—bodily and spiritual—*intrusion.*[16]

Rights here are objects, but ones that retain their unattainability because of a certain knowledge of a world of unremediable violation. *This* right that Williams speaks of is an aim of desire more than a proper object of desire. Rights as aim, or said another way, the performative of rights, clarifies and critiques both the commonsense and critical theoretical assumption that the legal value of rights is coterminous with their effective or symbolic value. The distinction, then, between rights as aim of desire, and rights as object of desire, allows us to further distinguish in the arena of political life, between desire and demand. While demands for rights can be met either by the benevolence of the state or by a revolution of the people, desire for rights threatens to keep burning by its own inexhaustible drive, an "immense alchemical fire."

Brown's Many Times

Let us now look more closely at *Brown*,[17] the principal case of the modern Civil Rights Movement. It is true that the case, as a matter of black letter law, overrules the doctrine of "separate but equal." But it is also true, as a matter of its authority through citation, that the decision to enforce racial equality brings together the times of slavery, segregation, and integration into one doctrinal event. *Plessy v. Ferguson* (1896), as *Brown*'s segregationist antecedent, and *Parents Involved in Community Schools v. Seattle School District No. 1* (2007), as its "post–civil rights" descendant, constitute *Brown*'s many times.[18] This plural temporality is given in each of these cases' dependence on a present tense of the fantasy of colorblindness, and the settlement of racial equality's horizon in universal equality. There is not one colorblind ideology enacted and enforced over time that narrates law's language across *Plessy, Brown,* and *Parents Involved.* Rather, there is a tightly woven braid of presents consisting of the differential iterability of the fantasy of colorblindness in each case. In this way, *Brown* is not merely a landmark decision of the modern Civil Rights Movement but is an always present doctrinal event.

The confluence of law's address to slavery, segregation, and integration in *Brown* suggests a structuring desire around which the partial objects of history, social reality, and civil rights are organized. In the lesser-known 1955 decision attending the 1954 decision declaring separate-but-equal doctrine unconstitutional, Chief Justice Warren ordered that local and state officials should desegregate their public schools "with all deliberate speed."[19] For many, the gradualism imposed on the abolition of formal segregation was too slow to respond to the urgency of racial hostilities accumulating at the time. And for others, it was too fast for resistant states paranoid about the paternalism of federal authority.

Over half a century after *Brown*'s established time of judicially ordered desegregation, in *Parents Involved* the Supreme Court ruled that local districts' continued use of race to integrate public schools was unconstitutional. While acknowledging the persistence of racial segregation, Chief Justice Roberts installed another temporal frame for desegregation, when he observed that "the way to stop discrimination on the basis of race is to stop discriminating on the basis of race."[20] In contrast to the gradualism of *Brown*, the presentism of *Parents Involved*'s temporality appears as an antithesis to "deliberate speed." Against a more tactful (but of course, no less violent) approach to reform, Roberts's abruptness displays a flippant authoritarianism of the fantasy of colorblindness. While the fantasy of colorblindness in *Brown* is an eventual integration, in *Parents Involved* integration is already a reality but for a certain liberal obsession with race. The point is that these varying times of racial equality—one reflecting timid willingness and the other cruel asceticism—are simultaneous in the recursive citational structure that *Brown* is at the center of.

The fantasy of colorblindness that mediates our reading of *Brown*'s significance stalls an encounter with both the structural reality of segregation's persistence and the legal reality of its internally produced aporias of racial equality. We are generally familiar with the first type of circumvention, but less familiar with the second type. The irreducible temporal dissonance of *Brown* is just one example of the second type, and the chapters that follow address a number of others. They together create an idiom of a foundational legal aporia produced by and against claims of racial inequality in modern American law. Race in law is a *constitutional aporia*, and the fantasy of colorblindness is what fills this negative space of law.

This idea of race as a constitutional aporia is obviously anathema to classic understandings of the rule of law as the development of positive rules into a rational, uniform, and balanced system of governance. And yet, this constitutional aporia can be read across the various areas of law where claims of racial inequality are made, including in criminal procedure, property law, civil rights law, voting rights law, civil procedure, and immigration law, to name a few. Given this, it is all the more curious that this idea has not been subject to sustained examination by scholars of race and law, who once were the vanguard of questioning precisely how the culture of the rule of law seems always to rationalize racial inequality. That is, the inconsistencies, contradictions, dissonances, and illogics evident in cases deliberating claims of racial inequality have for the most part been approached only as law's inevitably varying effects, instead of as its general condition. And by this elision, cases that raise the claim of racial inequality have been treated as a fringe or specialized area of law, instead of as the generative source of law and its interpretive world. If we are to encounter race as a constitutional aporia of the law, we can no longer accept colorblindness as a (neo)liberal and (neo)conservative political ideology absent a fantasmatic core. Subsequently, this book challenges the dominant understanding of colorblindness as an ideology in contemporary critical race theory by elaborating the implications of the fantasy for how we engage the law's formal presentation of propositions, histories, doctrines, and rhetorics.

Again, *Brown*'s doctrinal eventfulness is illuminating. We find that successive failures to achieve the mandate to desegregate have not issued more elaborate legal mechanisms to address racial inequities in society. There have not been recommitments to *Brown*'s clear judicial priority of intervening on racist social relations through the abolition of formal segregation. *Parents Involved* is the official statement on this failure. Rather, there has been only an overwhelmingly mournful remembrance of *Brown*, or to put it another way, an increasing fantasmatic investment in an ever-abstracted promise of colorblindness.

Brown's image in political discourse is one of failed promise and eulogized memory. Interestingly, however, *Brown*'s formal structure of judicial reasoning cannot be completely grasped along these terms. We have only to note that the most controversial issue *Brown* presents for American law today is not whether school desegregation must be regulated in some way or another. Rather, it is whether *Brown*'s ruling was legally sound to have accepted the Clark doll experiment as dispositive evidence of the harmful psychological effects of segregation on black children in the South.[21] In the legal academic literature, many have debated the merits of the doll experiment in proving injury in a system of racial segregation, as well as the larger theoretical question of the status of social scientific data in judicial processes. However, what this legal literature fails to come to terms with, as leading scholars on *Brown* have observed, is the relative evidential weakness and ultimately unknowable influence of the psychological studies on the Supreme Court's decision in this moment of national political upheaval.[22] What lingers of the historical memory of these dolls is their curious relationship to the law's attempt to acknowledge and intervene on American racist culture.

Thus, even if we cannot know for certain how dispositive the doll tests were in producing the ruling of *Brown*, we do know through the text of *Brown* that the Court cites the study, and by this citation directs a certain attention to the real effects—if complex and ultimately immeasurable—of racial fantasy. Whether or how accurately the Court interpreted and judged the black child's fantasy and its significance for decision on the legal issue of racial segregation is not of concern here. Such a concern would only reproduce the spurious scientific discourse on black pathology and rehabilitation.[23] Instead, what is more significant about *Brown* is the indelible stamp, through citation, on American law with a question about the real force of racial fantasy.

This is no small gesture, and its critical importance is further underscored by the fact that legal scholarship has recently been fixated on filling in the question of fantasy posed in *Brown* with cognitive and social scientific data to reductively argue that various psychological dimensions of racism should be legally actionable or regulated by policy.[24] Against this trend to reduce the question of racial fantasy to an issue of producing psychological evidence of racism, I want to hold open *Brown*'s citational recognition of racial fantasy as a social fact we must center in theorizing race and law. For evidence of racial disproportionality, that is, today's ur-fact of racial inequality (whether validated by historical experience, social position, or political power) accumulates without a necessary critical relation to racial fantasy.

So against or alongside such evidence-based petitioning and filing, we might more intentionally follow *Brown*'s citational gesture and consider how the dolls are for modern American law what Freud called a "screen memory."[25] In *Brown*, the nation produces a displaced memory (the doll tests) in order to avoid the trauma of de jure and de facto Jim Crow law; at the same time, the screen memory must protect the coherence of the story that the nation tells (and would continue to tell) itself. That story is about the ultimate triumph of American legal universality: *Brown*'s overruling of *Plessy*'s majority rule that segregation is not inconsistent with equality and its implicit affirmation of *Plessy*'s dissenting rule that "our constitution is color-blind." At the same time, underwriting this double movement of American law's transcendence from segregation, and its simultaneous rejection of segregation and affirmation of colorblindness, is a constitutive lack of meaningful legal change in the name of abolition.

National (mis)recognitions of past racial injustice, then, are always already mediated by a "screen memory" taking any number of echoic forms of multiculturalism obscuring the trauma of the origin of the United States as a slave society. As Anthony Farley has argued, "Slavery is screened by segregation and segregation is screened by neosegregation and so it goes on and on and on from slavery to slavery to slavery."[26] *E pluribus unum*, we might say, is the interpretive schema of the mystical foundation of slavery. The glaring omission of the word "slave" in the original Constitution; the supremacy of state sovereignty against the institution of universal civil rights in the aftermath of chattel slavery; the lynch mob below the surface of Fourteenth Amendment equal protection and due process jurisprudence—all such legal obscurities set the fantasmatic space for the pursuit of racial desires through law, a zone of *jouissance* opened up by the originary trauma of slavery in the modern world.

The mythical triumph of colorblindness through *Brown* is not a failure of the advocates for equal citizenship and civil rights, but is, to borrow Joan

Scott's term, a "fantasy echo" of a capacious American national movement toward self-consciousness unmoored by law from its constitution in slavery and conquest.[27] Williams zeroes in on "a shape, a hollow, an emptiness at the center" of American law,[28] and against which any identification or disidentification with *Brown*'s dolls offers no protection. Instead, those dolls, standing in as a fact of law's inseparability from fantasy, continue to return in legal scholarship and constitutional doctrine as a problem for standard interpretations of evidence, culture, and history. In a democratic system in which deliberation is distributed by the universal imposition of standard procedures of interpretation and enforcement, the dolls refuse the law's tendency to reduce social desire to legal petitioning, the latter of which is then taken as a sign of consent to be governed. As evidence, the dolls are a screen where racist culture and the rule of law merge to raise the question of the real fantasy of colorblindness organizing *Brown*'s reasoning. And by this internally riven issuance, a de-constitution flourishes.

The Dreamwork of the Law

The eclectic field of critical race theory that has emerged in the last half-century crystallizes what I take to be the most important intellectual engagement with the problem of race and law. Most vividly presented by Williams, critical race theory as I attempt to engage it in this book is the performance of the idea that to lawyer toward unconditional freedom is to cast into poetic relation ideas, words, bodies, and histories that the structure of legal reason repeatedly severs (such as "racial" from "equality"), or obdurately binds (such as "equal" with "protection," or "We" with "the People").[29] What makes critical race theory critical, in my mind, is its essentially theoretical orientation to law as a form and practice of writing.

At this register, the field unsutures law and reason by a certain lawyerly dissection and rearrangement of law's *écriture*. Lawyering in this sense resembles dreamwork more than the production of counterfantasy. This is not an explicit argument put forth by critical race theory, but more a demonstrative practice of critical race theory as a form of thought that improvises the professional activity of lawyering. It can be found in the most incisive texts of critical race theory, as I have been elaborating through *Alchemy*, and radically splays the torque and force of the foundational principles of legal universality sedimented in the law's language, which are especially evident and obscured in the canonical legal cases addressing racial inequality. The cases I read are, then, a doubled return to, and a double affirmation of, the truth of law's writing on racial inequality that Derrick Bell revealed in his theorem of "the permanence of racism."

So in order to revisit critical race theory together with the central cases identified there loosely as the canon of American law on racial inequality, we are compelled to think more expansively about what something like a "racial jurisprudence" might be. A more obvious generic definition of racial jurisprudence elevates the racial identity of the claimants. This genre symbolizes the political efforts of claimants demanding to be treated equally—for example, *Rogers v. American Airlines* (1981) and *Pigford v. Glickman* (1999); or demanding the privileges of whiteness—for example, *Gong Lum v. Rice* (1927) and *Fisher v. University of Texas* (2013). A slightly wider generic definition elevates the adjudication of a "nonracial" policy that reproduces racial inequality and discrimination. This genre symbolizes the law's reproduction of racial inequality through its regulatory function—for example, *Yick Wo v. Hopkins* (1886), *Brown v. City of Oneonta* (1999), *Brown v. Plata* (2011), and *Arizona v. U.S.* (2012). The first genre of racial jurisprudence is identity based and the second is sociologically based.

Both these genres are plagued by positivist notions of race and legal subjectivity that cannot do justice to the whole of race in the American legal archive. They are tethered to the endless task of cataloguing racial identity and fact-checking racial injury (however reductive or nuanced) without calling into question the racial logic of the split between the particular and the universal that structures the law's theoretical approach to racial inequality as a formal and social problem of inclusion/exclusion.

That said, the law's theoretical approach does not have to be our own. We might instead explore a new relation between the particular and the universal that inheres in the split itself. This might allow us to exposit the significance of the source from which the endless task of cataloguing and fact-checking is generated. We might think of this as coming down with a case of Derrida's "archive fever," which symptomizes a kind of attention to those peculiar cases that elude generic definition and punctuate (and puncture) the law's drift toward universality, especially through its promise of universal equality. I am interested in a notion of racial jurisprudence based on the general value of the antigeneric case. Racial jurisprudence is precisely the *case of the split* between the particular and the universal that law's language circles around. By extension, racial jurisprudence in this sense is concerned with the development of a capacity that illuminates the peculiarity of the particular (claimant) and the force of the universal (claim). This conception does not preclude identitarian and sociological understandings of racial jurisprudence, but moves through and beyond them. Indeed, the constellation of cases driving this book's reading of race and law—*Korematsu v. U.S.* (1944), *Bakke v. UC Regents* (1978), *Prigg v. Pennsylvania* (1842), *Plessy v. Ferguson* (1896), *Dred Scott v. Sandford* (1857), *Lawrence v. Texas* (2003), *Bowers v. Hardwick* (1986), *Procunier v. Martinez* (1974), and *Overton v. Bazzetta* (2003)—can be made to stand for these two genres, but are not subsumable by them.

In other words, the general value of the antigeneric case is not reducible to generic definitions of case law, just as racial jurisprudence is not reducible to the instrumental value of judicial rulings. And this irreducibility is that toward which lawyering in the widest sense writes, and that which requires us to dwell in what of law's language brings our imagination of freedom to the originary limit of modern American law in and against slavery. Stretching law's language to this limit, my notion of racial jurisprudence is defined by those traces that are, in fact, singular definitions of the whole of modern American law. This is the real threat of racial jurisprudence, as we will see in the chapters that follow.

This concept of racial jurisprudence, undertheorized in critical race theory, is nonetheless present in the thought. So in this book, while offering readings of cases, I also highlight how we might read critical race theory within this conceptual frame. Across the chapters, I provide further theoretical scaffolding to one of the most radical arguments produced by critical race theory about what is at stake in the critique of law's racial politics. It is not simply about the possibility of political resistance by the disenfranchised subject against de jure and de facto discrimination. Rather, it is the possibility of a being in practices of making the impossible case, preparing for a hearing, attending (to) the scene of pleading, and overturning by overflowing the law's architecture of precedent. It is the assertion of a fugitive law of freedom by the an-authorized, against which the law is blindly guarded in every case.

Holding onto this possibility, the law's words take on an afterlife in dreamwork that we must engage on their own terms, and for their strange leaps of association between those objects the words stand in for. Stated another way, to broach the dreamwork of the law through the lingering forces, phrases, arguments, and acts contained in and by legal reason is to encounter an enigmatic time, logic, and history of the fundamental aporetic structure of race in law.

This aporia is littered with the claim of a being whose law is the pursuit of unconditional freedom against, in the words of Frank Wilderson III, "the infinite trajectories of freedom that emanate from Humanism's hub [that] are anything but infinite—for they have no line of flight leading to the Slave."[30] These freedoms woven from the loom of Kant's categorical imperative are the signs of an unfree ethical subject on behalf of which the proper lawyer stages a diversity of performances with the state as its audience.[31] This average understanding of lawyering is prone to an understanding of law and social movements that carve lawyering up into ethnic-specific historical and sociological narratives of conflict and uneven incorporation.

I want instead to think of the claims of racial inequality emerging in the dreamwork of the law as the force of a kind of lawyering that exists precisely as the excessive insistence of and against the categorical imperative by which freedom and rational will are conflated.[32] In other words, the enigmatic force of racial jurisprudence is imprinted on legal judgment as the lawyering of a "gratuitous freedom."[33] This force is not abstract or ephemeral if one is able to read racial jurisprudence beyond generic lines and for the antigeneric case as the trace of lawyering toward unconditional freedom.

We might consider, for example, the indivisibility of Angela Y. Davis's practice of thought across, on the one hand, her opening defense statement made during her 1972 trial at the Santa Clara County Superior Court, and on the other, her "Unfinished Lecture on Liberation—II" in her 1969 UCLA course "Recurring Philosophical Themes in Black Literature." To discern this indivisibility, we must be able to read a legal argument across these two texts that improvises through and beyond a generic distinction between litigation and philosophy. Here is where we enter: "In this opening statement, members of the jury, you will be given a skeletal outline of the evidence with which we intend to contest the prosecution's contentions. This will be the skeleton, so to speak—the flesh will be added to the bones as the trial progresses."[34] She goes on to elaborate "the flesh" to come, asking, "[P]recisely what will the evidence show about my association with the struggle to free the Soledad Brothers?" In answering, she presents the legal argument: "You will see that because of my own commitment to the struggle to achieve freedom for all oppressed people, upon learning of the plight of these three men, I along with others took steps to build whatever support we could for the movement around them, around other political prisoners and prison conditions in general."[35] What emerges here is a case of and for the movement of "the struggle to achieve freedom." "The flesh" is all the legal evidence that was already there in the law, in her/their opening, that proceeds to lay out those crucial legal facts of the fact of black freedom struggle.

In her UCLA "Unfinished Lecture," we learn that the material status of the slave requires "a transformation of the principle of freedom into a dynamic, active struggle for liberation."[36] Certainly, we can consider Davis's opening defense statement as an historical example of "a dynamic, active struggle for liberation." However, in her courtroom statement, she avows her commitment to "the struggle to achieve freedom," and *not* the "struggle for liberation." In this regard, Davis's "Opening Defense Statement" is not an accurate translation of the philosophical ideas contained in her UCLA "Unfinished Lecture" into a legal case. Perhaps this failure of translation is the effect of a pragmatic tempering of a radical philosophic language. But this would be an average explanation, which presupposes different degrees of repressiveness between law and philosophy. I instead prefer another explanation in which the two texts are of a piece of a certain facticity of black freedom struggle that is always and variously opening because it is an unfinishable argument (or is it the other way around?) for everything that generates a "transformation of the principle of freedom," or what she specifies in her "Unfinished Lecture" as "the ability to strive toward the abolition of the master-slave relationship itself."[37] Liberation is not a higher order of freedom. Rather, the break between the idea of "freedom" in her statement and the idea "freedom" in her lecture is precisely what delivers to us the indivisibility of a freedom against freedom impressed on the law as the *legal reasoning* of her defense against the state's prosecution of her, and also and more important, against the very freedom to be criminally judged as guilty or innocent.

We might understand "lawyering" here as a certain abolitionist tradition of inventive practice that knows no other freedom than the struggle against it. And its form across the many spaces of this legal practice appears in what I call a *poetics of the plea*. At stake here is the possibility of a sociality whose case, by virtue of bearing the cost of freedom, has no claim other than a continuous movement of opening to black freedom struggle. Indeed, the opening of a case, as a matter of legal procedure, is called "pleading," and as performed here by the "we" of Davis's statement, reveals a pleading that is an opening onto a movement of what Nahum Chandler identifies as the "more-than-one, of the double, of the peculiar and problematic sense of world."[38] This form of pleading—the practice of making a case with no actionable claim, or the drive of the impossible claim—constitutes all the statements of a defenseless defense that are what make the case.

By this poetics of the plea, we are faced with an ultimate decision. We either receive civil rights to give them away as an illimitable capacity of invention, or we begrudgingly contextualize civil rights as only ever the exclusive historical property of the law and its subjects. This book decides for the former because the nature of the plea, in itself, and for itself, is already given in any thought of civil rights today, despite critical attempts either to conservatively hoard or progressively distribute them. For the poetics of the plea that generalizes civil rights is, to return to Chandler, a "non-simple form," that must be understood to be what it has always been: the "problematization" of law's existence.[39]

From this theoretical vantage, critical race theory is not only a critique of the social effects of legal exclusion, or an interdisciplinary examination of how the law is implicated in the social construction of identities and categories. Critical race theory is also not only a critical discourse on the law's racist past or a prescriptive knowledge of how to pursue structural change either through or against the law. Such interpretations of critical race theory together risk imposing the thought with a political movement toward inclusion and equality that is far more coherent than its most prominent texts reveal. Instead, critical race theory, as this book approaches it, is the place in law where a poetics of the plea persists as a beautiful and horrifying descent into the law's language and the dreamwork that emerges there.

In this way, critical race theory unhinges law's language from everything (history, culture, science, sociality, philosophy, and politics) its sweeping authority relies on to challenge the law at the level of its essential everyday materiality. The truth of critical race theory's critique of legal exclusion inheres still in a question about the practice of a freedom beyond freedom at the elemental level of the law: words. The challenge of lawyering toward unconditional freedom then rests precisely in the question of how in practice to bring words to life through what Veena Das has described as the "iterability of writing" and the "the citability of its utterances."[40] It is to find words, speak them, write them, hear and feel them—but words always with, to think with Hortense Spillers, a "vestibular" capacity that reflects and is indebted to New World slavery as the scene of modernity's repeating departure and return.[41]

Derrick Bell has called this kind of legal work with words—both characteristic of the civil rights lawyer, but as well of a more undercommon variety forged between people and rules through wishes, expectations, demands, and other nonformal mobilizations of legal rhetoric—an ethics of racial realism. In his essay, "Racism Is Here to Stay: Now What?," this ethics is invested not with a drive toward transparency, self-interested inclusion, or sociohistoricity, but counterintuitively, with imagination, the insistence on impossible arguments, a generative refusal of law. The resistance Bell theorizes is a notion of black freedom struggle that is precisely a struggle for freedom because of the endlessness of struggle. Bell must be recalled at length here:

> All now acknowledge that hopes for *Brown v. Board of Education* and the civil rights laws and precedents that followed were too optimistic. Few may agree with me that our racial equality goals may never be realized. . . . [But] deep down, most of us working in civil rights know this is as true as is the seldom acknowledged fact that each of us is going to die. Indeed, one finds a revealing similarity between how individuals deal with death and how civil rights activists deal with the minuscule

> possibility that "we shall overcome." . . . This is neither a prescription of despair, nor a counsel of surrender. It is not an approach without risks, quite like those we must face as we seek the salvation in life that comes when we accept the reality of death. . . . We need to recognize that a yearning for racial equality is fantasy. . . . [H]istory and personal experience tell us that any forward step is likely: 1) to drive blacks backward eventually, and 2) to contribute to the reinforcing myth many white and some black Americans embrace that theirs is an ultimately successful (read humane) existence.
>
> You will note a seeming inconsistency that plagues my argument. On the one hand, I urge you to give up the dream of real, permanent racial equality in the country. On the other hand, I urge you to continue the fight against racism. One experiences an understandable desire to choose one or the other as valid. . . . But it is not a question of pragmatism or idealism. Rather, as a former student discerned it, it is a question of both recognition of the futility of action . . . and the unblinking conviction that something must be done, that action must be taken.[42]

For Bell, legal work as the mobilization of words is the always possible abolition of racism as neither ends nor means. It is the invention that obtains only upon accepting that the state gives no shelter and issues only violence by rule and exception.[43] It is a provocation to fully enter the dreamwork of the law, or in Fanon's words, read through David Marriott, to make the "real leap" of self-creation.[44] And by a certain decomposition and recomposition of the signs these acts leave behind as the letters of the law, the "floating signifiers,"[45] as Williams puts it, irrupt from the pull of the fantasy of colorblindness and perhaps allow us to continue writing that dreambook that is critical race theory's always unfolding text.

Letters of the Law

We arrive, then, at the question: How to read the law today? Or better asked, following Hortense Spillers, "[Do] we look with eyes, or with the psyche?"[46] What protocol of reading is made available by focusing on the fantasy of colorblindness and the dreamwork such fantasy guards against?

This book hopes to offer a protocol that is based on the trace of law's internal memories of slavery and black freedom struggle, which is to say, those unmemorializable events of both individual and collective experience for which the fantasy of colorblindness stands in. Their antinarrative trace stages a problem of race in American modern law that cannot be resolved by political analysis or historical contextualization. It can only be approached as the staging of a question.[47] Whatever knowledge or insight might be revealed by "legal methodology" carries this question along to inoculate itself against it, and as such, the legal methodologies of doctrinal analysis and formal legal reasoning, the ones prioritized in this book, must be passed through fully in order to get to the question and "reclaim" it anew.

The *trace*, then, is this putting of the question in the many instances of law's writing, and concurrently, requiring the law to be read simultaneously as a set of rules, a disciplinary regime, a material history of political traditions, a symbolic system, a form of reasoning, and a literary genre of interpretation. As a protocol of reading that attempts to broach this expanse of law as a language is the suggestion made by the title of this book, *Letters of the Law*. This is the horizon of reading that any extralegal (which is not to say unimportant) knowledge brought to bear on law must strive.

The vastness of a possible new reading of the relation between race and law need not succumb to groundless proliferation of abstraction and meaningless differentiation that afflicts a certain "law and . . ." trend that American legal theory has witnessed in recent decades.[48] For the relay between Williams's provocation that "rights are to law what conscious commitments are to the psyche" and Spillers's question, "[Do] we look with eyes, or with the psyche?" suggests that there is a common theoretical presupposition that can ground such an expansive reading practice. Certainly, sociological, historical, linguistic, literary, philosophical, and semiotic importations to legal studies are in the backdrop for both. But the possibility of critically arranging these importations for a reading of racial jurisprudence is grounded by their shared argument about the reality of unconscious desire. Together they suggest that if there is *any* reading to be had of law, it is through the primary scene of law's "profound intimacy of interlocking detail" that obtains at the point Spillers identifies as the "zero degree of social conceptualization."[49] Democratic political life governed by law is conditional to law's language that in every instance of its written investment in its most prized values—interpretation, judgment, national history, reason, due process, individual autonomy, and so forth—uses words, phrases, images, and affects that are cathected signs of the unmemorializable events of slavery and black freedom struggle. This incandescent presence of absence in law's language, the Real of the law's fantasy of colorblindness, demands nothing less than a protocol of reading, always at the limit.[50] And because *this* limit is, in fact, a trace discernible everywhere in the law, the protocol of reading must be of the letters of the law.

One might be disappointed in what follows if looking for an account of the racial politics of legal subjectivity, though I hope the implications of my reading of racial jurisprudence would be highly relevant in this regard. For theorizing legal subjectivity without a deeper understanding of the constitutional aporia of race appears to be too fixated on illusions of political agency that Bell argues are beside the point, at least at the ethical point of the struggle for a freedom beyond freedom. On the one hand, the words of law must be held to the "letter of the law." On the other, the words of law possess an aura of what Gayatri Spivak, in her look at law, calls "morphogenic innovation—innovations leading to new forms."[51] Bell's legal realism accepts both the conservative and felicitous nature of law's language, and insists that black freedom struggle is the struggle against this dialectical legal structure of liberal freedom.

Thus we delude ourselves with critical engagements of law that generally mistake this legal dialectic as a valid choice between either working "with the law" or "outside the law." This is not a choice we can make, not only because it is impossible to do either purely, but also because it is an outright mystification of what the law is in reality. As we have seen in the dominant empirically determined approach in critical race theory, producing more scientific evidence of racial inequality, whether through the law's terms or beyond to sociological, historical, or demographic terms, cannot challenge the fantasy of colorblindness.[52] We would do better to squarely face this dialectical frame as a forced choice and invent a practice of freedom that struggles against it by affirming both, which is to say, by attempting to fully inhabit the law's language.

Each chapter, then, attempts to arrive at and amplify the constitutional aporia of race in law through the divergent paths of the formal doctrinal conventions that structure the fantasy of colorblindness. They each put pressure on the hallmark doctrines of racial jurisprudence, including the citizen's right to equal protection, the sovereign's right to judicial review, the individual's right to privacy, and the criminal's right to freedom of expression. The social issues implicated by each of these doctrines range from affirmative action and desegregation, individual liberty and national security, sexual freedom and racial profiling, and rehabilitative punishment and civil death.

Each chapter's arrival at the racial limit of these various doctrines and social issues attempts also to render the expansive horizon of reading each doctrinal convention invites. Racial limits are given in each chapter, as the unassimilable time of slavery in the law's history of multiracial citizenship, a racial animus that escapes the justificatory logic of judgment, the impossible affirmation of racial privacy by due process rights, and the prisoner's epistolary life as a form of civil death. These limits are registered as the presence of an absence: the time of slavery is given in the form of a decompositional right; racial animus in an echoing plea; racial privacy in constitutional interpretation; and civil death in letters of the law.

Although the chapters are sequentially designated, I wish them to be handled as together creating a knot of legal reasoning in which the fantasy of colorblindness and the Real objects of race are bound and unbound. With respect to the latter potentiality, I make a number of relevant arguments across the chapters that together emerge to support the general claim I have been making about the necessity of developing a new protocol of reading race and law. In Chapter One, "Decompositional Rights," I argue that the black claim to civil rights not only fails to achieve the status of an affirmative recognition of a citizen subject, but that its force as a right decomposes the philosophical interdependence between citizenship and civil rights in Fourteenth Amendment equal protection jurisprudence. The black claim to civil rights does not write an effective attachment between rights and people. Instead, it is a legal form that decomposes liberal modern citizenship's reification of civil rights as objects of (dis)possession.

I further argue, in Chapter Two, "Colorblind Judgment," that this decompositional right that unhinges the possessory relation between citizenship and civil rights lives in the form of an echo where the law admits a certain helplessness of judicial review in the face of its founding violence in racial difference. My focus in this chapter is to animate the abyssal shape of universal legal reason through the echoic form of the black claim. To theorize the black claim as such is not to say that the black claim simply negates the promises of democracy and its multiracial history. It is, rather, to say, that the black claim is the materialization of desire that appears as a form of writing. This writing scandalizes the compositional form of legal reasoning by staging an inhabitation of the infinite regress of law as an always contingent (but no less violent or vicious) authority given in its specific mode of governance through word. This inhabitation is what I call the poetics of the plea immanent to colorblind judgment.

The aurality of the poetics of the plea takes the form of an enduring echo in the formal topographical structure of judicial review. In Chapter Three, "Racial Profiling," I explore legal interpretation as a kind of apostrophization of this plea, or put another way, as the positive rendering and regulation of the violence of slavery in written rules of writing and reading law. The Constitution, as an authorizing boundary around the creative capacities of legal interpretation, is no more and no less than the repetition of this authority over this domain of legal writing, or what we might call, following Spivak, a "graphematic structure."[53] And this constitutional interpretation, what I call racial profiling in a deconstructive sense, takes as its "unendorseable"[54] origin the catachrestic recording of slavery across its archive, and the haunting of the slave's fugitivity in the law's various protections of personal sovereignty.

I conclude the book with Chapter Four, "The Purloined Prisoner," by arguing that the repressive conditions of punishment, secured precisely by constitutional interpretation, have produced a lifeworld of the letter that perhaps stages a new political terrain of desire that underscores the relevance of the book's general aim. I explore how racial privacy as that which cannot be protected by legal interpretation is perhaps given in prisoner First Amendment rights jurisprudence and letter-writing as its internal limit. Civil death runs up against this limit of expressivity that is neither extinguished nor sheltered by law and its punitive administration through the system of mass incarceration. Illuminating this limit in the lifeworld of the letter shores up the necessity of reading law both to the letter, and for its letters. Inhabiting this lifeworld requires a kind of reading in descent—neither a reading of dissent, nor a dissentious reading, but a falling with she who is given in the name of the prisoner.

The Dead End of Racial Jurisprudence

The recent 2013 Supreme Court ruling on the constitutionality of affirmative action policy in higher education, *Fisher v. University of Texas, Austin*,[55] underscores the urgency of deconstructing the fantasy of colorblindness. Indeed, we have only to scratch the surface of the decision to do this. On first glance, the majority opinion, written by Justice Kennedy, appears like a proceduralist avoidance of deciding substantive matters. By this initial reading, the decision vacates the Fifth Circuit Court's ruling that Texas's policy was not in violation of the Equal Protection Clause as elaborated in *Grutter v. Bollinger*,[56] reasoning that the appellate court had not sufficiently reviewed whether the policy was "narrowly tailored." And because of this procedural error, a decision on the substantive issue of affirmative action's constitutionality would have to wait.

Agreeing with the majority's judgment of the procedural inadequacy of the appellate court's ruling, Justice Thomas nonetheless wrote separately to emphasize the pastness of the history of slavery and segregation, and thus, its irrelevance for a future deliberation by the Court on the substance of affirmative action. It is here, in this relay of agreement between Kennedy and Thomas, that we should pause. For it bears an enfolding of the majority's colorblind measuredness and a concurrent color-conscious impatience. The decision simultaneously waits for a more precise application of Equal Protection doctrine on affirmative action and cannot wait to be done with it altogether. It is, in one decision, the progressive time of *Brown II* and the presentist time of *Parents Involved* redux.

This temporal recursivity, however, is not, and cannot be acknowledged as such. Instead, it proliferates in the baroque marginalia of dicta. At the end of Kennedy's opinion, we are left with such a play on words, which should not distract us from their seriousness as the navel of truth about the relation between race and law. There he opines that ideal judicial review would be neither "strict in theory, but fatal in fact" (quoting *Adarand Constructors, Inc. v. Peña* [1995], and *Grutter*) nor, adding his own gloss on this famous dicta, "strict in theory, but feeble in fact."[57] We can put our own gloss on Kennedy's play of dicta here to understand Thomas, who in his turn, is anguished that judicial review of affirmative action policies continues to entertain any compelling interest that recognizes racial difference, including the compromised interest of diversity first affirmed in *Bakke*. Thomas's impatience, in other words, is with the fact that judicial review, in the face of the history of race and law, has only ever been "strict in theory, *and* feeble in fact," instead of "strict in theory, *and* fatal in fact."

Seemingly, to wake judicial review from its zombie-like commitment to diversity and its infinite policing of acceptable and unacceptable policies regulating racial difference, Thomas resurrected, true to form, the interdiction of all legal interdictions with the hopes of scaring judicial review straight. This interdiction is given in the specter of the forever-standing claim (as in, open-ended, or indefinite) never fully reaching proper legal standing in the wake of slavery's formal abolition and during the consolidation of a Jim Crow America.[58] The truth of race and law is in this internal point of law's regress into its own words, and where the interdicted claim comes to life. Of course, Thomas is not concerned to actually hear this claim, let alone argue for its rightful standing to be adjudicated. Instead, Thomas's indignation insists that affirmative action's historical tradition is that of the "slaveholders"[59] and the "segregationists."[60]

He calls to law's rational mind, the sentimental discourse of slavery that imagined itself as a modern institution of enlightenment for the "black race";[61] and also recalls the paternalistic discourse of segregation recorded in legal history by cases such as *Briggs v. Elliott* (1952)[62] and *Bolling v. Sharpe* (1954).[63] Here, he declares, are our proper negative examples by which to reinvent strict scrutiny doctrine in affirmative action cases, if not all race discrimination cases brought under the Equal Protection Clause.

But the interdicted claim Thomas resurrects is not the slaveholder's or segregationist's. It is, rather, a fundamentally problematic being in law, the "black race," around which such sentimental and paternalistic discourses came to life back then, and is given new life by Thomas now as he recites that discourse as a negative example. That is why, as hard as Thomas works in his legal argument to make recourse to this claim as a negative example, as a claim without ground, it ineluctably asserts its timeless vestibularity. Neither he nor the law can escape it.

I am specifically referencing the arrival in the *Fisher* opinion, in the strange place of Thomas's hell-bent reasoning against affirmative action, of the figure of W. E. B. Du Bois as the towering intellectual figure of modern thought's fundamental critique of a world built on slavery and capitalism. Here is where Du Bois enters:

> A century later, segregationists similarly asserted [as with the slaveholders] that segregation was not only benign, but good for black students. They argued, for example, that separate schools protected black children from racist white students and teachers. See, e.g., Brief for Appellees in *Briggs* 33–34 ("'I have repeatedly seen wise and loving colored parents take infinite pains to force their little children into schools where the white children, white teachers, and white parents despised and resented the dark child, made mock of it, neglected or bullied it, and literally rendered its life a living hell. Such parents want their child to "fight" this thing out,—but, dear God, at what a cost! . . . We shall get a finer, better balance of spirit; an infinitely more capable and rounded personality by putting children in schools where they are wanted, and where they are happy and inspired, than in thrusting them into hells where they are ridiculed and hated'" (quoting Du Bois, Does the Negro Need Separate Schools? 4 J. of Negro Educ. 328, 330–331 (1935)).[64]

We can easily reveal the segregationist defendant's gross use and abuse of Du Bois in *Briggs* to stand their ground against the kind of national structural changes the Fourteenth Amendment promised as the echo of the slave's claim to freedom.[65] And I find it necessary here to reproduce what is so strangely cut from Du Bois in this legal history Thomas continues to write by his citation to *Briggs* as negative example. Here is the prescient Du Bois in his article referenced by Thomas: "I know that this article will forthwith be interpreted by certain illiterate 'nitwits' as a plea for segregated Negro schools and colleges." And to these "nitwits," like the *Briggs* defendants and to all, including Kennedy and Thomas, who would fail to understand the fundamental issue underlying the black struggle for education, he plainly states, "It is not. It is simply calling a spade a spade."[66]

What, then, is the spade Du Bois is calling a spade? It is the false choice of segregated or integrated schools determining and protracting the possible development of a knowledge based on "the fact that American Negroes have, because of their history, group experiences and memories, a distinct entity, whose spirit and reactions demand a certain type of education for its development."[67] Defending this "certain type of education" that he argues is more possible in committing to black schools than in litigating school integration, he specifies, "In history and the social sciences the Negro school and college has an unusual opportunity and role. It does not consist simply in trying to parallel the history of white folk with similar boasting about black and brown folk, but rather an honest evaluation of human effort and accomplishment, without color blindness, and without transforming history into a record of dynasties and prodigies."[68]

Ultimately, it is the possibility of "Sympathy, Knowledge, and the Truth" that black schools promise, where "children are treated like human beings, trained by teachers of their own race, who know what it means to be black in the year of salvation 1935."[69] And the political ramifications of developing this form of education, he explains, are clear and urgent, both domestically and abroad.

> Here, we have in America, a working class which in our day has achieved physical freedom, and mental clarity. An economic battle has just begun. It can be studied and guided; it can teach consumers' cooperation, democracy, and socialism, and be made not simply a record and pattern for the Negro race, but a guide for the rise of the working classes throughout the world . . . . [Knowledge of] modern civilization would not only help them [Negroes] find their place in the industrial scene for their own organization, but also enable them to help Abyssinia, India, China, and the colored world, to maintain their racial integrity, and their economic independence. It could easily be the mission and duty of the American Negroes to master this scientific basis of modern invention, and give it to all mankind.[70]

This is only the most basic sense of Du Bois's radical political recommendations in the context of the legal struggle for equal education that is cropped away by his necessarily partial appearance in *Fisher*. The least we can do after reading *Fisher* is to echo Du Bois's own insistence against the "nitwits" of history.

In addition to this, however, this book is after a more difficult task, which is to understand what about the radicalism of Du Bois's critique requires the segregationist and the neoconservative to reference him at all—just as we might ask why Thomas does not (not just in *Fisher*, but many other opinions he has written on the issue of racial discrimination) simply leave slavery and segregation to the dustbins of history and argue as a matter of doctrine why the diversity rationale does not qualify as a compelling interest under the Equal Protection Clause? What about the conservative course of doctrinal development in racial jurisprudence is not enough to rest one's arguments in, and instead, compels the recitation of the history of slavery and segregation?

The central argument of this book, highlighted now with this direct and contemporary reference in the law to Du Bois's radicalism, is that the only way to think ourselves out of the dead end of both liberal and conservative legal development is to insist, as did Du Bois, on the claim of the slave that is always there, even in the most unlikely places, including Thomas's opinion in *Fisher*.[71] That is, perhaps Thomas's resurrection of the slave and her claim (for sure, only to degrade it) tacitly avows its truth as the law's foundational challenge. Thomas's recalcitrance toward the claim of the slave is a rejection that ultimately requires a latent phobic recognition of it. In *Fisher*, this takes the form of Thomas's citation to a text in which Du Bois is faithfully asserting this claim unburdened by the limitations of the legal and political context of his day. "I am no fool,"[72] Du Bois warns, and by this warning echoes an historical reality in which the slave's claim rings true by every partial and failed address made to it. The slave as *the* irreducible legal personality of modern American law, by virtue of its foreclosed claim to freedom, is not simply an image that might potentially wake the law from its belief in multicultural diversity, as Thomas wishes. We might instead approach this legal personality as a legal fact to the extent that it tends always to return in law, and carries with it the whole of freedom struggle that Du Bois has the penchant to perform in his political analysis, knowing full well the various political resistances to this performance.

The claim of the slave surfaces today still, and even in perhaps the most pessimistic doctrinal arenas where legal efforts to promote racial equality have historically taken place and seemingly exhausted their transformative potential. At the dead end of this racial jurisprudence, in fact, is a horizon of escape illuminated by this claim. For if the claim of the slave in *Fisher* makes clear that legal reform stagnates in a cesspool of various commonsense articulations of constitutional law, the claim nonetheless leaves trails of its own disappearance. Its endurance is not in its opposition to history, or politics, or experience. It is in its inhabitation of a legal present apposite to the unasked question of how its disappearance is required by a constitutional law reconstituted in the wake of the Civil War so that no form of governance—no matter its jurisdictional authority, its function within a federal democracy, or history of political leadership—would undo the law's decision to rewrite itself in a truer image of a universal equality lifted from its social foundation in slavery.

The Free Right, or Civil Rights to Come

A new theoretical relation between rights and law emerges from Williams's scene of irreducible splitting between aim and object "black desire" produces in modern American law. This scene of law's language is one in which, she says, we "*give* them [rights] away."[73] Of course, rights are privileges bestowed on the people by the state, and rights are fictitious inventions of political practice. But rights are also felicitous, in the most radical sense of a performative, that cannot know or will in advance what right will obtain from law's reading and writing. That felicitousness, which has little to do with legal enforcement or political recognition, and more to do with a desire for rights as an aim, is a *free right* in and through—extimate to—law's language that is beyond the regulative-critical impulse that would restrict the economy of rights to relations of possession and dispossession.[74] The free right marks a legal relation of giving what one does not and cannot have, by a one that cannot and will not have, including the fact of the giving.

In a particularly speculative moment in *Alchemy*, Williams allows us to encounter something like this free right. The overall narrative structure of Williams's autobiography as one of rule-imposed silence and rule-breaking speech is interrupted by a dream about a kind of hearing. In that dream, she recounts, "I hear myself speaking: *Voices lost in the chasm speak from the slow eloquent fact of the chasm. They speak and speak and speak, like flowing water*."[75]

What she hears, literally, is something other than her own voice that comes from some outer acoustic scene. Her enforced silence in real life, or her symbolic lack, arrives in a nonhuman voice, "flowing water," she hears as herself. The colon that separates the two sentences illustrating her dream grammatically doubles the voice, or marks a certain excessive generativity of unconscious desire, as she stands to the side of herself to hear herself speaking, and materializes that nonplace with an image of a distinctive sound that emerges from a dark void. This voice is perhaps the sound of drowning as the envelopment of human voices by water.

Williams's hearing is not merely a representation of the empirical reality of human speech falling on the law's deaf ears. It is theoretically suggestive of a knowledge of voice as *objet a*, or the ground of desire.[76] Voice in this sense enters Williams's narrative here to present the question, again, of "black desire," as the condition of possibility for the thing, the voice, that neither she nor any particular other already possess, and that comes from a place that is nothing more than a divide. "[T]he slow eloquent fact of the chasm" dilates not into a parable of reclaiming a personal voice in the face of racial exclusion, but a theoretical assertion of the materiality of unconscious desire that is always there, as in the hearing in Williams's dream, and in a possible reading of Williams's speculative law. The free right, or the right aiming at equality, then, is law's zero-point, just as the voice is phonology's.[77] It is the object-cause of a certain "ani*materi*ality,"[78] to use Fred Moten's concept, of law that precedes and exceeds the symbolic discourse of race and rights and its fantasy of colorblindness.

The ongoing study of race and law must, like Williams, continue to pursue the Derridean problem of an essentially "unpresentable" justice.[79] Indeed, from

Hugo Grotius to Patricia Williams, we see that modern law has always reflected a certain nondisciplinarity or antidisciplinarity, respectively, that transcends the disciplines and professional schools today that proliferate so many interdisciplinary efforts of legal reform. These efforts are programmatic for public interest legal scholarship, but it is an unstated value of critical theory. One need only note how much critical theory depends on a critique of law that has not read the law's language. So while it is easy to either condemn or celebrate the civil rights that any legal reform must incorporate in the name of justice, it is more difficult to understand the fundamental entanglement of civil rights with a radical history of American modern law.

For Derrida, it is *only* by approaching law as a foundational paradox that we can hope for the "possibility of justice."[80] Indeed, he proposes that "deconstruction takes place in the interval" between the "deconstructibility of law (*droit*)" and the "undeconstructibility of justice."[81] According to this proposition, we should interrogate the limit of the rule of law's social reality as an empirical object of study, and thereby reveal the law's absolutely contingent dimension in its basic form as the "ruin of signature,"[82] be it the state's or any other sovereign figure's. Its forcefulness lies less in its *enforcements* of social hierarchy, but in the essential violence of an imposition of *contingency*, of which law-as-enforcement is but a reification. This contingent essence of constitution, "founding violence," that has no form, is the predicate for law-as-enforcement that gives this formless law form. And thus, modern American law as a history of legal reform is the incomplete institution of Enlightenment ideals of democratic life as failures of writing that are otherwise mystified by the Habermasian procedural concept of democracy.[83]

The *possibility* of justice appears in failures of writing. But what about justice itself? Derrida has this to say: "Justice as the experience of absolute alterity is unpresentable, but it is the chance of the event and the condition of history. No doubt an unrecognizable history, of course, for those who believe they know what they're talking about when they use the word, whether it's a matter of social, ideological, political, juridical or some other history."[84] The very "use" of the word "justice," or the confinement of the word to the use-value of legal meaning, is precisely what forecloses justice from taking place. We must note here that Derrida is not saying that justice has no place, just that the presence of justice is conditional to the "experience of absolute alterity."

This might be something akin to a position from which justice rushes forth by the urgency of "now" and fails to have meaning beyond that singular event. It might also mean that the experience of absolute alterity can only be accessed retroactively by an event that *would have* taken place, and so even this is "'justice'" but not "justice." I strike the quotation marks to emphasize Derrida's nonquoted reference to justice to recognize his attempt by omitting quotation marks to mark the *différance* of justice freed from legal referentiality and subjectivity.[85] What Derrida constantly defers is an idea of an unmediated experience of justice, and thus even in his gesture toward the "experience of absolute alterity" he must signify through a play of quotation marks its noncorrespondence with "justice."

At the same time, in his drive toward a thought of justice in a deconstruction of law, a certain blindness is written into deconstruction. And that thing to which a deconstruction of law is blind, is what Moten argues is the precondition or the ground of an "improvisational materiality" upon which Derridean deconstruction proceeds. This is where Moten would take Derrida, who desires to get there but can't quite do it, not with literature according to Moten, and I would add, not with law. Derrida's law never gets down with the "legalese," never quite goes "vernacular, where everything + n(othing) is named, where everything + n(othing) is said."[86]

So even if it is just to render a decision in the midst of a certain proper persistence in the differential between "'justice'" and "justice," one misses the chance to ask that question that Moten echoes as "*Uncle Toliver*," and his "strange arrival" through and against history. This is a question of the simplicity of the not-so-simple matter of the slave through the "violent imposition of silence that marks slavery."[87] Asking "[h]ow is this strange arrival possible?"[88] Moten answers:

> It arrives through various arrangements of the story of Uncle Toliver, the story of a man who could not tell his story as a matter of law, and as a matter of the materiality of his life and death. But the mediation that gives us that story does not obscure the position and situation spoken through his silence. It is spoken so profoundly that the entirety of the Enlightenment tradition and its critical other is invoked, re-opened, revised, improvised. The mediated and reconstructed voicing of the slave speaks through the vernacular and for freedom.[89]

Moten goes on to explain that this mediation is an ensemblic form of knowledge "*figured in and improvised through the ethical mediation of the Enlightenment's critical opening of the whole.*"[90]

This same question that Moten asks of the literary writing of history, one could ask of law's writing (for law and literature share a common material: words). Extending Moten's echoing question within the realm of law's language, what strangely arrives by a notion of Derridean "justice" circling around American constitutional law is none other than the free right audible as the poetics of plea.[91] Reading the letters of the law is to call attention to a poetics of the plea as an ensemblic improvisation of a knowledge of the free right contained in civil rights discourse that perhaps "allows a fundamental reconstitution" of modern American law. The "free right" appearing through a reading of the letters of the law disperses over and beyond the entire field of law's vision and blindspots, and breaks in on and down the deathly opacities of the fantasy of colorblindness into what Moten identifies elsewhere as "a certain chromatic saturation that inhabits black as that color's internal, social life."[92]

The free right, ultimately, poses the question of what a natural law of abolition, or a fugitive law of freedom, might be. I am not suggesting that an answer to this question become the basis of a positive law for a new form of democratic governance; *I pose this question precisely because we do not know where it could take us.* Affirming the free right, an elsewhere *in the law* to be read *from law*, need not be only a matter of base survival or service work. It is also a matter of inhabiting the knowledge that civil rights have never been present, a radical attention to a civil rights to come, and the question of the "first-person-plural" already here in the play of free rights. So while some might profess that we are in a post–civil rights moment in order either to absolve the state's responsibility for equally enforcing civil rights or to reinvest the state with moral conscience, I find this declaration of our contemporary moment strangely anathema to the law in its broadest sense. No, we are not in a post–civil rights moment. We are in a free right movement. Let us put aside the reflex to condemn or celebrate the law and to read the law more carefully. All we will find there is that we are locked in a centuries-long civil rights dance.

Here the law's language opens up onto something like a free rights jurisprudence, the writing of what Williams lyrically describes as "the bizarre and undecidable litigation of 'something happened' versus 'nothing happened.'"[93] Indeed, Williams's scene of writing "black life blooming within white" across *Alchemy* is not some revision of a phallic contest of racial progenies, but the tracing of a life that "disappear[s] into the middle of her own case."[94] Another law is given in that which is necessarily vanished in every present to preserve the law's fantasy of colorblindness, but by a certain excessiveness to this disappearance a fleshly remainder in the words of law is also always there to be encountered by those who would desire to read them.[95] At the dead end of racial jurisprudence, where there is nothing but the free right that demands our reading of the letters of the law, so begins our preparation for a hearing with no end.

CHAPTER ONE

Decompositional Rights

> The oscillation between then and now distills the past four hundred years into one definitive moment. And, at the same time, the still-unfolding narrative of captivity and dispossession exceeds the discrete parameters of the event. In itemizing the long list of violations, are we any closer to freedom, or do such litanies only confirm what is feared—history is an injury that has yet to cease happening?
>
> —Saidiya Hartman, "The Time of Slavery"

Saidiya Hartman wonders in the epigraph above whether a distinction can be made from "the long list of violations" between "freedom" and "history [as] an injury that has yet to cease happening." This same question can be put to civil rights discourse in American legal history and begs the further question of how, ultimately, we might understand the law's promise of equality given an essentially knotted relation between freedom and captivity? Does the enduring black struggle for civil rights work toward liberation, or does it fatally rehearse the "still-unfolding narrative of captivity and dispossession"? And, how does the time of slavery require a wholesale rethinking of the normative understanding of citizenship as a legal capacity to bear rights (usually civil rights)?

One way to begin an answer to these questions is with a certain latent skepticism toward civil rights that surfaces by the "litanies" of claims to civil rights. At the same time, this skepticism emerges also as a *question* about what is at stake when civil rights in American legal history are reduced to either a narrative of freedom or dispossession. In particular, the black claim to civil rights—exceeding the organization of the American legal archive into identity-based constituencies or periods of civil rights reforms in the mid-nineteenth and twentieth centuries—suggests that this narrative binary is neither necessary nor adequate to the task of rethinking the relation between race and law. Both post–civil rights critiques and defenses of civil rights bear the mark of this theoretical acquiescence, specifically by continuing to reduce the force of the black claim to the identity of its claimant or its historical impact on the development of civil rights law.

Taking a step back from these debates, we might ask instead: What *is* this claim on civil rights that forever gives the lie to the law's history of equality? What is this claim that in its repetition at once drags down the ideal of democratic citizenship and resurrects it in an always already colorblind vision of political community? Contrary to Hannah Arendt's argument that "the nation-state cannot exist once its principle of equality for the law has broken down,"[1] Hartman's sense of history suggests that the nation-state exists precisely because the principle of equality has always been broken. The United States as a nation-state is constituted by a permanent condition of inequality between blacks as the descendants of slaves and an always-plural community of citizens. Within this scene, the black claim to civil rights compels us to ask how such broken equality becomes constitutional, as well as how such constitution is escaped.

I offer some provisional answers to these questions in this chapter by tracing the force of what I call a decompositional right, which upon its pleading decays the assurances of equality and civil rights proffered by legal rationality. It is a form of right that recursively un-writes the various types of rights the law has developed to define citizenship. And it surfaces in legal reason by what Derrida calls a "degenerescence" of the presumed effective relationship between civil rights and citizenship. "Degenerescence" is one of the names Derrida gives to what he calls "an essential disruption" of law "within the heart of the law itself" (whatever type of law—in his particular piece, the laws governing genres).[2]

Accordingly, I examine how the law maintains a taxonomy of rights in the face of the black claim to civil rights. This taxonomy orders categories of civil, social, and political rights, assigns various levels of legal protection for and enforcement of them, and becomes a theoretical matrix by which rights-based claims are adjudicated. I am interested specifically in how the black claim splays this generic taxonomy of rights from which the classic rights of citizenship are engendered. In what follows, we enter into the degenerescence of this taxonomy through perhaps the most exhausted topic of racial jurisprudence: affirmative action in higher education. There we find that the decomposition of the law's principle of equality into what the Supreme Court tepidly reaffirmed in 2013 as the "educational benefits of diversity"[3] is merely an elapsed half-life of the law's inverted image of black citizenship. By exploring the foundational cases adjudicating the issue of black citizenship—*Plessy v. Ferguson* (1896), the *Civil Rights Case of 1883*, and *Dred Scott v. Sandford* (1857)[4]—we find not a legal personality to be incorporated into universal citizenship, but instead, one who must be endlessly demoted from citizenship. Ultimately, what we will find by tracing the decompositional right through these cases is a form of noncitizenship that I call "dispossessive citizenship."

The Colorblindness of Multiracial Citizenship

The question of citizenship and race appears in contemporary racial jurisprudence obliquely. Outside of the de jure and de facto racial politics of naturalization and immigration law that many have recently criticized for excluding foreign nationals and regulating their kinship networks, racial jurisprudence and its focus on discrimination engages issues of citizenship through constructions of a colorblind national history. This fantasmatically establishes the origin of American citizenship not in racial exclusion, but in a racial inclusion that citizenship professes to have always strived for. And in the spirit of racial inclusion, affirmative action in higher education remains an important area of racial jurisprudence where that origin story of an inclusive multiracial citizenship lives on.

Consider the Supreme Court decision, *Grutter v. Bollinger* (2003),[5] decided in the wake of three decades of right-wing assaults on race-based affirmative action policies, particularly in higher education. This case confirmed the persistence and persuasiveness of the origin story of American multiracial citizenship in what affirmative action jurisprudence calls the "diversity rationale." This justification, which validates race-based affirmative action policies with the goal of creating a diverse learning environment, arises from the Court's recognition of the university's First Amendment right to academic freedom. Reiterating this rationale to the exclusion of other possible justifications advanced by proponents of affirmative action, Justice O'Connor reasoned,

> [The] benefits [of diversity] are not theoretical but real, as major American businesses have made clear that the skills needed in today's increasingly global marketplace can only be developed through exposure to widely diverse people, cultures, ideas, and viewpoints. . . . What is more, high-ranking retired officers and civilian leaders of the United States military assert that, "based on [their] decades of experience," a "highly qualified, racially diverse officer corps . . . is essential to the military's ability to fulfill its principle mission to provide national security."[6]

As telling as this discussion is of the law's increasingly neoliberal investments in diversity, *Grutter* simply clarifies the effect of the landmark decision, *UC Regents v. Bakke* (1978),[7] where the diversity rationale was first established. In this case, Allan Bakke alleged that the university's affirmative action policy discriminated against him as a white medical school applicant. What is more interesting than the political power Bakke successfully mobilized by asserting a civil rights claim based on his white identity is how the decision fantasmatically reconstructs an inclusive multiracial history of citizenship to arrive at its ruling on affirmative action. That is, of the four compelling interests the university presented in *Bakke* to defend its affirmative action policies, all but the diversity rationale were rejected. Reducing under-representation of minorities, ameliorating the effects of "societal discrimination" against certain minority groups, and improving delivery of public services to underserved minority communities were all rejected as compelling reasons for affirmative action. And because of this, any discussion of affirmative action in education has since, as demonstrated in *Grutter*, been ruthlessly constrained by *Bakke*'s historical delusion, both about the law's capacity to remedy racial injustices of the past and to recognize the historical specificity of slavery and its vestiges.

How does *Bakke* reason away the historical impetus for Fourteenth Amendment Equal Protection jurisprudence, the spirit of which the university's affirmative action policies were argued to embody? Justice Powell, writing for the majority, made a decisive analytical move by conflating the history of slavery and racial segregation with the history of new immigration; in Powell's analysis, the latter history wins pride of place. It is, in his view, the more persuasive and, as the story runs, demographically accurate account. Justifying the Court's departure from the original intent of the Reconstruction Amendments, which was to provide the recently emancipated slaves with the rights of citizenship, Powell writes:

> It was *no longer possible* to peg the guarantees of the Fourteenth Amendment to the struggle for equality of one racial minority [because] the United States had become a Nation of minorities. Each had to struggle . . . to overcome the prejudices not of a monolithic majority, but of a "majority" composed of various minority groups . . . that shared a characteristic . . . willingness to disadvantage other groups. As the Nation filled with the stock of many lands, the reach of the Clause was gradually *extended* to all ethnic groups seeking protection from official discrimination.[8]

Note the double slippage here: first, from "newly freed Negro slaves,"[9] a restricted and singular definition implied in the above passage as "one racial minority," to "minorities," a category that is malleable and expansive; and, second, from the social phenomena of slavery and segregation in particular to the amorphous term "discrimination." Just as *Bakke* would become emblematic of the reverse-discrimination claim, so too would a vision of American citizenship in a multiracial national history become a never-ending source of slippage from slavery. As this chapter progresses, we will see how the reasoning in *Plessy,* the *Civil Rights Cases of 1883,* and *Scott* had already laid precedent for this historical slippage. But for now, we should note that the multiracialization of a general national history away from the specific history of slavery and segregation is the basis for *Bakke*'s invention of multiracial diversity as the only constitutionally valid reason for affirmative action.

More important, the multiracial diversity rationale appears during the upswing of American diversification prompted by immigration policy shifts of the mid-1960s, and it echoes a fantasmatic history of transnationality. This history recasts the originary aporia of slavery with the glow of America as a "Nation of minorities," concealing the internal racial limit of the Constitution and its first and second Reconstruction Amendments. As if recoiling from the historical stink of the centuries-long flows of transatlantic human cargo, what *Bakke* does doctrinally with the diversity rationale figures into the Court's fantasmatic history of a progressively transnational United States.

The temporality of Powell's progressive narrative about the multiracial demographics of the United States—"As the Nation filled with the stock of many lands"—not only provides a type of harmony between the ideas of America as the "Land of Opportunity" and a "nation of immigrants." It also poses another type of harmony between transnationality and diversity that is found in their etymological meanings. "Trans" in Latin means "across," "through," or "beyond"; and in conjunction with "nation," it signifies a crossing through and beyond difference that unifies a Nation from/of "many lands." "Diversity" in its Latin origin, *diversus,* is the past participle of *divertere,* meaning "divert." What we have with the harmony of transnationality and diversity, then, is a history of multiracial nation building that, in Powell's rendering, diverts history away from the problem of slavery and segregation as the context for the Reconstruction Amendments.

Specifically, Powell goes on to list a host of cases identifying this "stock of many lands": Irish, Chinese, Austrian, Japanese, and Mexican American.[10] Diverting the history of the Fourteenth Amendment through the legal precedent of the New Immigrant, there is an *absolute silence* as to the "land" from which the black minority migrates. References to a black minority in this opinion are not connected to any origin whatsoever: not a foreign nation, a distant land from whence they came, or a distinct historical culture to which they belong. African Americans are Negroes, former slaves, the slave race, or blacks. *Bakke*'s fantasy of colorblindness obtains in a multiracial citizenship that casts the time of slavery outside history, including histories written by and into law.

To be clear, my point is that *Bakke*, and then *Grutter* and *Fisher*'s affirmations of *Bakke*'s diversity rationale, require a progressive history of a multiracial transnational citizenship that fixes slavery's pastness to the exclusion of slavery's ever-presentness. Affirmative action jurisprudence exemplifies the cultural reality of slavery Hartman describes as an "oscillation between then and now." Indeed, Hortense Spillers argues that "every generation of systematic readers is compelled not only to reinvent 'slavery' in its elaborate and peculiar institutional ways and means but also, in such play of replication, its prominent discursive features."[11] She goes on:

> This field of enunciative possibilities—its horizon, its limits, its enabling postulates, and its placement in perspective with other fields of signification—constitutes the discourse of slavery, and as concretely material as the "institution" was, as a natural historical sequence and as a scene of pulverization and murder, "slavery," for all that, remains one of the most textualized and discursive fields of practice that we could posit as a structure for attention.[12]

What Spillers is pointing to here is the possibility of thinking about the racial significance of historical diversion the diversity rationale produces. The diversity rationale is precisely the law's reinvention of slavery as an event always lost to history through a "play of replication" and "placement in perspective with other fields of signification"—namely, multiracial nation-building. The absolute past tense of slavery in the law's historiographic narrative of citizenship is so far passed that it does not qualify as a memorializable event in contemporary national multiracial history. Instead, it appears as the stage for the commencement of history, and specifically, a history of multiracial citizenship.[13] In "post–civil rights" affirmative action cases, the discrepancy between the time of citizenship and the time of slavery is there, in the letter of the law, but is remarkably overlooked as the break in historical progress that it is. Instead, the temporal discrepancy recedes from view as the law's colorblind promise of equality is repeated through a fantasmatic history that depicts a transnationally forged multiracial citizenship as the assumed path out of slavery.

However, the law's narration of national historical progress in affirmative action jurisprudence through multiracial citizenship, which reduces slavery to a barely mentioned detail of the past, is not merely an issue of historical interpretation. It is symptomatic of a structural limit within legal rationality where black citizenship appears as a terrifying oxymoron, and subsequently, the perfection of the universal promise of equality becomes a permanent preoccupation of law in the first instance.

Thus, should we be tempted to write off Powell's multiracial citizenship simply as a historical gloss on a controversial legal issue, we must remember that Powell's sense of historical possibility had been explicitly considered by one of the towering intellectuals of modern American democracy. Returning to Alexis de Tocqueville's nineteenth-century commentary on democracy and slavery in the United States, *Democracy in America* reads like a founding text of this fantasmatic multiracial history that defends the law from the profound difficulty of incorporating the time of slavery into history.

In the particular section "The Principle of the Sovereignty of the People,"

Tocqueville writes tellingly about the fictitiousness of citizenship. He characterizes the uniqueness of citizenship under American democracy as that which is "unencumbered" by previous fictions of citizenship "thrown over," or veiling, European forms of monarchy or oligarchy.[14] The fiction of citizenship Tocqueville speaks of is an ineffective citizenship, one that fails to translate popular will into meaningful political representation, whether due to arbitrary and uneven distribution of political power, coercion and despotism, or "uncivilized" social conditions antithetical to Enlightenment ideals. Here, Tocqueville's image of a true democratic institution of citizenship emerges against the failures of European sovereignties.

American democracy is distinguishable from its European counterpart because it grants "universal suffrage." This is, of course, at the time of his thinking, less a reality and more his aspiration for democracy. Tocqueville's design of democracy through the developing United States is *ficto figura veritatis*: fiction that takes on the veneer of truth. Citizenship in American democracy, by Tocqueville's own account, is underwritten by an implicit fiction we continue to refer to as American democracy.

Yet this fiction, like *Bakke*'s fantasmatic history, is not unburdened by the question of slavery. For if Tocqueville begins with a celebration of American universal suffrage in comparison to European political systems of representation, he ends with speculation about what he perceives to be an impossible equality between future black freedmen and a future multiracial transnational citizenry. This impossibility renders American democracy not as the realization of citizenship, but portrays it as historically unfinished and unable to do away with the trace of slavery. And it is precisely because of this difficulty of imagination that the racial project of slavery becomes inextricable from the national project of establishing universal citizenship. Tocqueville muses, "There is a natural prejudice which prompts men to despise whomsoever has been their inferior long after he has become their equal; and the real inequality which is produced by fortune or by law is always succeeded by an imaginary inequality which is implanted in the manners of the people."[15] No amount of formal guarantees to individual liberty, political and civil rights, or freedom from prior conditions of servitude can reconcile this "imaginary inequality" that constitutes the symbolic network of American citizenship.

Tocqueville can find neither historical precedent nor a viable source of empirical support for a *black* citizenship. Instead, writing some thirty years before the Civil War and the Amendments to the U.S. Constitution declaring the legal abolition of slavery in the American republic, Tocqueville goes on to provide us with an interesting speculation. Because the ideal of American citizenship can do nothing about this "natural prejudice" that becomes institutionalized in an "imaginary inequality," the abolition of slavery would require either total biological assimilation or demographic separation—in either case, not social or political integration—of the freedmen. Black citizenship in Tocqueville's America is posed as a question regarding whether and how the legal personality of a black citizen can emerge in the interstices of slavery and democracy, whether national subjects can be made of a minority group that crossed not from one national territory into another, but remained trapped between the Atlantic Ocean and a settler multitude. Spatially locating the soon-to-be freedpersons, Tocqueville explains, "on the continent, the blacks are placed between the ocean and an innumerable people."[16]

In other words, if Tocqueville understood American citizenship as the transformation of national subjects in voluntary or coerced transnational passage to the New World, he also understood "the blacks" somewhere in the midst of, but not participating in, this traffic. Rather than entering the frontier of one sovereign state from another, descendants of African slaves are caught between the nonground of the ocean and the emergent place of a multiracial democracy, between nature and political community. Racial exclusion from citizenship for blacks "on the continent" is to remain between ocean and people; just as it is to remain between an absolute past and the evolving multiracial national history performed in *Bakke*. It is as if the event of slavery has forever drowned continental Africa in the Atlantic and the cruel journey its waves gave witness to. Thus, even if it is true today that the history of immigration expands the frame of contemporary racial politics in the United States—offering more ethnic groups with their own demands—this expansion only reaffirms the political and legal difficulty of squaring black citizenship with the multiracial citizenship identified by Tocqueville and *Bakke*.

A failure to engage this difficulty—whether by minimizing its force in the present or adding other histories of oppression to it through analogy—narrows our understanding of the relationship between American democracy and citizenship. Tocqueville and *Bakke* reveal that the racial limit of citizenship is not the uneven remaking of heterogeneous national subjects into American citizens or enemies. This unevenness is the history of the development of U.S. multiracial citizenship. Rather, the racial limit is a structural problem of American democracy as such, or what Tocqueville unwittingly identified as the particular "imaginary inequality" of black people in contradistinction to all other groups, and which he forecasts will forever elude legal or historical change.

Toni Morrison's insight on popular culture confirms Tocqueville's speculations on this score. In her article "On the Backs of Blacks," she addresses precisely the mistaken belief that transnational histories of immigration can adequately attend to this racial limit of democratic citizenship. She writes:

> Popular culture . . . is heavily engaged in race talk. It participates in this most enduring and efficient *rite of passage* into American culture: negative appraisals of the native-born black population. . . . *Whatever* the lived experience of immigrants with African Americans—pleasant, beneficial, or bruising—the rhetorical experience renders blacks as *noncitizens*, already discredited outlaws.[17]

Morrison's observation makes plain the oblique philosophical and legal language of multiracial citizenship: to become American, as such, structurally requires a negation or discrediting of the native-born black population. This is no optional encounter or simple matter of conscience and goodwill. She is identifying a symbolic mandate issued universally by popular culture to U.S.-bound immigrants; an inexorable, forced choice that holds out not only the Pyrrhic promise of "becoming American," but, more important, the concomitant injunction to accommodate antiblackness. This symbolic mandate is not the contamination of law by culture, but is a law of democratic law that appears in its investments in multiracial citizenship.

Imagined Inequality at the Limit of Civil Rights

My argument thus far has been that this enduring fiction of black inequality emerges through references in racial jurisprudence to the time of slavery. How, precisely, do we approach this enduring fantasy of an irreducible antagonism between multiracial citizenship and blackness that spans various historical shifts, from Tocqueville's time to our purported postracial present? How do we understand the black claim to civil rights given the intractability of what Tocqueville recognized as an unassimilable imagined inequality of black people?

I now turn to these questions by examining how the time of slavery is contained in the legal reasoning of the central cases on black citizenship, *Plessy,* the *Civil Rights Cases of 1883*, and *Scott*. The primary form of containment across these cases is the law's taxonomy of civil, social, and political rights. For the most part, we accept that the law should regulate civil and political rights, but not social rights. This commonsense taxonomy of rights emerges, significantly, through the question of how to understand black citizenship, and, more specifically, how rights do or do not signify the equal citizenship of black people.

Let us examine these cases in turn, beginning with *Plessy* as the place where the actual signifier "color-blind" appears for the first time in a landmark Supreme Court case on race. While most read the case as the inaugural articulation of an ideology of colorblindness, the mere presence of the signifier "color-blind" does not actually introduce a new ideology in legal discourse, even if it establishes a more formal relationship between the two. Rather, the signifier is a particular condensation of the aporia of race that transcends national history. It requires the law to redirect the problems it encounters in meeting its universal promise of citizenship to a repeated assertion of a natural order of rights—civil, political, and social—that are to be variously given or withheld.

Justice Harlan famously declared, "Our Constitution is color-blind . . ."[18] in his dissent against the ruling that separate-but-equal railroad accommodations for blacks and whites did not violate the Equal Protection clause of the Fourteenth Amendment. He was arguing for the formal recognition and enforcement of equal civil rights of African Americans, which included the right to be free from discrimination by public agencies. Reading the majority and dissenting opinions together, *Plessy* appears to be the law's reduction of the black struggle for citizenship to a matter of formal racial categorization in the face of Jim Crow segregation. This despite the fact that it was the *social* logic of antiblack racism (Tocqueville's "imagined inequality") that excluded African Americans from the political sphere classically represented by the institution of citizenship.

Specifying *Plessy*'s rearticulation as "racial formalism," Cheryl Harris has argued that *Plessy* "not only installed colorblindness as the *dominant metaphor* animating understandings of equal protection, it *encrypted racial hierarchy* within the framework of colorblind analysis."[19] If the polysemic nature of the metaphor of colorblindness facilitated the dissemination of equality as a formal legal principle into the national culture, in its "shadow," according to Harris, there is an "encrypted racial hierarchy."[20] To encrypt something is to put ordinary language into code. We might understand the idea of formal racial equality as *code* for what is ordinarily understood as an absolute social division between white superiority and black inferiority. One speaks in code, but the intimacies of this code convey ordinary meanings. (Again, Tocqueville's "imagined inequality" reveals itself as an exacting phrase.)

The crucial point is that this is precisely how the signifier "color-blind" emerged. Harlan, as we will recall, proffers the signifier or code word "color-blind," while unabashedly assuring the nation that social inequality remains outside the purview of judicial interference or legislative regulation. Thus, as a matter of the Tocquevillian truth of "imagined inequality," he states, "The white race deems itself to be the dominant race in this country. And so it is, in prestige, in achievements, in education, in wealth, and in power. So, I doubt not, it will continue to be for all time, if it remains true to its great heritage, and holds fast to the principles of constitutional liberty."[21]

The "citizen" guaranteed "color-blind" equal protection by the Fourteenth

Amendment at issue in *Plessy* becomes a legal subject in contradistinction to a general social condition of blackness. To invest in "color-blind" equality is to accept a compromise. On the one hand, its ordinary meaning rests on a commonsense assumption that equality between whites and African Americans can eventually be legally negotiated by enforcing only their civil rights. But on the other hand, its coded meaning rests on a philosophic assumption that the social condition of blackness is absolutely outside of any sovereign regulation of law. The law permits itself to regulate and enforce civil equality by creating civil rights, but it prohibits itself from doing the same with social equality, by either creating social rights or using civil rights toward socially equal ends.

This compromise also plays out in Harlan's other famous passage that stages a curious apposition of blacks and Chinese:

> There is a race so different from our own that we do not permit those belonging to it to become citizens of the United States. Persons belonging to it are, with few exceptions, absolutely excluded from our country. I allude to the Chinese race. By the statute in question, a Chinaman can ride in the same passenger coach with white citizens of the United States, while citizens of the black race in Louisiana . . . who have all the legal rights that belong to white citizens, are yet declared to be criminals, liable to imprisonment, if they ride in a public coach occupied by citizens of the white race.[22]

Harlan's comparative commentary on racial assimilation qua formal legal status, in which the foreignness of the Chinese is asserted, seems to be Harlan's *explicit* line of reasoning. However, even if Harlan compares the legal status of blacks and Chinese according to the formal criteria of citizenship, we cannot forget on this count that the ruse of colorblindness, as elaborated by Harris, is its *formalistic* treatment of race in law. That is to say, if we displace this line of *formal* comparison with the question of *effective* legal status, then the logic of Harlan's comparison collapses entirely. The comparison cannot stand against the social reality of the disenfranchisement and state-sanctioned terrorism of Jim Crow that both blacks and Chinese experienced to varying degrees and with no compunctions about whom the institution targeted. Its remainder can serve only the most anxious and contradictory rhetorical function here. For as Harlan argues for colorblindness—or a meaningful civil equality—by suggesting that blacks should at least be afforded the backhanded dignity of the Chinese, he cannot help but rearticulate the reality of the "imaginary inequality" of black citizenship as such.

In other words, as much as Harlan argues for a real civil equality between blacks and whites, his reasoning admits that the reproduction of racism occurs at the social level, as opposed to the formal level. Consequently, the affront that holds up "the Chinese race" as the standard bearers of national exoticism—a statement that is, of course, not without its own irony—is subsidized by a *practical capacity* to enjoy forms of social mobility that blacks cannot. Meanwhile, blacks remain, absurdly so according to Harlan's reasoning, socially outcast even as the law gives them formal civil equality.[23] Thus, the sentimental *presumption* of formal black citizenship proffered by Harlan's dissenting opinion in *Plessy*—the decree of "universal civil freedom"[24]—indicates the indispensability of an "imagined inequality" to his plea for a "color-blind" Constitution.[25] Multiracial citizenship defined by colorblindness reveals through its very anxious innocence its antiblack foundations.

We are dealing here with a kind of colorblind talk as a de facto naturalization policy that goes beyond the legal recognition of political status. In *Plessy*, we see the affirmation of Tocqueville's prediction that universal citizenship in the United States, threatened to be haunted in perpetuity by the "imagined inequality" of blacks, would require a certain transcendence from the formal recognition or extension of black civil rights. The rhetorical gestures that attach to biographically transnational subjects like "the Chinese," whom Harlan referenced to ultimately underscore the intractability of black social inequality, demonstrate the fantasy of colorblindness at work in the establishment of a more general capacity to become American: not so much by proximity or similarity to *whites*,[26] as by distance and difference from *blacks*.[27] It reveals the capacity of rights to effect (not necessarily effectively) the civil and social equality of diverse nonblack groups, while raising the conundrum of a certain mootness of rights to black civil and social equality.

Let us not then be distracted by the signifier "color-blind" and the multiracial scene through which it is staged in *Plessy*. When Harlan announces, "Our Constitution is color-blind," he establishes that the rules of national membership in a political community do not apply to the social arrangements of racial inequality. Colorblindness is the abstraction of multiracial citizenship from the racial disorder of the *socius*. There is no coincidence here between the civic domain of a nation and a racial *socius*; there is only an unbroachable disjuncture between the particular status of blackness as a never-ending "imagined inequality" and its intrusion on and in the civic life of the nation. Put another way, the fantasy of colorblindness mobilizes both the idea of universal distributions of civil rights (including to black claimants), and Tocqueville's "imagined inequality" of a people between the "ocean" and "the continent."

It might appear on initial reading that Harlan, in his moral march toward colorblind multiracial citizenship, is tossing a bone to the segregationists by assuring them that social relations will not be effected by the abolition of Jim

Crow. But what I am suggesting is that this apologist tone is not mere rhetorical embellishment on the legal argument for equal citizenship. It is, rather, a condition of possibility for the fantasmatic trajectory of citizenship more generally. In fact, Harlan articulated this assumed split between civil and social equality attending the idea of universal freedom much more clearly in his dissenting opinion in the *Civil Rights Cases of 1883*, which struck down a provision of the federal Civil Rights Bill of 1875 that criminalized racial discrimination in certain quasi-public venues. Here we find the same argument he is most known for in *Plessy* but without the apologist gloss. I will explore the majority ruling in more detail below, but for now I would like to draw out the importance of understanding Harlan's disagreement in the *Civil Rights Cases of 1883*, precisely for its more sober assessment of how exactly the Reconstruction Amendments reformed the Constitution as the fundamental law of civil rights and liberties.[28]

While Justice Bradley, writing for the majority, would strike down the Civil Rights Bill because the venues under federal regulation in his opinion were private and not an incident of slavery, Harlan argued that the venues were private corporations serving a public interest and discrimination by them were incidents of slavery. Based on this, Harlan concluded that such private venues fell within Congress's regulatory power under the Thirteenth and Fourteenth Amendments.[29] But the more significant disagreement between Bradley and Harlan hinged on an interpretation of law, not fact. Harlan is very clear that the Thirteenth and Fourteenth Amendments, and then the attendant Civil Rights bills of 1866 and 1875, were enacted to abolish slavery as well as what he calls the "race line."[30] Contrary to the majority opinion's position that the only thing the Thirteenth Amendment authorizes Congress to do is legislate against formal enslavement, we find here that Harlan has a much deeper understanding of slavery as a racial institution. Here is his argument about the spirit of the Thirteenth Amendment:

> I do not contend that the Thirteenth Amendment invests Congress with authority, by legislation, to define and regulate the entire body of the civil rights which citizens enjoy, or may enjoy, in the several States. But I hold that since slavery, as the court has repeatedly declared, was the moving or principal cause of the adoption of that amendment, and since that institution rested wholly upon the inferiority, as a race, of those held in bondage, their freedom necessarily involved immunity from, and protection against, all discrimination against them, because of their race, in respect of such civil rights as belong to freemen of other races. Congress, therefore, under its express power to enforce that amendment, by appropriate legislation, may enact laws to protect that people against the deprivation, *because of their race*, of any civil rights granted to other freemen in the same State.[31]

He goes on further to ground his interpretation of the Reconstruction Amendments in the long-established precedent in federalism doctrine that "Congress, in the absence of a positive delegation of power to the State legislatures, may, by its own legislation, enforce and protect any right derived from or created by the national Constitution."[32] He asks, "If, then, exemption from discrimination, in respect of civil rights, is a *new constitutional right*, secured by the grant of State citizenship to colored citizens of the United States—and I do not see how this can now be questioned—why may not the nation, by means of its own legislation of a primary direct character, guard, protect and enforce that right? It is a right and privilege which the nation conferred."[33]

Just as the Constitution would become the supreme written law of the federal democratic republic independent from its colonial sovereign, for Harlan, the Reconstruction Amendments' declaration of a "new constitutional right" is the supreme written law of a postbellum nation no longer divided between master and slave, or white and black. This new constitutional right, in abolishing the constitutional property right of the master, installs a constitutional civil right of the "colored citizens" to be free from slavery. We must retain the specificity of Harlan's argument here. This new constitutional right, which can be claimed generally (as we see from *Bakke, Grutter* and *Fisher*), was nonetheless specifically written into the Constitution with the federal intent of addressing the particular condition of the slave.

This federal source of a "new constitutional right," which could have become the basis for a fundamental antidiscrimination law conceptualized by Harlan, is curiously overlooked in both critical and traditional histories of contemporary Fourteenth Amendment racial antidiscrimination doctrine. Harlan's idea of colorblindness that cloaks the division between universal civil equality and natural social inequality has become a foil for attributing the cause of persisting racial discrimination and violence across various realms of social life to the mere mention of civil rights in political discourse.

But reading Harlan's arguments in *Plessy* through his discussion of a "new constitutional right" in his dissent to the *Civil Rights Cases of 1883*, we sense that arguing against the continued relegation of the freedmen to civil death through segregation is as difficult as arguing against the naturalized social inferiority of black citizens underscored in his comparison of blacks and Chinese. As Harlan introduces the signifier "color-blind" into antidiscrimination law, its referent, "the new constitutional right" of the freedmen to be free from racial subjection, immediately vanishes. And here, in Harlan's very defense of the civil rights of the freedmen and his invention of a symbolic traffic in colorblindness and multiracial citizenship, we see the discrepancy of the time of slavery surface again. This time, however, it is in the necessity of slavery's continuing abolition by this "new constitutional right," but a right that is always under erasure by the fantasy of colorblindness. Indeed, as Robert Cover reminds us, "Law is the projection of an imagined future upon reality."[34] Colorblindness is the projection upon reality of the imagined future of this "new constitutional right" that promises, still, to abolish slavery.

The Inversion of Black Citizenship

In my reading of affirmative action cases, the time of slavery surfaces by its elision in the historical narrative of transnational multiracial inclusion informing the diversity rationale. In reading Harlan's dissenting arguments for equal citizenship in *Plessy* and the *Civil Rights Cases of 1883*, the time of slavery surfaces in segregation-era cases in the way that the "new constitutional right" of the former slave always vanishes under the sign of "color-blind" equality. Here I would like to explore why the time of slavery in racial jurisprudence seems barely readable as a fact that is either already addressed by the law, or beyond the law's address. I want to further pursue how the time of slavery challenges multiracial citizenship in the two landmark cases on black citizenship, the *Civil Rights Cases of 1883* and *Scott*. These two cases bookend the growing political and legal controversy over the fundamental Tocquevillian question of how to overcome the imagined inequality of blacks, especially as the specter of formal emancipation would become real with the Civil War and the Reconstruction period. Let us look at them in turn for the remainder of the chapter to come back full circle to the main idea of the decompositional right.

The Civil Rights Cases of 1883 dealt in more detail with how the Reconstruction Amendments related to each other with respect to the formal recognition of blacks as American citizens. Issued just twenty years after the Emancipation Proclamation, the Supreme Court held unconstitutional the federal "Civil Rights Bill" of 1875, which criminalized discrimination against anyone based on "a particular race or color, or who had been in a previous condition of servitude" from enjoying "accommodations, advantages, facilities and privileges of inns, public conveyances, and theaters."[35] The Court reasoned that because the Fourteenth Amendment only prohibited racial discrimination by states and not individuals, and because the Thirteenth Amendment only prohibited formal slavery and not discrimination based on racial conditions of slavery, Congress had no constitutional authority to enact such expansive legislation.

This opinion gave rise to quite stunning language that strangled the possibility to derive effective civil rights from the Reconstruction Amendments.

On Bradley's reading, the Fourteenth Amendment cannot apply "directly," but rather, the civil rights of due process and equal protection "are secured by way of prohibition against State laws and State proceedings affecting those rights and privileges, and by power given to Congress to legislate for the purpose of carrying such prohibition into effect, and such legislation must necessarily be predicated upon such supposed State laws or State proceedings, and be directed to the correction of their operation and effect."[36] Note here the embedded mechanism of reasoning: federal civil rights legislation must be predicated on state action, and subsequently, the mode of federal intervention can correct only state deprivations of civil rights by reinstalling the foundational prohibitory principle of the Reconstruction Amendments. Federal civil rights protections are negative protections—a guarantee by the federal government ensuring only that states will *not* engage in certain behavior—and even then, such federal protections are never independent propositions, but dependent emendations.

Whenever civil rights issues arise in the law, then, we are to take them as a sign that the prohibition against state discrimination was transgressed. Civil rights emerge from the Fourteenth Amendment as enforcements of a prohibition. This for the most part is not an intuitive or commonsensical understanding of civil rights. Critiques of how the Reconstruction Amendments are flawed because they do not give Congress a positive power to provide civil rights to freedpersons are many and absolutely necessary. We saw in the prior section how Harlan made his argument against this now-dominant position, even if his arguments would have their own particular lethal implications.

But how exactly does the law turn these Amendments' negative power into a positive source of civil rights violations? By virtue of drawing a line between federal and state authority, Bradley must contrast what may not be against what is. As he labors to describe the Amendments' proscription of state discrimination, he also describes what remains beyond the proscription. Bradley explains:

> [It] is proper to state that civil rights, such as are guaranteed by the Constitution against State aggression, cannot be impaired by the wrongful acts of individuals, unsupported by State authority in the shape of laws, customs, or judicial or executive proceedings. The wrongful act of an individual, unsupported by any such authority, is simply a private wrong, or a crime of that individual . . . . An individual cannot deprive a man of his right to vote, to hold property, to buy and sell, to sue in the courts, or to be a witness or a juror; he may, by force or fraud, interfere with the enjoyment of the right in a particular case; he may commit an assault against the person, or commit murder, or use ruffian violence at the polls, or slander the good name of a fellow citizen; but, unless protected in these wrongful

> acts by some shield of State law or State authority, he cannot destroy or injure the right; he will only render himself amenable to satisfaction or punishment, and amendable therefor [*sic*] to the laws of the State where the wrongful acts are committed.[37]

Here, what remains beyond the Amendments' proscription is the freedom of private acts—murder, slander, and harassment—and, as well, we must not forget the particular private acts at issue in the case: contracting, buying and selling, and lodging. The faith that Bradley displays in criminal law's commitment to punish private acts of racial terror is nothing short of incredible. But what is more important is the appearance of an entire social world of private acts and omissions (the jurisdiction of criminal and commercial relations) that issue from Bradley's attempt to hold the jurisdictional line between the federal government and the states in his interpretation of the Reconstruction Amendments.

Within Bradley's unwitting scene of social terror and dishonor, we should dwell on the key word "may," repeated throughout it. Of course, Bradley's intended meaning indicates a sense of possibility for future action. Perhaps he could just as likely have used "might" in this sense (to think at the level of hypothetical that the legal mind is trained toward). Since "might" connotes a past-ness to a possibility, perhaps "may" appeared more appropriate for this particular rhetorical turn. Yet, whatever his calculations of word-choice, "may" in the stronger (however unintended) sense indicates permission, a concession, a certain freedom to act. In its legal sense, "may" connotes a command; and in its religious sense, "may" connotes wish or desire. Reading Bradley's reasoning again with this stronger sense, the passage becomes an affirmation of private violence and discrimination toward freedpersons. It is an unauthoritative authorization of racial terror and dishonoring that takes place on a jurisdictional line between federal constitutional civil rights and state criminal law.

The contrast between the appellation "freedperson" and the authorized freedom to commit privatized racial violence in this passage is remarkable enough. But there is more to the negative power of the Fourteenth Amendment. Bradley goes on to explain that if it is clear that the Fourteenth Amendment only regulates state action, it is equally clear that the Thirteenth Amendment does directly regulate private acts, but only those that "fasten" a "badge of slavery" on an individual.[38] Moving on to discuss the Thirteenth Amendment, he asks, "Can the act of a mere individual, the owner of the inn, the public conveyance or place of amusement, refusing the accommodation, be justly regarded as imposing any badge of slavery or servitude upon the applicant, or only as inflicting an ordinary civil injury, properly cognizable by the laws of the State and presumably subject to redress by those laws until the contrary appears?"[39]

Bradley holds that such acts cannot be an imposition of the badge of slavery. He does this by recalling the Civil Rights Bill of 1866, by which under the authority of the Thirteenth Amendment to abolish slavery and its incidents, Congress meant only to "vindicate those fundamental rights which appertain to the essence of citizenship, and the enjoyment or deprivation for which constitutes the essential distinction between freedom and slavery."[40] Those essential to "civil freedom" included the "right to make and enforce contracts, to sue, be parties, give evidence, and to inherit, purchase, lease, sell and convey property as is enjoyed by white citizens."[41] These legal, contract, and property rights were, in Bradley's mind, of a different nature than what he called the "social rights of men and races in the community,"[42] which Congress declined to formalize, and thus equalize. Since the discriminatory acts at issue in the case did not involve deprivations of contract, legal, or property rights because the acts of refusal to contract were committed by private citizens, they were "mere" deprivations of social rights, which did not fall under the protection of the Thirteenth Amendment.

The neatness of Bradley's categories of rights (and Harlan's for that matter) should not stop us from inquiring further into why such categories would seem so obvious in the first place. For if Congress in 1866 had not recognized what Bradley called "social rights," then it was recognizing them in the 1875 legislation at issue in the case, and adding on to (and not contradicting) its prior legislative intention. So much for pointing out this obvious inconsistency in the Court's reliance on Congress's intent to give meaning to the Thirteenth Amendment. Bradley, as if anticipating this critique, goes on to explain why the Court could only partially defer to Congress's clear authority to legislate "social rights." He cautions in what has become a timeless rejoinder, "It would be running the slavery argument into the ground to make it apply to every act of discrimination which a person may see fit to make . . . ."[43]

Here we see the Court worry that a sound legal argument is being abused, that something of the merit of the Thirteenth Amendment is so misused and overused that it is at risk of being destroyed. He invokes an image of slavery's reparation threatened with sabotage by virtue of the repetition of claims made in the name of it. In the law's effort to undo the damages of a society built on racial slavery by providing for a more expansive social equality—between white and black citizens and the essential civil rights they share, but also between the various kinds of rights (civil, political, social) recognized and enforced by the law—the cause of action defeats the spirit of the initial emendations. Thirteenth and Fourteenth Amendment legal remedies beget a fundamental legal degenerescence in antidiscrimination law. The "new constitutional right" Harlan spoke of decays the moment breath hits air.

This is where we encounter a critical knowledge contained in the opinion, cushioned as it is in a certain cruel performance of legal reasoning. Bradley moralizes:

> When a man has emerged from slavery, and, by the aid of beneficent legislation, has shaken off the inseparable concomitants of that state, there must be some stage in the progress of his elevation when he takes the rank of mere citizen and ceases to be the special favorite of the laws, and when his rights as a citizen or a man are to be protected in the ordinary modes by which other men's rights are protected.[44]

The decompositional right is a species of writing that emerges through and against a law so blinded by envy toward what Bradley calls the "special favorite" that it inverts the positions of slave and citizen.[45] And by this inversion, the cause and effect of civil rights is reversed. Instead of seeing the cause for the development of civil rights as the need to undo centuries of subordination and exclusion, legal envy perceives civil rights as the cause for an unruly black exceptionalism. It is true, as many critics of racial jurisprudence have pointed out, that the problem with colorblindness is that it positions the abstract negative civil freedom of the racial minority above the actual positive social freedom of white citizens. But I would add that the fantasy at the core of colorblindness circles around this legal envy blindly urging that civil rights causes black exceptionalism.

The crucial point in our arrival at the spiteful heart of the opinion is that this inversion and reversal is not rectifiable, or subject to injunction, any more than the private racist impulses hypothesized by Bradley can be justly contained by state criminal legal systems. Rectification or injunction would only further prove the truth of the imagined arrogance of the black claim to civil rights. Instead, the fantasmatic mechanism of inversion and reversal is the essential reason—the condition of possibility—for the legal structure of civil rights that judicial interpretations of the Thirteenth and Fourteenth Amendments institute. It is what propels the simultaneous building up and rolling back of civil rights law that, since *The Civil Rights Cases of 1883*, has produced not a slow legal progression toward equality, but an insistent rationalization that the mere exercise of black citizenship necessitates that civil rights be shorn from it.

This means that today, when we identify the inversion of racial inequality from white over black to black over white, we cannot simply try to set the record straight about who really dominates whom. It is clear from *The Civil Rights Cases of 1883* that, between the deracialization of "slavery" in the Thirteenth Amendment and the prohibition against the "denial of equal protection of the laws" in the Fourteenth Amendment, the imagined legal personality of black citizenship is always subject to dethronement.

Law that presents itself as both an objective and normative statement, like that presented in the *Civil Rights Cases of 1883* on universal democratic citizenship, embodies a wish for the future, and in that wish, admits an absence in the present reality. The argument that because blacks are citizens they should therefore possess no less—but more crucially, no more—than "those fundamental rights which appertain to the essence of citizenship,"[46] at once admits the absence of black citizenship in reality, and represses this absence through a boundless envy toward the figure of a free(d) slave. In this way, the case is not simply good fiction, but Tocqueville's *ficto figura veritatis* that continues to resonate in current racial jurisprudence.[47]

Here lies the most important point of this chapter: The fantasy of colorblindness represses the primal *jouissance* of envy behind the "mere citizen's" wish to deprive the "special favorite" black citizen of a freedom equal citizenship lacks. This *jouissance* drives legal writing and its pronouncements on "color-blind" civil rights, whatever the racial identity of the claimant might be. And thus, there was and can be no operative migration, in law or society, as Tocqueville observed, from the nonground of black social life to civic membership in a sovereign state, even if this nonpassage has been rearranged. By a complex maze of prohibitions, corrections, inversions, and reversals layered on top of this *jouissance* of envy, there would be no progressive time in which equality in black civil and social life could be legally recognized, let alone effectively protected. For the black citizen is fantasmatically endowed with too much freedom—so much freedom, in fact, that the purpose of antidiscrimination law is, Bradley argued, to ensure black freedom is always put in check. If the master needed the law to check slave fugitivity, then the citizen would need the law to check black freedom. As such, with the declaration of slavery's abolition, there was hardly a moment in which civil life for the emancipated slave could take hold.

The Decompositional Right of the Black Claim

The strange gift of emancipation comes from a form of citizenship experienced and adjudicated in law as a perpetually recanted offer, as an always-bungled recognition.[48] Who is this citizen whose claims are held with such contempt that she takes on the sneered-at image of the law's pet? A citizen whose imagined exceptionality elicits such envy, whose domination calls upon the law repeatedly to diminish her to something "mere," to an ordinary citizen; and thus, whose claim survives only as a "testamentary whimper"?[49]

I have read these questions of black citizenship through and beyond *Bakke*, to *Plessy*, to *The Civil Rights Cases of 1883*, and now, turn to *Scott*—however refracted this line of insight might be by the fantasy of colorblindness. This case considers whether Dred Scott, a black person who was born and held as a slave in Missouri, but had previously resided in a free state and territory for four years, could become a citizen within the meaning of the U.S. Constitution. Whether he had the capacity to become a citizen would determine whether he had standing to bring his civil claim of battery and false imprisonment against his owner in federal court based on diversity jurisdiction.[50] Chief Justice Taney, writing for the majority, finds that because Scott could not be a citizen within the meaning of the Constitution, the federal courts were unavailable to him.[51] In an opinion exceeding two hundred pages, Taney's ruling that black people—both bonded and free—do not have the capacity for citizenship, also ruled the Missouri Compromise unconstitutional.

Some have argued that this latter finding exceeded the legal question at issue in the case—that is, Scott's political status. However, upon a closer reading offered by Christopher Eisgruber, it becomes apparent that the question of Scott's capacity for citizenship and the legal future of the institution of slavery are intimately entangled.[52] According to Taney's reasoning about why Scott was not a citizen, slavery is as much a result of a political economic necessity to formally exclude blacks from citizenship, as it is a limit of political imagination regarding the capacities of the black claim to have standing, which is to say, to stand in as a sign of a legal subject. In other words, this opinion is not about what superficial or complex biographical criteria one must meet in order to be included in U.S. citizenship, but rather, whether blacks meet the threshold of the abstract legal subject, a threshold that precedes any given citizenship criteria designed to sort such abstracted persons according to various national or cultural affiliations.

In deciding Scott's political status, Taney's analysis falls along two lines of inquiry. First, he analyzes whether Scott could be a citizen if he were free. Second, Taney analyzes whether Scott could be a citizen if he were not free. Finding the Missouri Compromise unconstitutional falls within this second line of inquiry, wherein the constitutionality of the Compromise was a predicate for Scott's claim that he was free, having resided in Missouri, then a free territory under the Compromise.

Attention to both lines of inquiry is absolutely crucial for understanding the racial significance of this case. With respect to the first question, the Court finds that because citizenship is not synonymous with whether or not a person holds the rights of citizenship, the fact that Scott (and legally free black people within the jurisdiction of free states and territories) held and exercised a number of political and civil rights did not prove his fitness for inclusion in the nation. Segregation of blacks in free states is taken as a case in point.[53] Further, Taney contrasts Scott's hypothetical free status against that of white women and children, who are regarded by the law as citizens, or members of the nation, even though they do not possess political or civil rights.[54] Thus, racial exclusion from citizenship has less to do with whether or not one has rights but whether black people could be imagined as members of this political community, or, more precisely, whether they could be imagined to have the capacity to become members of any political community.[55]

With respect to the second question, the Court found that because a slave is an object to be owned, she is not a part of "the people" within the meaning of the Constitution, and therefore is not a citizen. Scott, hypothetically represented as chattel, occasions the priority of the Fifth Amendment Due Process Clause, which protects private and state interests in property, over and above any specific congressional enactment or general political intent to curb the expansion of the institution of slavery into the Western territories. Here, Taney overturns long-standing customary and doctrinal precedent on the power of the free states to protect the legal status of former slaves (escaped or manumitted), and the power of slave states to claim their property rights over slaves pursuant to the Fugitive Slave Clause. This reasoning—emphasizing the impossibility of incorporating an object of property within the meaning of "the people" for which the institution of citizenship stands—is perhaps the dominant image of *Scott* in popular and critical discourse, although it is certainly only a partial image of how Taney explains Scott's racial exclusion from citizenship.

We must take both lines of inquiry together because they complicate how the law actually negotiated the civilly dead status of free and enslaved blacks. It is not only because Scott was chattel that he was found to be incapable of citizenship. It is that Scott was both categorically without capacity for political belonging *and* chattel. Here a curious double negation emerges from the two analyses determining the relationship between blackness and citizenship in the case: if Scott were free, he could not be a citizen because rights in and of themselves did not signify a capacity to become a citizen; if Scott were not free, he could not be a citizen because he was an object of property.

This double negation is not simply a result of Taney's originalist interpretation of the Constitution, limiting citizenship to whomever the Framers intended to include at the time of drafting, and the Naturalization Act of 1790, limiting naturalization to "aliens being free white persons."[56] Rather, it is also the result of Taney's insistence on a form of political lack that remains unchanged by any customary or natural rights that might or might not attach in social practice to black life. As Taney asserts in his attempt to historically contextualize the legal matter, "They had for more than a century before been regarded as beings of an inferior order, and altogether unfit to associate with the white race, either in social or political relations; and so far inferior, *that they had no rights which the white man was bound to respect*; and that the negro might justly and lawfully be reduced to slavery for his benefit."[57]

Immediately we can hear a resonance here with Tocqueville's "imagined inequality." As well, Taney's assertion of the truth that "[the negro] had no rights which the white man was bound to respect" is also resonant with the social inequality that Harlan would protect from his efforts to enforce universal civil freedom, and that Bradley would acknowledge as the complicity between states' police power and private citizens. But we must also attend to the specificity of Taney's wording. It suggests that anything resembling rights that black people might possess were canceled out in their encounters with whites. Like the target of envy that must be constantly reduced in the *Civil Rights Cases of 1883*, Taney's specter of black citizenship is a figure whose legal standing promises a constant cancellation of civil rights. This legal relation of endless taking between black and white citizens paints a picture of civil death less as a movement of legal subjectivity from political participation to disenfranchisement, and more akin to the temporality of torture.

This description of the social scene of slavery contains at least two possible interpretations. On the one hand, there is the more obvious reading: that blacks do have rights, but none that whites must recognize. On the other hand, there is a less obvious reading: that there is a form of right before and undeterminable by citizenship. What are these rights that blacks are assumed to "have," *before they are stripped by whites, and then asserted against this stripping to be legally enforceable as civil, political, or social rights*? They must be rights that fantasmatically exist prior to and in excess of the taxonomy of civil, political, and social rights elaborated across *Scott*, the *Civil Rights Cases of 1883*, *Plessy*, *Bakke*, and *Grutter*. We might call them ante-rights, which have no other authority aside from the form of a claim that threatens the law's entire taxonomic order of civil, social, and political rights.

Subsequently, the black claim to civil rights must be understood with an emphasis on the claim, and a particular question about the nature of an unauthorized authority. The whole of the black claim to civil rights is not simply reducible to a desire for legal recognition or the statement of injury.[58] It incites the divisions among, and resonates across, civil, political, social, *and* ante-right rights. The decompositional right, then, is the ensemblic form of the claim that sweeps across and reconfigures any taxonomic reasoning for distributions or withholdings of civil rights. The decompositional right is the plural manifestation of that unknown right that would become the endlessly un-righted citizen.

Suffice it to say that *Scott*'s twinned rationales of blackness as the mark of objectified life and of un-righted civil life was neither addressed nor overturned by the Reconstruction Amendments—the Thirteenth abolishing forms of slavery and bondage; the Fourteenth granting citizenship and equal protection of the laws to all people born in the United States; and the Fifteenth granting the newly freedpersons the right to vote. In fact, *Scott* reveals a certain senselessness to the Reconstruction Amendments. If *Scott*, as the most explicit judicial statement on black citizenship, announced the impossibility of black citizenship because any claim to it could only be made in the form of a right whose function is to be taken away, a form that decomposes rights, then the Reconstruction Amendments, in formally conferring civil rights to the freedmen, only expanded the terrain of dispossession. They created new modes of recantation through formal delineations of civil rights and a form of noncitizenship I would call a "dispossessive citizenship," by which the citizen is recognized not by the conferral of rights, but by the revocation of rights.

A dispossessive citizen's claim does not invent new rights, but new decompositions of rights. *Scott* lays bare that what is at stake in the break between slavery and freedom is this revocative mode of citizenship, which is then cast variously across the historic *Civil Rights Cases of 1883* and its murderous envy; *Plessy* and its birth of the "color-blind" signifier as code for a permanent black social inequality; and today's affirmative action cases and their diversionary rationales of diversity. The fantasy of colorblindness that the decompositional right evokes requires the law to write against its founding liberal principles of civil rights, at the same time that by this writing the law's language slips in and into the form of a runaway claim that belongs neither to the claimant nor the judge, but to the essential temporal difficulty of the black claim—the only place where we can begin to read civil rights again, and anew.

CHAPTER TWO

Colorblind Judgment

In reality, we know nothing,
since truth is in the abyss.
—Democritus (460–400 B.C.)

While the previous chapter explored the canonical Supreme Court opinions on black citizenship for the affective structure of the fantasy of colorblindness, my interest in this chapter is to explore the fantasy of colorblindness through the formal structure of the judicial opinion on racial discrimination. The judicial opinion is the primary written text in which the fantasy of colorblindness surfaces and, simultaneously, recedes as rhetorical embellishment or ideological obfuscation of the reality of enduring racial inequality. The judicial opinion is a representation of a position within law on a social conflict. But the judicial opinion is also a formal act, meaning that this representation within law is simultaneously the creation of law according to formalized protocols of legal reasoning. The judicial opinion is always both judgment and rule, and this coeval vocation provides another entry point into deconstructing the fantasy of colorblindness.

Legal judgment takes the form that many know today as the "strict scrutiny" level of judicial review applied to racial discrimination claims brought by individuals or classes against state agencies. As we will see in this chapter, this form of judgment is not without its own unresolvable ethical questions about whether something like racial justice is deliverable by the "distributive" logic of modern legal reason.[1] Under what conditions might such judgment be just? Can the law issue a judgment in favor of racial equality given its formal, psychical aggression toward the black claim to civil rights? If the black claim to civil rights does not elicit the law's recognition of a nominal or potential citizen but instead recursively unravels the chance for such recognition, then how are we to understand legal judgment?

The modern legal reason assumes an idea of judgment that generally separates rule and rhetoric when applying doctrine to legal conflicts. And although this line of separation is admittedly amorphous and subject to interpretation, one of the specific purposes of legal judgment through judicial review is to be able to make authoritative distinctions between rule and "dicta." Legal judgment as an objective and neutral procedure of evaluating legal conflicts—even, or especially, in the context of resolving racial antagonisms—engenders the fantasy of colorblindness as a formal defensive mechanism extending the transcendental promise of racial equality. But how does this defensive formalism work? And against what does it defend? To begin answering these questions, I now turn from the prior chapter's focus on the racial *jouissance* of civil rights to the primary defensive structure of legal reason in the face of this perverse affective core by taking a closer look at the language of strict scrutiny doctrine.

The Deathly Language of Judicial Review

The U.S. Supreme Court's ruling in *Adarand Constructors, Inc., v. Pena* (1995) is a watershed moment in antidiscrimination law. Where there had previously been some deference given to federal affirmative action policies using "benign" racial classifications,[2] *Adarand* formalized colorblind judicial review as a general approach in racial jurisprudence by ruling that all federal affirmative action policies would now be subject to "strict scrutiny." As the most demanding of judicial review, in brief, strict scrutiny doctrine holds that if the state has a compelling objective for racially discriminatory action, and the action taken is narrowly tailored to achieve that objective, then it is not based on racial animus and is thus constitutional. *Adarand*'s universalization of strict scrutiny would require proponents of affirmative action to produce airtight justifications for the use of racial classifications. Needless to say, the effect of such judicial cynicism toward affirmative action stoked the fire of "reverse-discrimination" claims brought by white plaintiffs against local and national affirmative action policies.

Adarand's universalization of colorblind judgment presumes equality between individual claimants of racial discrimination, irrespective of historical, social, or racial position. It also presumes equality between all types of laws regulating racial difference. *Adarand*'s colorblindness allows no judicial distinction between a reverse-discrimination claim brought by a white plaintiff, as many have critically discussed, and a disparate-impact discrimination claim brought by a minority plaintiff. Further, it does not allow any judicial distinction between a remedial policy or a bigoted policy. The fantasy of colorblindness formalized in *Adarand* takes shape in the universalization of strict judicial review. This colorblind judgment assumes not only the liberal principle that "all men are created equal," but that all race-based laws are, too.

The fantasy of colorblindness, in its formal procedure of judgment, demands that the law treat racially different individuals the same, and that laws regulating racial difference receive the same level of review. Interestingly, perhaps uneasy about this illiberal universalism informing *Adarand*'s drive toward colorblindness, Justice O'Connor added curious dicta that contain a fascinating defense of strict scrutiny doctrine. Addressing proponents of affirmative action who worried that this extension of constitutional law's most stringent level of review would effectively mean that all affirmative action policies would be ruled unconstitutional, O'Connor added a "wish to dispel the notion that strict scrutiny is 'strict in theory, but fatal in fact.'"[3] Taken for its ruling and this rhetorical flourish, then, *Adarand* reveals the universalist drive of strict scrutiny and a curious desire that judicial review would not in fact do what had been, in reality, already well underway since the *Civil Rights Cases of 1883* (as we saw in the previous chapter).

Far from exuding confidence and resolve in colorblindness, this wish that haunts strict scrutiny actually marks the law with a profound anxiety through such fatalistic language. The wish in *Adarand* instantiates a deathly dimension in racial jurisprudence. This is evidenced by the jurisprudence's failure to provide for effective civil rights, or what Ruth Wilson Gilmore would call a failure to protect against "premature death."[4] But it is also evidenced by an anxiety accompanying the judicial language that extends strict scrutiny doctrine to all laws using racial categories. How does this fatalism unfold in law as it strives toward colorblind judgment? What kind of deaths are imagined, feared, protected against, mourned? And for what kinds of lives and futures are the broken promises of colorblind judgment renewed?

O'Connor's unconvincing insistence of a future for affirmative action and for race-based remedial laws more generally provides an entry point into a deeper interrogation of the psychical structure of the fantasy of colorblindness. Her wish encapsulates what we might take as the post–civil rights maxim par excellence, wherein the belief that strict scrutiny is not "strict in theory, but fatal in fact" is an admission along the line of a psychosocial symptom.[5] And it is this admission at the heart of *Adarand* that reveals the entanglement in racial jurisprudence of the fantasy of colorblindness with the specter of some sort of ruinous return of, as we will see in the next section, what is referred to as the "abyss" of racism. Read through the looking glass of *Adarand,* strict scrutiny doctrine and dicta trace a law forever circling, whether anxiously or resolutely, in a vortex of failed civil rights revolutions of the nineteenth and twentieth centuries.

Let us now turn to *Korematsu v. U.S.* (1944),[6] the case in which the Supreme Court affirms formally for the first time the strict judicial review of racially discriminatory policy. Here we find how the deathly language of strict scrutiny that flowers in *Adarand* is initially sowed in racial jurisprudence.

The Ugly Abyss of Racism

In 1984, the Supreme Court affirmed Fred Korematsu's writ of *coram nobis*, which set aside his original criminal conviction at issue in the famous 1944 *Korematsu* case. In 1942, Korematsu was found guilty of violating a local law excluding people of "Japanese ancestry" from remaining in particular areas of the West Coast, including his city of residence, San Leandro, California.[7] Some forty years after the internment of Japanese American citizens, the Supreme Court ruled that Korematsu's conviction was based on a grave and unconstitutional deprivation of due process. Here is how the Court reflected on the meaning of Korematsu's 1942 conviction, which it ultimately retracted:

> *Korematsu* remains on the pages of our legal and political history. As a legal precedent it is now recognized as having very limited application. As historical precedent it stands as a constant caution that in times of war or declared military necessity our institutions must be vigilant in protecting constitutional guarantees. It stands as a caution that in times of distress the shield of military necessity and national security must not be used to protect governmental actions from close scrutiny and accountability. It stands as a caution that in times of international hostility and antagonisms our institutions, legislative, executive and judicial, must be prepared to exercise their authority to protect all citizens from the petty fears and prejudices that are so easily aroused.[8]

The Court's memory of *Korematsu* here is striking. It is focused on the lesson *Korematsu* taught the nation: that no amount of military necessity and international hostility should lead the nation astray in protecting its citizens.

Yet, in its articulation of this lesson, the historical event *Korematsu* will forever stand for is couched in two disavowals: first, that the legal precedent produced by internment has limited application despite its permanent mark on legal history; and second, that the "petty fears and prejudices that are so easily aroused" against minority groups during times of international and national emergencies are not shared by and do not emanate from the government and its various institutions, which are presumed instead to "protect all citizens." While admitting in the 1984 opinion that Fred Korematsu's conviction was the result of a severe miscarriage of justice—that the government violated his right to due process—the Court simultaneously retracts this admission by denying that the law is racist. The way that the Court's memory betrays its judgment and displays a profound ambivalence with respect to the law's racist past raises the question of what terrible truth this ambivalence negotiates. This question is especially pressing given the fact that *Korematsu* has had far-reaching applicability in civil rights law by setting "strict scrutiny" as the standard of review for race-based state action.

The fact that this standard originates in the 1944 *Korematsu* case is no simple matter.[9] There, the Supreme Court used a strict scrutiny framework to find that policies interning Japanese Americans were constitutional. It explained that the U.S.'s war with Japan was a compelling reason for removing Japanese Americans to internment camps, and that the way in which the government pursued this interest was narrowly tailored so as to rule out the possibility that the policy had racist motivations. Since then, when the Court is faced with circumstances in which government policies explicitly use racial categories, and this type of state action deprives a racial group of its civil rights, the Court will review the policy with "strict scrutiny" to determine its constitutionality. The government must show that its policy is justified by a "pressing public necessity,"[10] or "compelling state interest,"[11] in contemporary language, and that the action is "commensurate with the threatened danger,"[12] or "narrowly tailored."[13] If these two conditions are shown, then the Court will find that the race-based government action is not motivated by "racial antagonism,"[14] or, as expressed another way later in the opinion, by "racial prejudice."[15] In Justice Black's words:

> It should be noted, to begin with, that all legal restrictions which curtail the civil rights of a single racial group are immediately suspect. That is not to say that all such restrictions are unconstitutional. It is to say that courts must subject them to the most rigid scrutiny. Pressing public necessity may sometimes justify the existence of such restrictions; racial antagonism never can.[16]

Korematsu remains authoritative in two divergent fields of constitutional law. The first is Fourteenth Amendment antidiscrimination jurisprudence, commonly known as "civil rights law," which concerns race-based state action and inequality. The second is executive wartime jurisprudence, commonly known as "national security law," which concerns the regulation of executive power during times of emergency. The first branch of *Korematsu*'s legacy, which establishes the constitutional foundation for prohibiting race-based state action through the doctrine of strict scrutiny, has been deformed to the extent that the rule has provided little or no relief for racial minorities. This was precisely the anxiety we saw emerge in *Adarand*. The second branch of *Korematsu*'s legacy, however, which defers the constitutional protection of American civil liberties to the constitutional mandate for executive action to protect the nation, is a mainstay of authority for various legal reforms made during times of war, including the present moment. This bifurcated doctrinal afterlife of *Korematsu* sets the law's treatment of race and nation down two separate doctrinal paths.[17]

Yet, this split is unfaithful to the relationship that the text of the opinion establishes between race and nation. Reading the opinion closely, race and nation in the Court's strict scrutiny analysis are, in fact, so entangled that it seems an interpretive wrong to carve up *Korematsu*'s doctrinal legacy as such. How does the either/or relationship that *Korematsu*'s split doctrinal legacy presents—between the problem of securing the nation against a foreign threat and the problem of prohibiting discrimination among a nation's racially diverse citizens—compare with the way the two are related in the rhetoric of the case? Where and how do we locate what is "compelling"—the work of compulsion within and/or beyond the nation—in the structure of justification that *Korematsu* sets for the development of contemporary civil rights law? If national defense—during wartime, and a World War at that—would set the bar for what would constitute a good governmental reason for using racial classifications, one wonders how any other interest would compare.

Nonetheless, strict scrutiny in *Korematsu* holds out the possibility for balance between the defensive excesses of sovereign power and the subjection of racial minorities under the *nomos* of the nation. Jed Rubenfeld argues that this "cost-benefit" approach to strict scrutiny is historically and logically incoherent, and "becomes a kind of logical monstrosity, a snake consumed by its own jaws."[18] It is as if national security and racial equality are set on opposite sides of the scale of justice, forever teetering and off balance, and the only way that the law can deal with this imbalance is to engage in an always inaccurate game of addition and subtraction to come up with an explanation for why the scale inevitably tips in favor of national security.

Discontent toward *Korematsu*, for the most part, only takes issue with explanations of this imbalance. For some, *Korematsu* stands for the adjudication of apparently contradictory constitutional values. The suspension of the civil rights of a racial minority in the interest of providing for a more expansive national interest is seen either as a reluctant necessity or a eugenicist duty. On this reading, whether opinion sways toward a condemnation of targeting American citizens based on racial identity without due process, or a total defense of expansive executive powers that mobilize racial classifications during national emergencies, there is an agreement that an essential conflict between protection of the nation and protection of racial minorities exists, and that the law can and should find a just way to negotiate this tension. The promise of balancing is not critiqued for its inability to be fulfilled.

For others, the problem of racial discrimination in *Korematsu* is subsumed under a prevailing and more fundamental legal tension between the civil rights of citizens and the executive powers of the nation representing those citizens.[19] Race, here, is understood as a contingency of an absolutely given national sovereignty. This suggests that *Korematsu* is more about conflict between nations, and less about conflict between races; that internment is more about the violence of war between nations than it is about the violence of peace between intranational racial groups. Here, the terms of the balancing are at issue, but nonetheless, balancing itself remains viable.

In reading the 1944 case's language carefully, however, we can see that balancing is decidedly beside the point. In conversation with Black, writing for the majority, a dissenting Justice Murphy asserts, "No reasonable relation to an 'immediate, imminent, and impending' public danger is evident to support this racial restriction."[20] In other words, there is no evidence showing a "pressing public necessity" that would "support," or balance out the race-based government action. The conversation between the two justices regarding the law is rather simple, and their two opinions regarding the persuasiveness of the evidence remains their most significant point of departure. They agree that there can be a balancing between race and nation. Murphy's disagreement with Black here is not about which level of judicial scrutiny should be applied in this case, or about the effectiveness of strict scrutiny in regulating racial discrimination, but about whether the facts support the majority's finding of justification that a strict scrutiny analysis is supposed to provide.

Let us also note that just as the two justices are in agreement that the interests of race and nation can be balanced, they share a similar theory of race. Although Murphy provides a more detailed framework for analyzing whether a group's racial characteristics have some "demonstrable relationship" to a particular "dangerous trait," Murphy's theory of race is, like Black's, based on a notion of race as ancestry and descent. Both Murphy and Black use the language of blood to describe Japanese Americans as a racial group, diverging only in their theories about what implication this has for determining that group's capacity to be loyal to the nation. Murphy states, "All residents of this nation are kin in some way by *blood* or culture to a foreign land,"[21] even as he goes on to reject internment advocates' "charge[s] relative to race, religion, culture, geographical location, and legal and economic status."[22] The point here is that whether or not Murphy is convinced of actual disloyalty among Japanese Americans, he is still concerned about and grants racial difference, both biological and cultural.

Most important for our examination of strict scrutiny, the two justices also share a theory of justification for race-based state action. Strict scrutiny as a mode of legal analysis designed to ensure that racial discrimination is adequately justified goes unquestioned by the dissenting voice. By centralizing judicial inquiry around the issue of justification, strict scrutiny preempts the question of whether racial discrimination can be justified in the first place.[23] Strict scrutiny's promise to justify, and the subterfuge of explanation (and critiques of those explanations) the promise sets in motion, diverts our attention from a more plainly obvious flaw in the doctrine. The problem is not that the law can only recognize two facets of identity that exist simultaneously in individuals, or that it privileges remediation only for national injury, and not racial injury. Rather, it is the conditional relationship the law poses between nation and race: if one, then not the other. The conditional logic established by strict scrutiny in *Korematsu* assumes that if there is a national interest that is served by a racially discriminatory policy, then we can be sure that such policy is not motivated by racial animus.

This conditional logic of strict scrutiny is not an either/or logic, or an exclusive disjunction. In adjudications of the constitutionality of race-based deprivations of civil rights, the conditional logic makes the denial of racism dependent on the affirmation of a national interest, but not the reverse (in which case it would then be a proper exclusive disjunctive). In other words, the strict scrutiny logic says that a positive finding of a need for national defense negates the presence of racial animus. However, it does not say that a positive finding of racial animus negates a finding for national defense. Strict scrutiny, as a matter of its logical structure, is more worried about nation than race.

If strict scrutiny as articulated in *Korematsu* did in fact establish an exclusive disjunctive relationship between nation and race, it perhaps makes sense to argue that *both* national exclusivity and racial animus worked together to produce the legal outcome of *Korematsu*. This is the premise of the concept of "racial foreignness" developed within critical race theory. Racial foreignness describes particular forms of racialization, including Japanese American internment, in the historical context of Asian immigrant exclusion from the *polis* and culture of the nation.[24] Policies prohibiting immigration from Asian countries, the marginalization of Asian American communities from equal participation in the economy, and the social representation of Asian cultures as outside or counter to Western values all have typically been historicized as a form of racial foreignness.

Notwithstanding this average definition of racial foreignness, what is crucial to take away from *Korematsu* is that the concept of racial foreignness does not entirely reach the most vexing aspect of the opinion. This obtains in the more fundamental function of the conditional logic of strict scrutiny established in the opinion's text and what its legacy allows us to understand about the hydraulics of race and the whole of antidiscrimination law in the United States.[25] More true to the text of *Korematsu* is the fact that the conditional logic of strict scrutiny establishes national defensiveness as a type of legal reason I would call colorblind judgment (to be distinguished from what many call xenophobia). As long as the state can plead a universalizable reason and efficient plan of administration, according to the conditional logic, legal judgment remains faithful to the principle of colorblindness. If colorblindness is the judicial ideal, strict scrutiny is its mechanism.

We arrive, then, at a more difficult legal issue that critical race theory has yet to address. If the law can, at best, only approximate a balanced relationship between state action that protects itself during times of national emergency and state action that protects its racial minorities from racism, then why did *Korematsu* pose this particular *conditional* relationship between the two? Why this conditional—if-one-then-not-the-other—logic that presumes that if racism is rational, justifiable, and calculated (thus constitutional), then it is not naked, compulsory, and emotive (thus unconstitutional)? What do we make of this overconfidence in the law, which insists that emergency obviates animus, that need eliminates passion, that justification negates compulsion?

These are not simply theoretical questions. They are questions about how we might more fully understand the force of legal reason that, left unanswered, leads to all sorts of inconsistencies in conceptualizing the relationship between race and nation in law. For example, Black accepts the idea that placing a selective burden on some for the good of the nation is justified by conditions of warfare, at the same time that he elides the logic's presumptive correlation of race and national threat—or discrimination against Americans based on race—by referring to Japanese Americans as "a large group of American citizens."

> [We] are not unmindful of the hardships imposed . . . upon a large group of American citizens. But hardships are part of war, and war is an aggregation of hardships. All citizens alike, both in and out of uniform, feel the impact of war in greater or lesser measure. Citizenship has its responsibilities as well as its privileges, and in time of war the burden is always heavier. Compulsory exclusion of large groups of citizens from their homes, except under circumstances of direst emergency and peril, is inconsistent with our basic governmental institutions. But when under conditions of modern warfare our shores are threatened by hostile forces, the power to protect must be commensurate with the threatened danger.[26]

At another point in the opinion, Black invokes the context of warfare to justify internment and defend the policy against the racial charge that it is a form of concentration camp. First, he disagrees that internment camps are concentration camps, a correlation he finds, apparently, unjustified.

> It is said that we are dealing here with the case of imprisonment of a citizen in a concentration camp solely because of his ancestry, without evidence or inquiry concerning his loyalty and good disposition towards the United States. Our task would be simple, our duty clear, were this a case involving the imprisonment of a loyal citizen in a concentration camp because of racial prejudice. Regardless of the true nature of the assembly and relocation centers—and we deem it unjustifiable to call them concentration camps with all the ugly connotations that term implies—we are dealing specifically with nothing but an exclusion order.[27]

Black then immediately disagrees that only race was at work, and instead claims that both race and nation were used to provide a justifiable explanation for imprisoning Japanese Americans, by referring to them as "citizens of Japanese ancestry."

> To cast this case into outlines of racial prejudice, without reference to the real military dangers which were presented, merely confuses the issue. Korematsu was not excluded from the Military Area because of hostility to him or his race. He *was* excluded because we are at war with the Japanese Empire, because the properly constituted military authorities feared an invasion of our West Coast and felt constrained to take proper security measures, because they decided that the military urgency of the situation demanded that all citizens of Japanese ancestry be segregated from the West Coast temporarily.[28]

I quote these passages at length so that we can better see how the presumption that racial discrimination can be justified inconsistently treats Japanese Americans as either categorically American citizens or a racial type within the category of American citizen. Because strict scrutiny grants that race can be subsumed under nation, it obscures this presumption. The obscurity of this presumption is troubling because the correlation between race and nation—"all citizens of Japanese ancestry"—remains unsubstantiated, arbitrary, and wholly illogical with respect to its difference from the racial "prejudice" and "hostility" that Black so adamantly denounces. The only difference, as Black would have it, seems to be that state action premised on race and nation is justifiable, and state action premised solely on race is not. He tellingly concludes his opinion with an attempt to protect the doctrine of strict scrutiny and its presumption by rejecting the use of context to reevaluate the Supreme Court's affirmation of internment: "We cannot—by availing ourselves of the calm perspective of hindsight—now say that at that time these actions were unjustified."[29]

My point is that the quibbling language between the majority and dissent is a series of misrecognized samenesses as differences. Yet the defensive tenor of the quibble should not escape our analysis. Murphy amplifies this tenor when he registers his uneasiness (not unlike O'Connor's in *Adarand*), and ominously warns that internment "falls into the ugly abyss of racism."[30] I am interested in this emphatic point, as opposed to his points of disagreement. Murphy's emphasis captures a notion of racism that strict scrutiny analysis leaves behind, and by extension, that colorblind judgment and universal legal reason also leave behind. This racism is evil, void, and immeasurable; unsightly, troubling, and embarrassing. One can think of no better realization in legal discourse of Derrida's meditation on the "force of law" where, in a crystalline moment of his famous article, he describes the mystical violence of law as "the moment in which the foundation of law remains suspended in the void or over the abyss, suspended by a pure performative act that would not have to answer to or before anyone."[31]

Korematsu, disabused of the history of its ethnic context, reveals then the logically unassimilable kernel of the racial discrimination claim in legal discourse, an internal limit to the hypothetical proposition a strict scrutiny analysis imposes on the letter of the law. As much as strict scrutiny and its development since *Korematsu* has attempted to make justificatory analysis more exacting and thorough, the unjustifiable is still present in its logic because absent evidence, or when the evidence simply fails to persuade, strict scrutiny unwittingly affirms the default: "the ugly abyss of racism."[32] Incapable of being offset by any context of foreign or national crisis, racism is that which persists when justification falters—when words fail and remain.

In the Cave of Colorblind Judgment

The racial abyss that opens up in *Korematsu* stirs feelings of insecurity about an unshakable racial animus in American legal history that exceeds the case's lessons on civil rights, citizenship, and war. And while these terms circulate now with a certain urgent novelty for political theory, they are a basic but insufficient part of how the law imagines the possibilities and limits of life in a multiracial society. Especially given the international community's refortifications against terrorism with its transnational declarations of "indefinite war," by returning to *Korematsu* for the racial abyss contained there, the doctrine of strict scrutiny glosses a general constellation of formal and informal rules of war that cannot completely resolve the aporia of race contained therein.

The case has international resonance precisely because of *Korematsu*'s omen of the ruinous return of racial animus, shrouded by the legal rationality of a form of judicial review that is preoccupied with national security. We should note that the abyssal in *Korematsu* is marked only to be denied when Black adamantly rejects Murphy's description of the Japanese American interment camp as a concentration camp. With this elision, Japanese American internment resonates on a global scene because it is debated as one of many forms of ethnic terror World War II infamously innovated and mobilized (namely, the Holocaust and the nuclear attacks on Japan).[33]

But *Korematsu*'s survival in antidiscrimination law through the doctrine of strict judicial review exceeds the history of global ethnic conflict that postwar human and civil rights regimes emerged from. *Korematsu*'s racial significance, drawn from my reading of its conditional logic of strict scrutiny, is the enduring problem of an as-yet unjustified priority of national sovereignty over claims to racial equality, and especially the black claim to civil rights discussed in the previous chapter. A closer examination of colorblind judgment established in *Korematsu* insists on a fuller understanding of what legal reason defends itself against. I have isolated and discussed this as what Murphy described as the "ugly abyss of racism," which I want now to recast as that against which an inclusive national sovereignty is constituted as defensible.

We might start with "inclusion" as the central logical problem revealed in *Korematsu*'s internal debate about the proper standard of judicial review of racial animus. But we must remember that "inclusion" has two senses. The first, which is the most commonly referred to in political discourse, is the act of taking in as part of a whole. Today we are rightly suspicious of the inclusions that attend politics of recognition, and the many forms of debt and exclusions that inevitably follow. More radical political thought today queries the paradox of democratic inclusion and exclusion in formulating human and civil rights campaigns.[34]

The second sense of "inclusion," however, and the one I would like to develop in our understanding of the abyssal in legal reason, derives more directly from the Latin, *inclūdĕre*, meaning "to shut in" or "enclose." "Inclusion" in this sense, most commonly referred to in scientific discourse, and most often used as a noun, is an effect predicated on confining or containing limits or space. This latter form of predication reveals a geometric sense of inclusion, as in an "included angle" that is created when two lines meet a common point. In other words, in geometry, the angle "∠ABC" can also be referred to as the "included angle of BA and BC." Translated into my prior discussion of the logic of strict scrutiny in *Korematsu*, we can think of the abyss as the included space created when the two orders of judicial review—blackletter law and dicta—meet at the common point of legal judgment.

In other words, the problem of inclusion that surfaces in the language of *Korematsu*'s decision is twofold. The first is a mereological problem of national division and aggregation: Who is a citizen? Who is an enemy? And when can racial identity be used by the state to divide and aggregate citizens and enemies? This problem is widely rehearsed in critical analyses of *Korematsu*, without satisfying resolution. And the second is a topological problem of spatial reference that is simultaneously a point of convergence and an opening of space: When legal reason and evidence meet, can the resulting legal judgment arrive at a truth about racial difference and the law? We can think of various ordinary versions of the angle, like a corner of a room, the projection of sight, or natural or artistic sculptures formed by movements of and against surfaces.

The shape of a cave as a type of inclusion comes to mind as a way to conceive of the remainder of judicial review that Murphy described as the "ugly abyss of racism." The cave offers one possible site where contemporary U.S. antidiscrimination law and political theory resonate in an imaginary space shrouded in a kind of blindness. That is, we might note an uncanny resemblance, in the philosophical problematic of a cavernous space of rational thought, between the judicial opinion on judicial review and Plato's cave in his *Republic.* Indeed, in Robert Cover's famous realist critique of legal interpretation, his scrutiny of the judge and his particular "dealings" of "political text in institutional modes of action"[35] calls to mind the secret space of the judge's chambers, and extends the uncanny resemblance of the abyss to the Platonic cave of political philosophy into a series of echo chambers in modern law.

Derrida's meditation on blindness and philosophical thought in *Memoirs of the Blind*, recalls that philosophic knowledge and judgment, staged as variations of "the Platonic speleology," is concerned from the outset with "all possible blindnesses."[36] The story of the prisoners' conversion from a dark nonknowledge, or what Derrida develops as "opinion,"[37] to a philosophic enlightenment is less a movement from blindness to sight than a story about the "*anamnesis* of blindings, so many dazzlements *en abyme*" that attend both the descent into and ascent from the cave. Plato's prisoners-cum-philosophers never "stretch out their hands towards the shadow (*skia*) or the light (*phôs*), towards the silhouettes or images that are drawn on the wall. . . . They converse, they speak of memory. Plato imagines them seated, chained, able to address one another, to 'dialectize,' to lose themselves in the echoing of voices."[38] The cave for Derrida marks the intimacy of blindness and echoing, darkness and sonic movement, nonknowledge and vernacular address.

We might extend Derrida's reading of the image of a cave of prephilosophic blindnesses to elaborate more fully on strict scrutiny doctrine in antidiscrimination law. The racial abyss carved into strict scrutiny jurisprudence enduringly marks a blindness that is essential to rational legal judgment. But the law does not emerge from this blindness through the deliberative sight of calculation and balancing. Rather, the law we only partially recognize as colorblind judgment continuously dwells in this collective echoic knowledge wedged between rule and dicta. We might say that whatever such a loss in the "echoing of voices" sounds like in the cave of colorblind judgment, it is a poetics of the plea that colorblind judgment at once includes within itself and defends itself against. What I have been developing as "colorblind judgment" is, then, precisely this *mise-en-abyme* of blindnesses between, on the one hand, the law's logocentric form of judicial review, and on the other, an entrapped plural echo of aural address.[39]

So even though the judicial opinion is not conscious of the fact that it imagines the people of its docket as characters in the mythical story of a nation birthed by the letter of the Constitution, it is nonetheless charged with the duty of judging whether the multiplicity of legal enactments addressing this docket of possible claimants abides by the universal mandate of the Constitution. Further, charged with interpreting multiple and conflicting forms of executive and legislative laws, even as they disavow the political force of doctrinal hermeneutics, judges must wait for the abyss of race to appear to begin their interpretive work (this is called, in constitutional law, justiciability, which is the doctrinal backdrop for the next chapter). And thus, at least in American antidiscrimination law, because racial subjection persists through a *network* of formal state enactments and omissions of this abyss, the judicial opinion literally provides a surface on which we can begin to more fully understand a type of echoic life, or a returning life in the plea, precisely because of the law's desire for universal colorblind judgment.

That is, upon closer reading of the judicial opinion, the unjustifiability of racial subjection bored down into the doctrine is a cavernous space that predicates the law's commitments to create and balance distinctions between justice and injustice, humanity and inhumanity, morality and immorality. Racial discrimination, as that which cannot be justified, forces us, then, to consider how the claim of racial discrimination, as a lost cause, or as a futile form of litigation—to recall O'Connor's dictum in *Adarand*—nonetheless rings with pleadings of an entirely different order of judgment and opinion. By giving the abyss the topological conception of the cave, we can visualize the black claim's mode of survival in an echo chamber constituted by the letter of the law. The black claim must not be thought of as simply the formalization of a demand for freedom by colorblind judgment. The precise form that this formalization takes is key, and it inheres in a splitting of the black claim between a formal legal plea destined to lose its case and a poetics of the plea that always succeeds in returning a desire for freedom by virtue of this concave surface of the judicial opinion. The black claim here is both the foreclosed formal interpretation of pleading and the successive resonance of the plea.

Now we must ask how to conceive of the precise relation between the poetics of the plea and judicial rationality in the face of racial discrimination claims. Is it simply a relation of one against the other, with the poetics of the plea destined to lose against the merciless elaboration of strict scrutiny? In antidiscrimination law, are we witnessing a scene of dialectical war between the law's desire for universal colorblind judgment and the black claim's desire for freedom? Is this the final dismal Hegelian truth of the judicial opinion (on judicial review of state racisms) that Murphy and O'Connor anxiously admit in their defensive rhetoric? Or can we find a way to allow this cavernous space in law, the only place within the judicial opinion where the poetics of the plea dwells, stand for itself? I take up these questions through Sophocles' play, *Antigone*, which has long represented the archetypal figure of ethical objection in the development of modern law and culture.[40]

Echoes in the Abyss

Antigone allows us to think in a more nuanced way through the various forms of living death the law produces. This is because of what I take to be Jacques Lacan's implicit theory of counter-biopolitics, which Joan Copjec reads in her chapter "The Tomb of Perseverance: On *Antigone*," in *Imagine There's No Woman.* My interpretation brings a Lacanian reading of *Antigone*, and the specific form of sublimation her position offers, to bear on a new approach to the judicial opinion. In elaborating this new approach, I wish to resist subsuming the judicial opinion into a general political instrumentalism of law that many now descriptively refer to as "the juridical." A Lacanian reading of *Antigone* also promises the possibility of allowing the abyss to stand for itself, or to put it another way, to avow the foreclosed desire for freedom as a fundamental structure of the law.

In his Seminar VII (1959–60), *The Ethics of Psychoanalysis*, Lacan describes Antigone as "the advent of the absolute individual."[41] Prohibited by Creon from burying her brother, and threatened not simply with death but with a sentence to suffer, Antigone is said to embody the peculiar existence of this absolute individual. The tragic hero Antigone embodies is fearless and pitiless—one who relates to sovereign law through both a fierce love and hate.[42] The tragic hero is subjected to "the situation or fate of a life that is about to turn into certain death, a death lived by anticipation, a death that crosses over into the sphere of life, a life that moves into the realm of death."[43]

This is what Lacan calls a "second death," denoting Antigone's crossing over into the realm of *Até*, a sphere beyond the realm of the human.[44] At this moment, she is likened to a bird and a lonely mother, both of whose cries and moans over lost children signify the metamorphosis of the human into something beyond.[45] Lacan's reading here is striking. The "fascinating image of Antigone herself,"[46] "Antigone in her unbearable splendor,"[47] for Lacan is manifested in the *sound* of this second death at the limit of modern sovereign power, municipal regulation, and moral good. Lacan is interested in how the passion of Antigone's bond to her dead brother and how her knowledge and disobedience of the law persist aurally through the retribution, doubt, rationalization, and prayers of the political community and family that surround her.

Antigone, then, embodies a kind of limit criminality that cannot be assimilated into the biopolitical regulation of life through historically contingent norms and their exceptions. Copjec, in her turn, asks not whether such unassimilability exists, but rather, what kind of structure supports it? What kind of limit does *Antigone* represent? The answer lays in Copjec's careful clarification of the psychoanalytic concept of sublimation, wrested away from the "commonplace misconception . . . that it substitutes a more socially respectable or refined pleasure for a cruder, carnal one."[48] She warns that we mistake the significance of *Antigone* for a tragic representation of a conscientious refusal to compromise the personal for the political. But then what would we need to grasp about sublimation, or what Lacan referred to as a "second death," in order to properly understand *Antigone*?

Copjec argues that the proper idea of sublimation inheres in its relationship to the "full paradox of the death drive."[49] She explains it in this way:

> [W]hile the *aim* (*Ziel*) of the drive is death, the *proper and positive activity* of the drive is to inhibit the attainment of its aim; the drive, *as such*, is *zielgehemmt*, that is, it is inhibited as to its aim, or sublimated, "the satisfaction of the drive through the inhibition of its aim" being the very definition of sublimation. Contrary to the vulgar understanding of it, then, sublimation is not something that happens to the drive under special circumstances; it is the proper destiny of the drive.[50]

Sublimation, we might say, is the practice of the death drive as an internal law of inhibition, and not the effect or symptom of some repressive social law, whether given by formal, informal, or personal sovereign authority. In other words, the desire expressed by sublimation in Copjec's precise sense marks a submission to another kind of law that is radically other to a set of social outcomes enforced by democratic rule, cultural custom, and personal morality. With this idea of sublimation we see an essential limit that is precisely not there; it is not to be enforced and transgressed, but, instead, to come into being, to allow the appearance of desire as object *a.* Copjec stresses this point, which Lacan already made in reference to the death drive as "creationist sublimation."[51] Commitment to, or more precisely, what Copjec develops as "perseverance" through, this other order of law is exactly what cannot be avowed as Antigone, the "terrible, self-willed victim."[52]

Let us now bring the Lacanian reading of *Antigone* back full circle to *Adarand*'s assertion that strict scrutiny is not "strict in theory, but fatal in fact."[53] On one level, it is not generally true that strict scrutiny is not "strict in theory." The doctrine's strictness comes from a perceived necessity to limit the demands of legal reason and the interpretive capacities of the letter of the law through formal judicial procedure. It also is not generally true that strict scrutiny is not "fatal in fact." The doctrine "in fact" destroys individual lives, civil rights claims, and more equitable distributions of resources that successful antidiscrimination litigation promises.

But on another level, *Adarand*'s dicta is generally true. To the extent that strict scrutiny doctrine is a defensive admission of an essential internal limit, it reflects in legal language in the precise psychoanalytic sense of an empty space that supports "creationist sublimation." The judicial opinion on judicial review of state racisms bears a certain unconditional perseverance in the black claim that takes place in a social world gratified by the dethroning of this claim through its legal recognition. Psychoanalytically, the black claim is impossible in and prohibited from judicial review in the same way that the real is impossible and prohibited from the symbolic.

Another way we can grasp the truth of strict scrutiny's dicta and practice is to approach it as an aesthetic performance of colorblind judgment. Lacan reminds us that the blinding affect of Antigone's image—the "violent illumination, the glow of beauty"—halts the audience's analysis of Antigone's situation and gives way to a feverish pitch of emotion.[54] Antigone's beautiful horror structurally positions the chorus in "essential blindness"[55] to Antigone's criminal being as "that place [in which] she can see [life] and live it in the form of something already lost."[56] And by this failure of witnessing, the chorus spills over into a realm of sound. So while conventional readings of Antigone's criminal being render her performance as a defense of some higher political principle or moral conscience, Lacan's focus on the aesthetics of her performance allows him to isolate the "splendor" of blinding beauty as a moment when her criminal defense of civil disobedience creates a feedback loop of desire.

Copjec clarifies that it is the particular aesthetic form of Antigone's blinding beauty that evacuates a predicated social or political order. This evacuation is expressed not through a "will to nothingness,"[57] but with "partial drives" satisfied by "small nothings," or what Lacan names "*objects a.*"[58] Copjec is adamant: "Some inherent obstacle—the *object* of the drive—simultaneously *brakes* the drive and *breaks it up*, curbs it, thus preventing it from reaching its aim, and divides it into partial drives. Rather than pursuing the Nothing of annihilating dissatisfaction, the now partial drives content themselves with these small nothings, these objects that satisfy them."[59] In Antigone's case, sublimation takes place via the small nothing of a ritual: her brother's burial and the choral frenzy that surrounds it. In antidiscrimination law, sublimation occurs via the small nothings of the plea—that is, the black claim and an equally frenzied logocentric legal rationality.

To be clear, the simulacra of "small nothings," whether in *Antigone* or in antidiscrimination law, are neither invisible nor silent. It is just that the justificatory calculus of strict scrutiny doctrine is blind and deaf in its logocentric practice of judgment. Justification both lags behind and runs ahead of the aneconomic structure of desire that persists through always-relativized, reasonable distinctions between good and evil, norm and taboo, and order and transgression. Justification cannot teach desire to obey the former over the latter, because as the judicial opinion reveals, despite its goal of universal colorblind judgment, its most troubling objects of desire are those that come into being through a law that is not predicated on anything other than those objects' inapposite appearances.

This is another way in which we can understand the poetics of the plea as a radical form of legal judgment. We should read not for the soundness of an opinion's reasoning or for a ruling's correspondence with an empirically given social conflict, but for a kind of encounter with legal reason that is internal to and independent of the social bonds and exclusions that give rise to the case and its eventual ruling. We can call this encounter with legal reason a non-justificatory justification, in the case of Antigone, and a "poetics of the plea," in the case of antidiscrimination law. To be clear, this poetics of the plea can consist in part of claimants' performatives, but it also consists of those "small nothings" of racial dicta and their differentiated returns. So, for example, we saw the racial dictum of *Korematsu* return in *Adarand*, and subsequently, its echo in *Grutter*. It is no small irony that we would see it return in the most recent Supreme Court decision on university affirmative action policy, *Fisher*, in which Kennedy would remand the case back down to the Fifth Circuit Court of Appeals on the reversed dictum that "Strict scrutiny must not be strict in theory but feeble in fact."[60]

Plea, we should note, shares etymological roots with "please" and "pleasure." The Latin root for these terms is *placēre*, meaning "to please" *and* "to be decided," apropos the theatrical flourish, "May it please the court . . ." that often formally opens each party's address to the judge. Retaining the etymological inseparability of plea and pleasure, we must be more precise, then, about just what kind of pleasure comes into being through a poetics of the plea. For through this precision, we can understand something more fundamental to the perception that what we witness in strict judicial review is a clash of desire between, on the one hand, the law's desire for colorblind judgment and on the other, the black claim's desire for freedom. How should we understand the difference between the law's desire and the black claim's desire? How can we understand their incommensurability as fundamentally different types of desire, regardless of how their expressions are symbolized in law?

We should return one final time to the concept of Lacanian sublimation and its specific focus on a "second death" or "creationist sublimation" that Lacan references as the real dimension of the object *a*. Alenka Zupančič has stressed that the object *a* is the "realization of desire,"[61] which is not to be mistaken for an emotional satiety in the attainment of the drive's aim. The "realization of desire" is the manifestation of lack as lack, and not the symbolic interpretation of lack. We are, in other words, talking about the transformation of a prohibited desire in the symbolic by virtue of its return in the real as that symbolic lack. This is in contrast to an endless interpretation of symbolic lack that can only reinscribe lack as absence. Copjec, in deceiving simplicity, affirms this notion of the real return of foreclosed desire, summarizing it this way: "If the symbolic must inscribe its lack of foundation in the real, the inaccessibility to it of some knowledge of this real, then, we are obliged to admit that it also thereby inscribes the real itself, since it is precisely there where we do *not* know, that enjoyment, *jouissance* (a pleasure in the real) arises."[62]

Here we arrive, then, at the fundamental difference between the law's desire and the black claim's desire. The desire for colorblind judgment is manifested at the symbolic level as the performance of the imaginary pleasure of judicial review and its variations of naming, ordering, and balancing all that has yet to be named, ordered, and balanced. However, the desire for freedom is manifested in the real as a performance of hollowing out the obscuring imaginary pleasures of judicial review. And in that very enactment of hollowing, the hollowing comes to stand in its hollowedness as some Thing I identify as the plea. Pleasures in the real that the poetics of the plea manifests cannot be eliminated by the symbolic pleasures of legal rationality, and in fact, they are the object-cause of the law's desire.

So, if colorblind judgment is a particular blindness toward forms of "death-to-come" life, those small nothings of the desire for freedom make up the real of legal language. Colorblind judgment can focus on all number of sociolegal issues like individual or group opportunity, institutional procedure, social constructions of reasonableness, temporal foreseeability, and empirical categories of injury. But just as the superegoic madness of Creon's persecution of Antigone could not guard against Antigone's desire, colorblind judgment cannot guard itself against an "other dimension"[63] of law that is there in the fracture *within* the judicial opinion.

The density of the fantasy of colorblindness takes form in strict scrutiny doctrine, consisting in the blurred sight of the judicial opinion adjusted by a feedback loop of all the racial discrimination claims that have not seen the light of day. If colorblind judgment's aim is a universal antidiscrimination law, the circling of desire around this aim is a *mise-en-abyme*, a legal experience of standing in a hall of mirrors with the "right to look."[64] Strict scrutiny is no solution to all the breached promises of law, and no final retort to the deathly hold of the fantasy of colorblindness on law. Yet, in its insistence on being a solution, it recursively continues to admit failed promise after failed promise, and by this recursive admission a radical inclusion within logocentric legal reasoning surfaces. We can know this inclusion as the negative space between doctrine and dicta. But we can also know this inclusion, *in itself*, as a poetics of the plea that takes form by the plea's very echoing endurance within. The poetics of the plea is an inconclusive reasoning that never arrives at a reason other than the *jouissance* of claiming the impossible claim as impossible. This is the abyss of race in law, the faces of Derrick Bell's well.[65] We must look down for the echoes it ineluctably returns to us every time words fail.

CHAPTER THREE

Racial Profiling

> [In] the interpretations of Laws, whether Divine, or Humane, there is no end; Comments beget Comments, and Explications make new matter for Explications: And of limiting, distinguishing, varying the signification of these moral Words, there is no end. . . . Many a Man, who was pretty well satisfied of the meaning of the Text of Scripture, or Clause in the Code, at first reading, has by consulting Commentators, quite lost the sense of it, and, by those Elucidations, given rise or increase to his Doubts, and drawn obscurity upon the place.
>
> —John Locke, An Essay Concerning Human Understanding

> In that regard, "slavery" becomes the great "test case" around which, for its Afro-American readers, the circle of mystery is recircumscribed time and again. This realization is stunning: as many times as we reopen slavery's closure, we are hurtled rapidly forward into the dizzying motions of a symbolic enterprise.
>
> —Hortense Spillers, "Changing the Letter: The Yokes, the Jokes of Discourse, or, Mrs. Stowe, Mr. Reed"

So far I have detailed how the colorblind fantasy of national history and judicial review has its foundations in slavery. Within this imaginative realm of racial jurisprudence, the black claim cannot register political belonging and takes the legal personality of dispossessive citizenship. Further, this dispossessive citizenship echoes in the abyss of judicial review as an infinitely returning plea. However, instead of inhabiting this racial limit of judicial review as the bottomless well of legal reason, the law is preoccupied with perfecting legal universality. This fantasy realm is written over and through the law's interpretive labors, and it is to this issue that this chapter now turns. How is legal interpretation implicated in the inversions and echoes of the black claim? And how does the black claim shape legal interpretation? If Locke posits an "obscurity,"[1] a certain shadow legal interpretation, then Spillers suggests that what has animated this shadow in legal language is the enduring question of slavery as the law's "great 'test case.'"[2] Thus, we should ask by what "motions of a symbolic enterprise"[3] the law reproduces itself in the interpretation of legal meanings and their necessary obscurities?

I will explore answers to these questions through the racial impasses of constitutional doctrine on privacy, which have been developed through the Fourth Amendment's declaration of the right "to be secure . . . against unreasonable searches and seizures"; the Fourteenth Amendment's Equal Protection right prohibiting denials of "equal protection of the laws"; and the Fourteenth Amendment's Due Process right to "life, liberty, or property." While Fourth Amendment law asserts that private space is protected from "unreasonable" police searches and seizures of persons and property, Fourteenth Amendment law protects personal autonomy over private matters from state regulation. Each of these notions of privacy revolves around the liberal assumption of personhood defined as a self in possession of a body, which Fourteenth Amendment equal protection law accepts as racially diverse but formally deserving of equal treatment.

Thus the legal development of personal sovereignty is articulated in strikingly nonracial terms. Privacy protections against policing and state regulation concern suspect bodies, biological bodies, and sexually desiring bodies, but they are marked as criminal, reproductive, and gendered, respectively, *to the exclusion of their a priori racial marking*. In other words, constitutional protections of personal sovereignty are curiously impervious to the racial mark of blackness that the law has consistently approached as that which lacks sovereign authority over self and body. Thus, examining legal interpretation through constitutional protections of privacy gets us closer to understanding how and why the law cannot give meaning to and protect something we can only oxymoronically refer to as "racial privacy." Here I seek to understand how and why black bodily and psychical integrity remains submerged, instead of dignified, by rights that protect personal sovereignty.

The Limits of Sexual Privacy

The most obvious place to begin an examination of race, sexual privacy, and equal protection may be *Loving v. Virginia* (1976),[4] in which the Supreme Court ruled an antimiscegenation statute unconstitutional. But the issue of racial discrimination and sexual privacy is not so obviously presented there. On this score, since *Lawrence v. Texas* (2003),[5] legal scholars have been particularly busy trying to articulate the interdependence of Fourteenth Amendment Equal Protection and Due Process rights in *Loving*'s discussion of the unconstitutionality of antimiscegenation laws. For example, William Eskridge has observed that *Loving* "relied on both the Equal Protection and the Due Process Clauses to invalidate the [antimiscegenation] law, which was an invidious racial discrimination and invaded a fundamental substantive due process right."[6] The challenge here is to precisely understand the "and" asserted in Eskridge's reading of *Loving*, against a dominant political discourse of marriage equality that reduces the *Lawrence* and *Loving* rulings to analogy.

In a general sense, Eskridge is correct that *Loving* discusses both the Equal Protection and Due Process Clauses in declaring the unconstitutionality of the antimiscegenation law. However, the opinion does not give each clause equal weight in its reasoning. Rather, the opinion's discussion of the antimiscegenation law's invidious racial purpose, *in itself*, is sufficient to find a violation of the Equal Protection Clause; and the Court's observation of the effect the antimiscegenation law has—depriving mixed-race couples the fundamental right to marriage—only strengthened the Court's Equal Protection analysis. In other words, the Court's discussion of the Due Process right to marriage is analytically extraneous to its dispositive reasoning that the Equal Protection Clause prohibits states from using racial classifications without meeting a "very heavy burden of justification."[7] (This is another example of the strict scrutiny standard of judicial review I explored in Chapter 2). The Court infers invidious intent from "[t]he fact that Virginia prohibits only interracial marriages involving white persons," and in this arbitrary prohibition "demonstrates that the racial classifications must stand on their own justification, as measures designed to maintain White Supremacy."[8]

I insist on reading the reasoning in *Loving* very precisely, not to minimize the Due Process right raised in the opinion, but to clarify that this right is implicated insofar as it affects a *white person's* Due Process right. Antimiscegenation laws generally regulated a white person's freedom to marry outside of his or her race, *not* a nonwhite person's right to marry another nonwhite person of a different race. This much is clear in what the opinion explicitly confesses about what it does not reach. In footnote 11 of the decision, the Court plainly states:

> While Virginia prohibits whites from marrying any nonwhite (subject to the exception for the descendants of Pocahontas), Negroes, Orientals, and any other racial class may intermarry without statutory interference. Appellants [the Lovings and the class they represent] contend that this distinction renders Virginia's miscegenation statues arbitrary and unreasonable even assuming the constitutional validity of an official purpose to preserve "racial integrity." We need not reach this contention because we find the racial classifications in these statutes repugnant to the Fourteenth Amendment, even assuming an even-handed state purpose to protect the "integrity" of all races.[9]

My point is that *Loving* reflects a racial formalism that turns on the dangers of laws based on racial classification because of how they interfere with white liberty—in this case, the right at issue is the right to marry *outside* of the white race, and crucially, not the right to marry *into* the white race. In this sense, *Lawrence* is suspiciously indebted to *Loving* for the expanded sphere of white liberty and sexual freedom that motivates the racial formalism of the opinion, but which nonetheless has gone unchallenged since then because the specific Equal Protection right of whites at the heart of the case has been erroneously displaced by a Due Process right to marriage as "one of the vital personal rights essential to the orderly pursuit of happiness by free men."[10] It is by this refraction, then, that I would now like to turn to *Lawrence* as a point of entry into understanding the particularly stubborn constitutional impossibility of protecting something we might call "racial privacy."

Reversing the 1986 Supreme Court decision, *Bowers v. Hardwick,*[11] which affirmed the constitutionality of antisodomy laws, *Lawrence* has been celebrated as the long-overdue recognition of equality between opposite- and same-sex couples, as well as one political step closer to legalizing same-sex marriage.[12] However, the celebratory aura of *Lawrence* obscures a seamier racial dimension of both the interpersonal sexual relationships and the police encounter initiating the case. Robert Eubanks, jealous of the interest Tyrone Garner and John Lawrence showed in each other one evening, decided he would punish Garner, then his boyfriend, by calling the police on him. To ensure a police response, he reported that "there was a nigger going crazy with a gun."[13] Eubanks's provocation of racist desire proved to be no small act of jealous rage; it set the question of the right to sexual privacy in motion, and would ultimately become the affirmative decision in *Lawrence.*[14]

If we recast *Lawrence* as a case about a lover's racist wish, where do we understand racial profiling to begin and possibly end? This question is meant to invoke the legal and political difficulties surrounding contemporary racial profiling claims and campaigns, caught as they are between Fourteenth Amendment Due Process, Fourteenth Amendment Equal Protection, and Fourth Amendment search and seizure doctrines.[15] From this vantage, *Lawrence*'s importance is less its affirmation of sexual privacy and more the evaded problem of racial profiling for which all of these three doctrinal areas were available to seek legal redress. The most personal of desires and the most cherished of fundamental rights are invaginated in the phone call to the police, such that making sense of sexual privacy within the terms of *Lawrence*'s ruling and public image is shot through with a certain impossibility of reading it also as a case on racial profiling. And as such, this impossibility and its striking presentation in

Lawrence are my points of entry for examining how the fantasy of colorblindness structures the social phenomenon of racial profiling.

The facts precipitating *Lawrence* suggest that the purported discovery of an illegal sex act would not have occurred but for the social practice of racial profiling. But also, and more compellingly, the language of the case's internal reasoning demonstrates that interpretation itself is a type of racial profiling. In this case, interpretation brings personal and social desires (equal privacy rights for same-sex couples) into symbolic existence at the level of the word by making recourse to blackness as an "imago" at the center of policing and adjudications of civil rights in the courts. Laplanche and Pontalis define the imago as an "unconscious prototypical figure" that "orientates [a] subject's way of apprehending others."[16] By specifically referring to the racial profile in legal interpretation as an imago, we might explore how a fantasmatic image structures a relation of escape and chase in the reproduction of legal meaning that broaches various formal and substantive limits differentiating the three doctrinal areas of constitutional privacy law.

In the prior chapters, we saw how civil rights are not only positive legal entitlements, but also signs of a general prohibition. The Tocquevillian negative "imaginary inequality" of blackness provides for a progressive history of multiracial citizenship, while this negation is doubled in a racial antidiscrimination law that protects against a fundamental aporia race introduces into legal judgment. Another way, then, to extend this analysis of the fantasy of colorblindness to racial profiling is to consider how multiracial citizenship and legal judgment share a common ground in legal interpretation mobilized around this black imago. Racial profiling is the originary projection of law over and against the imago at the heart of American legal interpretation. At this register of reading race and law, racial profiling has the power to make something out of nothing; it is the lasting source of slavery's symbolic productivity that Spillers identifies in the opening epigraph. Racial profiling, as an activity of real fantasy, bridges the aporetic relationship between the written and imaginative domains of the legal text found in our previous deconstructions of affirmative action jurisprudence and strict scrutiny doctrine.[17]

Let me be clear that I focus on the imago precisely to challenge the myth of black dereliction that lingers even in critiques of "negative stereotypes" of an essential black criminality. The imago is not a product or reflection of some social truth, but is a real unknowable cause of the fantasmatic structure of colorblindness. In fact, the experience of fantasy the imago introduces—and *not* the socially constructed stereotype of blackness—is more relevant to the maneuvers of colorblindness than critics of colorblindness realize. As an attempt in both function and form to disavow legal interpretation's reliance on this imago, the fantasy of colorblindness reproduces a certain never-ending deflection of guilt on to some other kind of criminal type that we see even in the most progressive liberal critiques of police profiling, whether of black, brown, or Muslim bodies. Instead of accepting this fantasmatic security of deflection, we might focus on how to render justice for the imago lurking in the word of law. We might read the imago as the generative ground of legal interpretation—embracing not Locke's complaints about this fecundity, but Spillers's affirmation of it. Tracing the force of the imago from the depths of a legal case's factual origins to the heights of constitutional law's loftiest pronouncements on equality, as this chapter does, is one attempt.

The Long Shadow of Racial Profiling

Contrasting the facts surrounding *Lawrence* with the ruling of the opinion, we see a disturbing trade: the potential to recognize the privacy violation of racial profiling is traded for the potential to recognize the privacy violation of heteronormative sexual morality.[18] The claimants are imagined in a purported legal stranglehold that forced them to challenge only the antisodomy statute enforced, and not the racial context of the application of the statute in the first place. And since a judgment can only decide issues raised by claimants, *Lawrence* is forced into using the language of same-sex and heterosexual intimacies in posing the question of equality.[19] Through this exchange, privacy in *Lawrence* becomes a discussion about the sovereignty of the individual to decide what kinds of interpersonal relationships she wants to have. And this privacy is precisely *not* about privacy in the policing context—how to designate a certain threshold of the individual's sovereignty as a limit to state enforcement of criminal law. This is despite the fact that the case could have addressed ineffective Fourth and Fourteenth Amendment limits on policing. Herein lies *Lawrence*'s "bad faith," what Lewis Gordon's theory of antiblack racism identifies as the ultimate existential form of irresponsibility.[20]

Ironically, it is in the Court's description of the claimants' position, and not an explicit argument raised by them, that we encounter the most compelling reason to read *Lawrence*. We are told: "The right of the police to enter does not seem to have been questioned."[21] Noting what is not questioned, the judicial opinion, and not the mainstream LGBT political campaign supporting the claimants, re-presents the lost opportunity to use a Fourteenth Amendment Due Process framework to raise circumstances and make claims that would challenge racial profiling and abuses of police power. This is no small gesture, for racial profiling, currently trapped between race-neutral Fourth Amendment doctrine and formalistic Fourteenth Amendment Equal Protection doctrine, is threatened by few if any constitutional doctrines that promise an effective check on racial discrimination in policing.[22]

Indeed, the broadened notion of Fourteenth Amendment Due Process privacy that should have been raised to challenge racial profiling in *Lawrence* had already been laid out in critiques of *Bowers*, the same case that *Lawrence* overruled. Kendall Thomas, in his article "Beyond the Privacy Principle," provides the most comprehensive overview and critique of dominant conceptions of privacy spanning the Fourth Amendment search and seizure doctrine, Fourteenth Amendment Equal Protection doctrine, and Fourteenth Amendment Due Process doctrine. He categorizes the types of privacy regulated by these doctrines as associational (for example, marrying someone of the same sex), decisional (for example, choosing how to end one's life), and spatial (for example, body cavity searches).[23] Against these categories, he argues that privacy should be guided by concerns for "bodily integrity, . . . a presumptive right to simple physical existence in and of itself."[24] This presumptive right, not insignificantly, could accommodate the kinds of claims made against police racial profiling and federalist excesses of state police power more generally. Under this theory, the claimants in *Lawrence* might have made a Fourteenth Amendment Due Process argument that probable cause based on an unsubstantiated assumption of black threat amounted to the degradation of Garner's bodily integrity and a reduction of his person to a fantasmatic image, and thus constituted a violation of his presumptive privacy right as theorized by Thomas.

The outcome, instead, was a curious splitting in constitutional doctrine on privacy. On the one hand, privacy expanded in Fourteenth Amendment Due Process doctrine, but on the other, it contracted in Fourth Amendment search and seizure doctrine. This split is no mere exception to the priority of legal uniformity, no mere glitch in constitutional law's progression toward consistency in its commentary on privacy. Rather, it is symptomatic of the absent presence of race in the case: the legal argument about police racial profiling that the claimants could have made; the "nigger" traded for a same-sex couple as the target of police aggression; and the nontranslation of Fourth Amendment privacy issues into Fourteenth Amendment Due Process privacy.

This aporia of race that emerges in *Lawrence*—a certain enduring escape from the long shadow of racial profiling—draws attention to just how illegible the injury of racially discriminatory policing is, while the imago's disavowal becomes the expanded legibility of sexual privacy. By rendering reality—real events, people, statements, gestures, and attitudes—into particular questions of law, legal interpretation writes over, rather than addresses (let alone redresses), racial injury. I am not suggesting here that reality should not be rendered for legal judgment at all. Rather, I am suggesting something more practical. The process through which reality is turned into word—the work of legal interpretation—should be taken as seriously as winning a favorable legal judgment, and valued independently of the legal instrumentalism of political movements. The significance of *Lawrence*, then, is not what it legally decides about anti-sodomy law, but what must not be argued in order for sexual privacy to be interpreted. It is useful not because it declares the policing of a certain form of interpersonal relation unconstitutional, but rather, because it bears the trace of a refusal to declare a certain method of policing unconstitutional. It is precisely the social reality of racial profiling that *Lawrence* must redact in order to be legally successful that gives this case political possibility—but only to the extent that the redaction can be duly claimed.

Lawrence reveals an additional troubled interpretive move that we might not otherwise recognize as such. This move is less about broaching fact and rule, and more about a formal structure of legal writing that depends on precedent and doctrinal consistency. Take the stronger point of the Court's reasoning in *Lawrence* for overruling *Bowers*. The Court observes a certain incongruity between state constitutional law and federal constitutional law on what comprises a privacy violation, and relies on judgments from five states that had rejected the application of *Bowers* to their substantive due process privacy doctrine. Of these five, the Georgia Supreme Court's decision in *Powell v. State* (1998),[25] in particular, leaps out of *Lawrence*'s archive of supporting precedence and citational practices.

In this case, the Georgia Supreme Court considered whether to overturn a defendant's criminal sodomy conviction based on his Fourteenth Amendment Due Process claim that the criminal law unconstitutionally infringed on his privacy right. The defendant was found guilty of sodomy, but not rape, since sodomy as a crime did not hinge on the issue of consent from the victim, the defendant's wife's seventeen-year-old African American niece. Heralding its state constitutional law on privacy to be the most expansive among other states and more inclusive than federal constitutional law, the Georgia Supreme Court ended up overturning the conviction because it reasoned that enforcing general morality was not a compelling state interest that could justify the regulation of consensual adult sexual intimacy.

Representing the facts of the case as "a non-commercial sexual act that occurs without force in a private home between persons legally capable of consenting to the act,"[26] the Georgia Supreme Court's majority opinion disavowed the scene of the case's origin—the incestuous rape of a girl veiled under the covers of family and racialized assumptions about consent. It never scrutinized lower levels of review, where unsurprisingly, the defendant's testimony that the niece had consented because she never uttered the word "no" settled the factual issue of consent.[27] However, contrasted with the Georgia Supreme Court's representation that "the State did not prove beyond a reasonable doubt that the act was committed 'with force and against the will' of the niece,"[28] the testimony of the niece, Quashana, indicates that the issue of consent was far from clear, or even resolvable. The silences, breaks, and lapses in her testimony, buried under the state's interpretations of its constitutional law, could never enter the judicial archive on their own terms.[29]

In both *Lawrence* and *Powell*, the implicit but fundamental issue is how to characterize the sex act in question in order to determine whether a constitutionally given privacy right exists.[30] Yet, the stabilization of sex through the law's interpretations of "consensual adult sex"—both in *Lawrence* and *Powell*—ultimately fails. This is not because "consensual adult sex" is a social construction or because the dissenting opinions raise valid concerns about enforcing sexual morality. It is because of the illegibility of Quashana's sexuality inscribed in *Lawrence*'s citational universe. Digging through layers of legal authority, we see in *Powell* that both sides cannot completely do away with this issue of incest and the sexual exploitation of girls by male family members, as well as the overwhelming obstacle that black women face when testifying against the presumption that to be black is to be always sexually available.[31]

As the majority opinion in *Lawrence* widens and domesticates the nature of the sex act in question by relying on the authority of *Powell*, it both retains and expels the scene of sexual violation in *Powell*. This profound ambivalence written into the finding of consent in *Powell* casts a shadow over *Lawrence*'s image of same-sex intimacy as consensual, monogamous, and loving. And this sedimentation of sex in law reveals that specified expansions of privacy are haunted by the more difficult issue of how the law is to redress not only Garner's violations, but Quashana's as well. A future anterior emerges, but not unburdened by a certain imago of blackness.

That is, *Lawrence* demonstrates how the interpretive trouble circulating around this imago is not about how to make a successful claim of racial injury, but how the possibility of making such a claim in the first place is factually, doctrinally, and citationally foreclosed. The positive rendering of a right to sexual privacy appears as a form of legal development that writes over the structural problem of policing, which, always there in the law, reduces the law's language and interpretive horizons to the grip of an imago of blackness. Thus, we should appreciate sexual privacy cases literally, for what they do and do not do in the text, precisely because they contain the limits of their own racial politics, and make possible a reading of racial profiling in and as the legal text.[32]

The Constitution's Founding Racial Profile

One might say that *Prigg v. Pennsylvania* (1842),[33] an antebellum case involving the criminal conviction of a slavechaser, Edgar Prigg, for kidnapping a fugitive slave, Margaret Morgan, is *the* foundational case for reading sexual privacy. *Prigg* is recognized as the first Supreme Court case to address the question of how expansively the Constitution permits the federal government to justify encroachments on civil liberties generally, and thus by implication, sexual privacy specifically, in the name of some state interest. Sanford Levinson notes that for Justice Story, the author of *Prigg*, the "[Fugitive Slave Clause's] status as a 'fundamental' linchpin of the constitutional structure made it important that the states be prevented from placing any burden on its effectuation." And for this reason, "*Prigg* may be, ironically enough, the debut in American constitutional analysis of the notion of a 'fundamental interest' that would be vigilantly protected by the Court."[34] In *Prigg*, that fundamental interest was private property rights to slaves, and in *Lawrence*, it was the right to sexual privacy.

That is, what is singular to *Prigg* becomes generalized and formalized beyond any delimited substantive or historical matter that the case immediately reflects. *Prigg* reveals that the structure of its constitutional question—arising from the singular position of a fugitive slave between federal and state laws—lives on despite the abolition of the legal institution of chattel slavery. For even if the subject matter of *Prigg* is no longer a formal legal issue in our present context, the form of the question is repeated well beyond legal decisions attempting to resolve the tension between slavery and the Constitution. Tracking this repetition, we find that the long shadow of racial profiling cast over *Lawrence* originates in slave law, where the always contingent guarantee of fundamental civil liberties, including sexual privacy, is a ghostly necessity to the elaboration and reproduction of constitutional law, the federal union, and the various kinds of rights through which its citizens come to identify with the national body.[35]

The question of law before the Court in *Prigg* was precisely this: Where the Constitution is silent on the relationship between congressional and state legislative authority over the subject matter of fugitive slaves, is the Pennsylvania Act of 1826, criminalizing the removal of a black person from Pennsylvania to a slave state, constitutional to the extent that it derives its authority from the police powers of the states and excludes procedural redress through Congress's 1793 Fugitive Slave Act?[36] *Prigg* resolved this complex federal issue by ruling the Pennsylvania Act unconstitutional.[37] Perhaps predictably, Story reasoned that if there was a conflict of law between Congress's Fugitive Slave Act as a nonexhaustive remedy for a positive right established by the Constitution, and Pennsylvania's act as an exercise of the constitutionally recognized police power of the state, then Pennsylvania's act was unconstitutional because Congress has exclusive legislative authority over the subject matter.[38]

In my interpretation, while Story's reasoning centralizes the language of property rights, his overriding preoccupation is with encroachments on federal jurisdiction, and not necessarily with injury to slaveowners' rights. Granted, there are a number of logical flaws in Story's reasoning, alongside sound evidence as to how the Court reasoned in service of a political choice to vindicate slaveowners' rights over the vision of abolition.[39] However, beyond these complications, what is striking is how the legal issue of injury to federal jurisdiction is repeated throughout the analysis.[40] That repetition reveals the centrality of the text of the Constitution in both producing the constitutional issue and providing an answer to that issue. Thus, when Yifat Hachamovitch asks, "Isn't a rule of the juridical gaze that it only comes to dwell upon its own reflection?, upon its own kind?, upon good copies, well-founded likenesses, pure genealogies?"[41] *Prigg*'s interpretive world answers affirmatively. Indeed, Story seems to be speaking explicitly to these questions when he stated, "No Court of justice can be authorized so to construe any clause of the constitution as to defeat its obvious ends, when another construction, equally accordant with the words and sense therefore, will enforce and protect them."[42]

The circularity of constitutional interpretation is secured, then, by twin loops of reasoning: the procedural mandates of the Constitution require that disputes over its fundamental rights find resolution through the federal government because the federal government was founded by the Constitution; and the substantive rights guaranteed by the Constitution require that disputes over their interpretation and enforcement find resolution through the federal government because the federal government founded the Constitution.

This tautology displays a curious fixation on the reparation of the Constitution's textual ambiguities through the more fundamental aporia of the federal government's origins in a constitutional compromise with slavery. The mythology of constitutional democracy underwrites the symbolic production and distribution of rights, liberties, and limited sovereign powers of states and citizens. More compellingly, however, the legal traditions of constitutional democracy are fantasmatically substantiated against the persistent return of the problem of slavery played out in interpretation. In order to resolve issues produced by legal interpretation's own obscurity, the self-referential hermeneutics of the Constitution calls into being a national body to police the always-disinterred presence of slavery. This national body is the federal government that Story refers to as the sole authority over the troubling presence of people of African descent in a white nation; a unified legal procedure through which white re-possessory claims to black bodies were to be properly redressed. But it is also the mimesis of Story's constitutional question, a repetition incarcerating the racial experience of the slave to the domain of fantasy on which the interpretive process of turning letter into law relies.[43]

This particular kind of internal image around which legal interpretation is organized, generated by what Tim Murphy calls the "eye of law,"[44] is what I have been theorizing as an imago, or what we popularly refer to as a racial profile. *Prigg* demonstrates this visual capacity, while the originary text of the Constitution disavows an internal image of blackness as a matter of symbolic representation. However, by this very disavowal, the development of constitutional law over time is secured through a repetition of this image's escape and capture (however unknowingly). Consider the actual language of the constitutional provisions at issue in *Prigg*, only one of which (Clause 3) is popularly known as the "Fugitive Slave Clause." Appearing in the section of the Constitution providing for the relation of states to each other, Article IV, Section 2 contains three clauses that together comprise the constitutional authority for the Fugitive Slave Law at issue in *Prigg*.[45]

> Clause 1. The Citizens of each State shall be entitled to all Privileges and Immunities of Citizens in the several States.
>
> Clause 2. A Person charged in any State with Treason, Felony, or other Crime, who shall flee from Justice, and be found in another State, shall on demand of the executive Authority of the State from which he fled, be delivered up, to be removed to the State having Jurisdiction of the Crime.
>
> Clause 3. No person held to Service or Labour in one State, under the Laws thereof, escaping into another, shall, in Consequence of any Law or Regulation therein, be discharged from such Service or Labour, but shall be delivered up on Claim of the Party to whom such Service or Labour may be due.[46]

The disavowal is located in the clauses' silence about the African slave, a silence positioned between the written words "Citizens" and "person held to Service or Labour,"[47] and the conspicuously unwritten word "slave."

We might say that these clauses together are an apostrophe marking the absence of the slave in the translation of the political debates about slavery at the 1787 Convention into the Constitution as founding text. Barbara Johnson discusses the notion of apostrophe as that which "involves the direct address of an absent, dead, or inanimate being by a first-person speaker." As a "form of ventriloquism," the "speaker throws voice, life, and human form into the addressee, turning its silence into mute responsiveness."[48] What this suggests with respect to constitutional law and legal interpretation is a certain co-originary constitution of law and the slave that we come to reference today as the racial profile, or as we might alternatively reference based on my reading thus far, as the Constitution's apostrophized slave.

That Clause 3 would later be stricken with the abolition of slavery does not, obviously, do away with the apostrophe that the entire Article IV, Section 2 denotes. And any legislation and case law that is established from the remaining Clauses 1 and 2—which continue to be the basis for federal jurisdiction over matters of interstate commerce, crime, and civil rights—are written from this grammatical authority.

Story's insistence—"[It] cannot be doubted, that [the Fugitive Slave Clause] constituted a *fundamental article, without the adoption of which the Union could not have been formed*"—recognizes how profoundly legal interpretation depends on the animating force of the apostrophized slave.[49] *Prigg*'s ability to give substantive meaning to the Fugitive Slave Clause takes as its condition of interpretive possibility the *mise-en-jeu* of pathos aroused by the absent slave in constitutional law—the silence as to the racial difference between citizens and persons, the conspicuously unwritten word that fixes the meaning of those that are written, that render the writing readable. Piercing this silence, the eye of the Constitution apprehends and substitutes the necessary absence of the slave in the word of law with an image in the law's fantasy life. In legal writing, absence and interpretation are two sides of the same coin, the coin being the racial profile.

Michael Foley has advised more generally that "it is precisely those unwritten components of a constitution that represent its most integral features and its most fundamental properties."[50] The racial profile as the Constitution's apostrophized slave continuously reappears through the foundational interpretive problem of textual silences. The relationship between the eye of the Constitution and the racial profile, then, is structured by a fantasy of a blackness escaping, a fleeting image the legal meaning must, but never can, capture in order to make sense out of its most troubling textual silences. *Prigg* is the ultimate proof of how the profoundly unwritten, if not unwritable, problem of slavery in constitutional law compels a constellation of indirect, digressive statements of law in response to what was not written.

In *Playing in the Dark* Toni Morrison calls this racial profile a "dark, abiding, signing Africanist presence," which "shaped the body politic, the Constitution, and the entire history of the culture."[51] She writes further, "Through significant and underscored omissions, startling contradictions, heavily nuanced conflicts, through the way writers peopled their work with the signs and bodies of this presence—one can see that a real or fabricated Africanist presence was crucial to their sense of Americanness. And it shows."[52] Where Morrison uses the language of racial restrictions and codes in law to argue for a similar structure in American culture and literature, she also suggests that to the extent that law is a literary form, this Africanist presence is crucial to the interpretive writing of law. Implicitly, then, constitutional law is a genre of writing in the American literary canon that Morrison critiques. For what form of writing depends on omissions, contradictions, conflicts, and "peopling" more than the law? As such, *Prigg* and the interpretive world of law it founds in the slave as constitutional apostrophe confirms Morrison's belief that this Africanist presence is "one of the most furtively radical impinging forces on the country's literature."[53] Indeed, Margaret Morgan, as the unnamable presence in *Prigg*, is the inspiration for Morrison's defining novel, *Beloved*.

This presence, this racial profile that haunts the literary imagination from which constitutional law is written, is a most urgent issue.[54] The silences of the Constitution give way to a visual field of legal interpretation.[55] In describing the racial profile as a visual impression I mean it in all senses of the word—as an imprint, impact, impersonation, and feeling. As such, racial profiling is not simply a neutral interpretive technique. Racial profiling is American law's core principle of interpretation.

Reading constitutional law from the unwritten legibility of Margaret Morgan, Quashana, and Tyrone Garner is always mediated by the "*bonds* of representation."[56] Not just fictional and real people, but also figurations of a constitutional imago, they remain imprisoned in a shape-shifting legal grammatical form beyond the symbolic world of the word of law. They are leashed to, and thus promise an unleashing from, the literary imagination of legal representation and interpretation. The racial profile moves somewhere between the categories of object and subject, thing and person, and fantasy and history—it is here that a radical rewriting of constitutional law and its foundations becomes possible. Here glimmers the possibility of a certain justness in law, which is to say, to render a transformative interpretation of it.[57]

Racial Profile, White Shields

Cheryl Harris's landmark article "Whiteness as Property," is an exceptional meditation on the aporia of race in law that I have been trying to outline through *Lawrence*, *Powell*, and *Prigg*. As an exemplar of critical thought on race and law, it suggests another scale of legal interpretation that, by its interrogation of the legal status of the slave, offers the chance for a transformative reading. Harris's article opens with an allegory about the history of passing in a white world. This is a history, Harris writes, about "not merely passing, but trespassing."[58] In contrast to the criminal existence of blackness under Jim Crow, Harris describes whiteness as a form of denial. "They [whites] remained oblivious to the worlds within worlds that existed just beyond the edge of their awareness and yet were present in their very midst."[59] Between black trespass and white denial, the modern discourse of property that Harris examines is a circumlocution of a secure, legally protected white racial identity. She refers to this as the "embrace of a lie."[60]

What is this lie, exactly, at the heart of the legal notion of whiteness as property? It is true that whiteness is a social construction protected by a law that treats it as a kind of property that can be possessed. Yet we can also read in Harris's theory a tacit acknowledgement of whiteness as a psychical formation organized by an unconscious relationship to blackness. Although the dominant tendency is to read Harris's piece as an analysis of how the legal ideology of property legitimizes the social privileges and powers that accrue to white identity, it is also perhaps an immanent theoretical engagement with race in the dreamwork of the law.

Let us look at this embedded theory more closely. Harris arrives at whiteness's resemblance to property through an exposition of the legal position of the slave as both thing and person, and how the law deals with the slave's resistance to this paradox. For purposes of political representation, the slave is both citizen and property; for purposes of commodity production, the slave is both thing and human; and for purposes of exchange, the slave is both money and person. Against the threatening capacity of humanity's "market-alienability,"[61] and against the universalizable "threat of commodification,"[62] Harris observes, somewhat in passing, "whiteness became a shield."[63]

We are dealing here with immaterial things like benefits, values, capacities, and expectations accrued to the social identity of whiteness.[64] Few have appreciated Harris's focus on how modern property law administers classical forms of property, including intangible things.[65] It is this focus that expands the notion of whiteness as property to include not only identity as a source of property interests (for example, that which is legally protected by a cause of action against defamation), but also as the very capacity and expectation to have a past, a community, and a future that the idea of ownership implies. But no one has seized upon an even more crucial insight in Harris's theory: under her legal metaphorization of whiteness as property is yet another literary move—not by metaphor but by a striking declarative. In writing about how property law enforces white identity and power, Harris's assertion that "whiteness became a shield" grounds the conceptual metaphor of "whiteness as property."

Thus we can extend Harris's formulation "whiteness as property" to "whiteness as property is shield." The resemblance between the syntagm "whiteness as property is shield" and Frantz Fanon's figuration of "white masks" is a suggestive overlap that emphasizes the fantasmatic structure of whiteness. For it was one of Fanon's tasks in *Black Skin, White Masks* to meditate on white culture's symbolic reliance on phobic fantasies of blackness.[66] On this extended formulation, when Harris finds that the "absence [of whiteness] meant being the object of property,"[67] her analysis of formally recognized whiteness is also an implicit analysis of the fantasmatic sense of threat, anxiety, and defensiveness crucial to white cultural life. As a shield protecting one from being made into an object, so the legal fantasy goes, whiteness as property provides the assurance of personhood itself. This shield of whiteness is inalienable, personal; it can be used and enjoyed; it is a marker of standing; and it is a mode of self-possession.[68] Most interestingly, this white shield is also a symbolic representation in law of the legal fantasy of personhood.

So when Harris writes further, "Owning white identity as property affirmed the self-identity and liberty of whites and, conversely, denied the self-identity and liberty of Blacks,"[69] we should pause at this precise problem: a racial position from which claims to various forms of value can be made, *and* from which representational acts can signify personhood—both for the world and for the self. Whiteness, as an object of law, is private property; and whiteness, as a representational act in law, "self-identity," is the cultural capacity to imagine oneself a subject of the law. Harris's analysis of the relationship between race and law exceeds issues of unequal access to the privileges of private property; it encompasses the larger legal problem of blackness as a form of life lived in the unassimilable depths of the law's language and its interpretive world of meaning. It points us to the possibility of understanding (or at least how the law understands) blackness as the experience of the law's rendering of social reality into words. Lacan calls this a symbolic death, where "the symbol first manifests itself as the killing of the thing," and thus, any mobilization of symbolic power always bears the trace of a murderous intimacy with "the thing," or a form of social existence irreducible to the symbolic life of the law.[70]

This brings us to the central legal case for Harris's text, *Plessy v. Ferguson* (1896), and an arresting recollection embedded in her discussion of it. In Chapter 1, I expanded on *Plessy*'s ruling that formal racial segregation is constitutional and its implications for thinking about a multiracial citizenship structured by the fantasy of colorblindness. It is worth revisiting *Plessy* through Harris's analysis because it, like *Lawrence* and *Prigg*, presents the racial profile through apostrophization. I am specifically interested in Harris's vital focus beyond the ruling on how Homer Plessy's lawyer, Albion Tourgée, rhetorically challenged Jim Crow. Harris quotes from Tourgée's filings, "Probably most white persons if given a choice, would prefer death to life in the United States *as colored persons*. Under these conditions, is it possible to conclude that *the reputation of being white* is not property? Indeed, is it not the most valuable sort of property, being the master-key that unlocks the golden door of opportunity?"[71]

Tourgée's larger argument here was about how the imprecision of formal racial categories applied to social practices results in arbitrary deprivations of property interests in racial identity. As Harris observes, the Court evaded this argument by simply asserting that Plessy's racial classification was clear. On my reading of this evasion, the problem with it is not the refusal to acknowledge the mishaps of due process in the application of formal racial categories. It is that the evasion admits a more disturbing truth about the function of formal racial categories. Toward this end, the Court pointed out that if Plessy was in fact a white man, according to Louisiana's rules of racial categorization, he could claim money damages for defamation.[72] And in this dismissive gesture, we witness the affirmation not only of whiteness as property, but also, the fantasy of a world where it is better to be dead than black.

"*Under these conditions*, is it possible to conclude that *the reputation of being white* is not property?"[73] By answering in the negative (that it is not possible to conclude that whiteness is not property), the Court by implication also affirmed the truth of "these conditions": that being black is worse than biological death. The black claim invokes the terror of being cast under the sign of blackness as "the thing" that the law protects itself and its subjects against. While the Court acknowledges the possibility of injury to Plessy's whiteness, it sees the injury of how this property interest materializes over and against the worse-than-death condition of being black, the realness of the fantasy of black life in symbolic death,[74] and of a black sociality beyond the boundary of any kind or form of representation.[75] Contained in *Plessy*, as well as in Harris's focus on this fragment of the case, is the truth of the relation between law and projection, between rule and fantasy: whiteness as property is a shield *against symbolic death*.

In *Lawrence*, overturning Lawrence's and Garner's convictions depends on the representability of same-sex intimacy as either consensual or deviant behavior. In *Prigg*, overturning Prigg's conviction pivots on the representability of Morgan as either person or property. In *Plessy*, upholding the railroad's segregation policies relies on the representability of Plessy's racial categorization as white or black. And yet, in each of these cases, because interpretation is limited by the literary imagination of the racial profile, only injury to whiteness can be given symbolic representation in the word of law. *Lawrence* apostrophizes an unquestioned black vulnerability to police surveillance and intrusion through its recognition of injury as state encroachments on sexual privacy. *Prigg* apostrophizes black persons as owned human beings through its recognition of injury as state obstruction of owners' rights to use and enjoy their property. And *Plessy* apostrophizes blackness as a symbolic death through its recognition of injury as the contamination of self-identity.

The metaleptic relationship between blackness and injury here is staged through the law's inevitable encounter with claims against and issued from an inhabited symbolic death. Against, but mobilized by, these claims, racial injury in the fantasy of colorblindness is always appropriated by the grievance of a (white) legal subject, and is always an exploitation of the spectacle of blackness haunting those most fundamental and most celebrated constitutional values that provide an endless source of legal issues for judicial interpretation. Given this, the symbolic foreclosure of black racial injury has less to do with the practical limits of legal interpretation, and more to do with the unstated fact that legal interpretation cannot address, let alone redress, the *thingly* form of the black claim. This is where acquiescing to the political sensibility of not arguing that which the law declares should not be argued (recall Kennedy's curious observation about the absence of a Fourth Amendment challenge in *Lawrence*) appears as a fundamental failure.

There are calculable claims for legal relief. And then there are things that cannot be argued because legal interpretation as a symbolic structure owes its reproductive capacity to the foreclosure of those things. Indeed, Plessy did not ask for personal compensation. His was not only a claim for legal relief. He argued the perversity of black exclusion and asked for an injunction on Jim Crow law instead. The Court's interpretive response to Plessy's plea was an admonishment: if Plessy was not Plessy, he could have asked the Court to compensate him for his property interests in whiteness. It was a mediated avowal of the fact that Plessy could not ask for anything from his position, let alone ask the Court to compensate him for his transgression from one biologically given racial caste into another. The Court's response to Plessy noted what could have been asked for, but in an impossible hypothetical situation. Still, in the Court's reproach that Plessy should not ask what cannot be asked for, it also admitted the reality of blackness as the thingly life of symbolic death. A devastating recognition if ever there was one.

Dreaming the Life of the Racial Profile

How then to address this mediated reality of blackness as the thingly life of symbolic death in the face of law? This is perhaps *the* civil rights question. Patricia Williams's *The Alchemy of Race and Rights* engages with this question in the struggle to pose an alternative relationship between the racial profile and the legal text. In this way, the form of Williams's writing and the truth it pursues is concerned, even obsessed, with what Robert Cover identified as the "jurisgenerative"[76] nature of *nomos*, and in particular how the racial profile that structures constitutional law's writing issues from a foundational "juridical mitosis" of the word of law.

One of Williams's most compelling discussions of the interpretive problem at the heart of racial profiling is found in her chapter "Fire and Ice (some thoughts on property, appearance, and the language of lawmakers)."[77] Analyzing the legal and media treatment of the 1984 police killing of Eleanor Bumpers, Williams argues that we must ask why some things appear so obvious to the law.[78] Why did Bumpers—an elderly, mentally ill, and poverty-stricken African American woman who refused to be evicted from her apartment—appear responsible for her own murder by the New York Police Department?[79] What is this fear behind the metalepsis of responsibility?[80]

For Williams, the source of this "obvious" need to take Bumpers's life emerges not through an interrogation of personal biases held by the police, but through her reading of the event and the various legal, official, and media representations that ultimately acquitted Bumpers's killers of any criminal liability. By reading the various logics of legal interpretation at work in the event, Williams scrutinizes the relationship between the written letter of the law and how its words are trafficked beyond the text. According to Williams, by disavowing this cultural dimension that is haunted by interpretations of the law's word, the law becomes a "punitive literalism," "the softened inverse of something akin to fascism," a "cool formality of language," a "sleight of tongue," and a "cruel form of semantic slipperiness."[81] Taken collectively, Williams's detailed descriptions of legal interpretation give a body to law's word and foreground the affective qualities of law as a cultural form.

Interestingly enough, based on this problem of *lex* absent *jus*[82]—of law without justice, or *lex-jus*—Williams does not proceed to prescribe what *lex* infused with *jus* would say. For her, writing about legal interpretation does not tend toward policy reform or doctrinal strategy (though we could certainly extend it in those directions). Rather, Williams's writing continues to press the interpretive problem of *lex-jus*, and by this pressure opens up onto a lurking racial profile in the midst of the law's dreamwork, where the law's cold word is just as chilling as the NYPD's purportedly necessary fear of Bumpers. The racial profile, both "something beyond" and "something about" her physical presence, the imago of blackness for which Bumpers is substituted, embellishes both police brutality and a law of police impunity.[83]

Williams's response, then, is to dream her relation to the law as much as the officials were hallucinating a response to the public about why the NYPD had cause to kill Bumpers.

> I dreamed about a black woman who was denied entry to a restaurant because of her color. In response she climbed over the building. The next time she found a building in her way, she climbed over it, and the next time and the next, and the next. She became famous, as she roamed the world, traveling in determined straight lines, wordlessly scaling whatever lay in her path, including skyscrapers. Well-meaning white people came to marvel at her and gathered in crowds to watch and applaud. But she never acknowledged their presence and went about her business in unsmiling silence. The white people were annoyed, angry that she did not appreciate their praise and seemed ungrateful for their gift of her fame; they condemned her. I stood somewhere on the periphery of this dream and wondered what unspoken rule, what deadened curiosity, it was that kept anyone from ever asking why.[84]

One is tempted to take this dream as an allegory of how the place of responsibility is reversed in Bumpers's death—how the law as *lex-jus* is unable to deliver justice because of a failure to intervene in the audience's perception of racial injury. However, the source of affect in the dream, and its correspondence with the metalepsis of responsibility in Bumpers's death, is the dream's narrative, but it is not its kernel.[85] This kernel, what the dream circulates around but cannot represent, indicates the more profound legal problem of a foundational aporia of race in the law.

The unfolding of affect from marvel and acclaim to annoyance and anger, then to betrayal and condemnation, begins with a statement of fact about a black woman's exclusion and her subsequent dazzling yet incomprehensible feats of magic. The evolution of racial envy, first sprouting from wonder and then lashing out as condemnation, goes unchecked by a social psyche that masks the founding ridiculousness of the scenario: that the law's citizens would watch and judge this figure defying all rules (civil and natural), but through a blindness toward the spectacle as a remnant of racial exclusion. White envy toward an ingratiating figure of blackness persists because some "unspoken rule" prohibits us from asking about the reason behind the "cynicism or rebelliousness that infects one's spirit."[86] The kernel of Williams's dream is not a law as the rule of law, or as the word of law, but instead, as a more fundamental racial prohibition against imagination. Here, the envy that produces the decompositional rights I discussed in Chapter 1 is not a result of moral corruption or a failure of will. Murderous envy fills a space in which imagination cannot take flight.[87]

This is the curious taboo Williams is left wondering about at the margins of her dream's spectacle. By this fundamental racial prohibition, white envy escalates as it continues to attach itself to an increasingly elaborate fantasy of black ingratitude. The result is, writes Williams, that "[t]he echoes of both dead and deadly others acquire an hallucinatory quality."[88] We would be remiss in too quickly passing over this conclusion. As in her dream, suggests Williams, the objects of social practices like police brutality are rendered into visual images—hallucinations—because law as an unstated taboo against imagination prohibits their echoes from becoming legible words; they are "wordless," like the woman of Williams's dream.

What would the consequence of transgressing this racial taboo against imagination be? Of committing the act of asking this spectacular woman of Williams's dream why she never returns her audience's (mis)recognition? Why the silence as she continues along her solitary and defiant path? One consequence might be the possibility of loosening hallucinated images of the woman from the imago of blackness gripping the law's fantasy life. Notably, this is *not* how the white spectators respond in Williams's dream. They mistake the ingratitude of the image for an essential black moral fallibility, instead of for the thing murdered in order for the image to "have" feelings (like ingratitude) of any kind. White envy is a failed recognition of the mystical image's metamorphosis in *fantasia* from an excluded person to a supranatural thing. It is a resistance to the invitation to imagine otherwise. It is the delimitation of the word of law as *lex-jus* that in its very differentiation between word and justice retains the possibility of a mediated exchange in recognition, restitution for a wrong, or distribution of responsibility between a *supra* legal personality and ordinary people. Yet, as *Lawrence*, *Prigg*, and *Plessy* through Harris reveal, this transformative unforeseeability is a permanent presence in the law, insofar as the imago of blackness precipitates a reading of law's plural aporias of race.[89]

To write of dreams and law is to pose the question of a free associative image animating the fantasy of colorblindness. It is to inhabit a thingly life in symbolic death. We might call Williams's writing the authorization of a "speculative law" that is faithful not to the associational, decisional, or spatial realms of private life, but to an *associative world* which the imago of blackness calls forth by virtue of its many intrusions. Divisions between text and vision, interpretation and imagination, as well as formal logic and free association are challenged by the imago of blackness Williams writes of and through.

So even as I have been laying out just how complexly permanent the foreclosure of black injury in legal interpretation is, and have been perhaps rendering the grim social phenomenon of racial profiling even grimmer, I want to stress that by writing (of) the law to contain the limit of its own racial fantasy, as Williams does, allows us to reimagine the possibilities for justice through our engagements with those limits. The problem with engagements with the law in the name of civil rights and social justice is not simply that we have conservatives and liberals on the bench, that grassroots organizations do not have enough resources, that the law has no higher authority to which it is held responsible, or that the terms of legal recognition are exclusionary. It is that the law's ability to change is bound by the literary imagination through which its hermeneutics—its writing and its rhetoricism—issue the word of law against the thingly life of the racial profile. Yet despite itself, the law's language gives us a glimpse of symbolic death, where a speculative law might proceed, and the chance for any case or cause to be made before the law is always held open.

CHAPTER FOUR

The Purloined Prisoner

Which words act as revenants, haunting the precincts of law?
—Colin Dayan, "Legal Slaves and Civil Bodies"[1]

In his essay "The Iconography of Nothing," Peter Goodrich returns to sixteenth-century Western art, where he finds some of the first images of the modern conception of law as written word. These images do not depict the actual words of law, but interestingly, depict law as a "blank space" on which words will come to be written. These depictions emphasize a contrast between the modern notion of law as written word with the classic one of "law as image."[2] He concludes, compellingly, that modern law is a system born from a vanished sign that in its blankness calls forth a writing.[3] Modern law is simultaneously a constitutive vacuity and all the written fantasies and fantasies of writing elaborated around it.

As Colin Dayan makes clear in the above aphorism of legal thought on slavery and incarceration, the written words of modern law matter because they conjure a legal personality whose incessant return raises the law's various fictions, otherwise taken as political truths and historical possibilities, *as fiction*. As such, readings of the law and its fantasmatic *écriture* evoke an unsettling feeling that no manner of legal interpretation, no amount of expert knowledge, and no capacity of faith in justice, derived from whatever source of law, can save us from the rule of law as a strange amalgamation of fiction and authoritarianism. Reading the law in this way is an attempt to understand a form of writing that is both material and immaterial, truth-making and truth-destroying, philosophic and pragmatic, and aesthetic and political. The words of law materialize an immanent politics of writing and reading that will have always been the case of racial jurisprudence before (in the sense of priority and pleading) American constitutional law.

So must we always renew our thinking about law as a matter of words, as I have been attempting to do. In this chapter, I wish to further build on the conceptual development of the poetics of the plea to dwell on how, in law's writing about racial inequality, it forever remarks on the twin birth of democracy and punishment in the United States. This chapter, then, is indebted to the published conversation between Angela Davis and Gina Dent, where they discuss "the impact of the prison as the paradigmatic institution of democracy," foreshadowed in Beaumont's and Tocqueville's research on the "new American penitentiary" preceding the publication of *Democracy in America*.[4] I lay out a set of political-theoretical questions based on their observations that the mass production of the prisoner through democratic governance depends on the material and immaterial territorializing activity of law's writing. Stated another way, if mass incarceration today is indicated by a class of people whose lives are determined by the seemingly unfettered administrative reach of the criminal justice system, then this immediately provokes the question of how to approach the complicity of law's writing in this expansion. How do we confront the law's validation of the obscene truth of modernity's dual political imperatives—democracy and punishment—at the level of its basic practice of writing the letter of the law on democratic and punitive governance?

What seems basic about the law as a practice of writing, and perhaps even too basic to deserve critical inquiry, to Goodrich and Dayan is the essential matter of law. As such, in this final chapter, my analysis descends into the plural forms of "letter" that signify formal rule (letter of the law), epistolary correspondence (addressed letter), the symbolization of speech's sounds (alphabet letter), literature (*belles lettres*), and learnedness (man of letters). The hope is that this descent outlines the fantasy of colorblindness as a world-making, territorializing practice that emerges through a collision of various forms of writing that compel the law to refine the Constitution's guarantee of free expression.

The Matter of Punishment

In *The Prison and the American Imagination,* Caleb Smith argues that "Prisoners are not beyond the embrace of law; they are mortified by it."[5] This idea is supported by the historical trajectory of mass incarceration, whereby the battle over constitutional guarantees of civil rights and liberties in the evolving legal architecture of slavery and formal racial segregation establishes the prisoner's precarious if not absent security in bodily and psychical integrity.[6] The racial and sexual vicissitudes of violence inherent in American mass incarceration defy notions of moral injustice, constitutional injury, or crime against humanity. They also escape explanation by references to racially or sexually disproportionate rates of surveillance and imprisonment, or even the historicization of what these calculations are taken to mean. Cassandra Shaylor aptly captures the difficulty of referencing this violence by conceptualizing it as "living in a black hole."[7] And though this violence is irreducible to legal, historical, or empirical terms, I nonetheless want to think about how it is contained in law. In other words, might the law as the constitutional signature of American democracy and punishment be the continual writing of this "black hole" in the world?

Given this scene of law's writing, then, we must trace the permanence of this void in the very writing of ever-changing (whether more conservative or more liberal) legal rules and doctrine. This is not because there is some truth to the anticritical cliche that "anything can be made to mean anything." Rather, according to Anthony Farley's meditation, it is because "[a]ll of it [the constitution of the world] is white-over-black, only white-over-black, and that continually."[8] The universalist ideals of equality and freedom shroud structural racism and misogyny in ambiguity, and thus the law is always implicated in maintaining this structure.

This suggests a more troubling issue than whether or not the deprivation of prisoners' rights (whether an effect of international or domestic forms of war) is constitutional. This deliberative calculation, whatever the result, is nonetheless wrought from the primordial blankness of the Constitution's guarantees, and produces other iterations of this ambiguity of legal meaning. However, this infinite regress of meaning always presents another chance for a decisive word to be spoken about the totality of constitutional law's writing of "white-over-black." The fundamental problem of the law's imposition of words from which punishment issues and by which state impunity is performed perhaps presents just this sort of chance.

By eschewing the pragmatism of the written legal decision, and instead focusing on the law's negotiation of undecidability and responsibility through writing, the social usefulness of punishment becomes a question rather than an unstated value. We are allowed to pursue a knowledge of punishment that does not (one hopes, at least) automatically become part of the culture of punishment. The materialities of punishment might surface more readily in their complexities. We can instead ask questions about what the relationship between punishment and expression, for example, is in the first place, before moving on to argue what it should be. Punishment is not only a system of signification whose purpose is to shape something outside of it. It is also, to the extent that it is a legally validated governing institution, a constitutional force of writing, coding, organizing, filing, reading, publicizing, and so forth. Similarly, punishment is not only an abstract term for specific historical and social policies of incapacitation, deterrence, or rehabilitation. It also bears a certain materiality of writing through which social identification, political imagination, and both mundane and spectacular statecraft are performed.

In short, punishment is paperwork. This complex surface of punishment allows us to approach practices and relationships beyond the value structures of the Beccarian social contract—around which the disciplines and legal study concerned with punishment are organized—and toward what Jacques Lacan called "literality."[9] The literality of punishment includes all the ways the relations of mass incarceration appear to us in our experience of it: legal, fictional, personal, administrative, epistemological, physical, bureaucratic, poetic, dreamt, erased, read, touched, and more. Literality suggests a "mode of being" in that the letter comes into contact with such varying levels of truth-making: personal, empirical, archival, legal, institutional, emotional, existential, and so on. It facilitates a confrontation with the structural implications of the law's writing by which prisoners' expressive rights have been whittled down to the single option (which is to say, a nonoption) of writing letters.[10]

Thus, because I am interested in thinking about how the coercion of language and the culture of punishment are negotiated in and by law, drawing from an empirically or historically bound archive of prisoners' letters seems less productive for my purposes. Rendering prisoners' letters into an archive calls them to order in a way that crops out their radical fecundity as a form of writing that reaches for (but does not necessarily arrive at) intersubjectivity from a state in which this is foreclosed in the interest of social and individual reform. To conceptualize prisoners' letters as an archive risks imposing an intersubjective relation between prisoners and history before we have asked whether and what kind of other ethical relation might come into view before or against their archival status.

In this way, refusing to archive prisoners' letters allows us to focus on their formal particularity as unfile-able. If we refuse to historicize them, their form takes on a certain infallible openness in and against time. The open letter written in 1971 by striking Attica prisoners is exemplary.[11] The five demands in this letter would develop into fifteen practical proposals to negotiate the end of the strike, and many of these proposals and the memory of the Attica prison uprising continue to inform radical prison activism today.[12] In *Romantic Correspondence*, Mary Favret argues that at the end of the eighteenth century we begin to see a shift in the association between the epistle and women's private writing with the birth of the "open letter," or what Baudelaire called the "treacherous letter"—an invitation, or an introduction into, a revolutionary movement and imagination.[13] Both the figures of the feminine and the mob enter the public sphere in an open letter that is the silenced voice of demand. The popular form of the open letter—a form that many political prisoners' letters take—is seditious precisely because of a feminine excess marked by their sentimentality, seduction, and sexual vulnerability. We might recall the collective volume, *If They Come in the Morning*, edited by Angela Davis during her confinement, and Bettina Aptheker and the National United Committee to Free Angela Davis and All Political Prisoners, also published 1971, not as archived materials, but as an open letter that begins with James Baldwin's "An Open Letter to My Sister, Angela Y. Davis," addressed "Dear Sister:. . . ."[14]

So instead of *in* the archive, I locate the prisoner's letter in the law, and more specifically in what Cornelia Vismann, in her book *Files*, identifies as a compelling disjuncture in legal language when "for a brief moment the act of exchanging and that of writing are fused, and things are translated into signs, *gramme* . . . a symbol in Lacan's sense."[15] Pursuing a genealogy of law through various file technologies, Vismann notes that "the law remains silent about its records. . . . Files are constitutive of the law precisely in terms of what they are not."[16] Files are not law, but its essential medium. She goes on, "They lay the groundwork for the validity of the law, they work towards the law," but crucially, "they establish an order that they do not keep. Files are, or more precisely, make what, historically speaking, stands *before the law*."[17] The prisoner's letter, or the convergence of letters in *If They Come in the Morning*, can be seen then as a piece in common with the files that constitutional interpretation depends on in order to file a case, and ultimately, in preparation for "a *hearing*."[18] And it is in this antelegal space that we might approach the idea that the law's writing is but a trace of such fugitive movements of body, spirit, word, and sound.

There is another way to think of this move, which is more directly reflected in the title of this chapter. It requires that we posit the prisoner's letter from the outset within a certain conceptual difficulty in thinking the totality of what Barbara Johnson identifies as "the scene of writing," in her reading of Derrida's reading of Edgar Allen Poe's *The Purloined Letter*.[19] That is, revealing Derrida's and Lacan's convergence in necessarily incompatible readings of "the scene of writing,"[20] Johnson prepares us to ask what the legal architecture of mass incarceration both hides in plain sight and explicitly objectifies in the container/cell/block. That which is hidden and objectified is, as we will see in my discussion of First Amendment law below, an absence of mastery over a primordial expressivity against which techniques of human deprivation are constitutionally sanctioned as political necessities. Here the humanity of the prisoner, marked by her limit capacity to write letters, is the object cause of the social punitiveness of racial inequality that finds institutional purpose in mass incarceration. And because of this, I am concerned with identifying how investments in the prisoner's irreducible humanity are mistaken for an empirical retort against the vicissitudes of civil death, instead of seen as a limit we must encounter and inhabit in order to have any ethical relation with the law.

So, we might ask, under the exigencies of confinement and surveillance in the prison, how are we to understand the formal attributes of the epistle, including the addressor, addressee, personal signature, sealed envelope, and postal destination? Prisoner letter writing, as we will see below in more detail, is less a specific mode of communicative writing and more a general condition of compulsory expression. Thus any archival value prisoners' letters might have decomposes in the cumulative mass of the letters' words, which peculiarly materialize the prisoner through and as her absence. In other words, if one of the distinguishing formal features of epistolary writing is that the letter comes to stand for the addressor who cannot be where the addressee is, then the letter literally stands for—a standing in and beyond the legal personality of the sentenced criminal—the absent prisoner's enveloped and enveloping presence. *This* letter, then, is what I am interested in tracing as a materialization of the prisoner's uniquely general, and not specific, condition before the law. *This* letter is, following Johnson's reading of Lacan's reading of Poe, "not a thing or the absence of a thing, not a word or the absence of a word, not an organ or the absence of an organ, but a *knot* in a structure where words, things and organs can neither be definably separated nor compatibly combined."[21]

Reading the prisoner's letter in constitutional law's administrative approach to deciding the issue of a prisoner's right *to the letter*, I want to work through the legal "framing"[22] that purloins the prisoner in and as a "black hole" of the law. The prisoner's letter in, by, and before the law reveals a certain unasked question about whether communicative writing is possible under the general condition of civil death. To be clear, I am not suggesting that writing is not possible under such conditions. I am, rather, more interested in simply holding out a space to ask a question about what such writing is, if it is not communicative precisely because sentencing a prisoner to civil death under contemporary conditions of confinement also sentences her to self-authorial death? I wish to follow Fred Moten's move in his essay "Blackness and Nothingness (Mysticism in the Flesh)" to "begin to consider *what nothing is*, not from its own standpoint or from any standpoint but from the absoluteness of its generative dispersion of a general antagonism that blackness holds and protects in and as critical celebration and degenerative and regenerative preservation."[23]

The long history of case law that sanctions the censorship of prisoners' expression has created a diffuse, transinstitutional space of noncommunication, or, more precisely, noncorrespondence. And by attending to these acts of noncorrespondence, a certain fluorescence of this mass scene of writing comes into view. The prisoner appears on both sides of the wall: not not communicating, not not corresponding, not not reading, not not writing, not not calling, not not wanting.[24] Rehabilitative punishment's perception of self-expression as a privilege appears as a strangely literal topographical rendering of enduring problems of language. There are so many letters (including all that are never sent, never arrive, only partially read, and so forth) highlighting so many prisoners' lostness, sentences barely read, a chorus of drowning chatter, filed away, and given hearings. We now turn to this vast negative space of communication across the prison as border.[25]

Words from Beyond the Grave

American law as a form of writing is an imperial presence in the international scene of modern legal development. As Paul Kahn elaborates, "The United States is the paradigmatic modern state: It was the first and remains the most successful state in the modernist project of collective will formation under the guidance of the new science of politics."[26] This new science of politics, or liberal political theory applied to nation-building, maps out the law's ever-expanding writing on social relations, and by this expansionist design, transnationalizes and renationalizes the constitutional fantasy of colorblindness.[27]

Part of what makes the logocentrism of American sovereignty successful is that the rule of law itself promotes a theological relation with the letter of the law. This is Kahn's most incisive point: that American sovereignty is a "vital civic religion, the fundamental tenet of which is that the popular sovereign is manifest in the production and maintenance of the rule of law."[28] Thus, the various militarily secured, globalizing forms of democratic governance that have been promising worldwide "freedom" over the last decade—Guantanamo Bay, shock-and-awe military strikes, Abu Ghraib, "Rule of Law" promotion campaigns, and drone surveillance in various "lawless" zones—can be taken as conversion missions to proselytize the word of modern law. Developing a practice of writing the letter of the law in this scene is a settler occupation, of which popular democratic governance is but an effect. American military actions (whether offensive, defensive, or humanitarian), then, are not extrajudicial or extralegal but are the territorial expansion of modern law's writing.

However, while we tend to look outside the geographical borders of the United States for examples of law's imperial drive, we have an equally compelling example from within. In 2006, the U.S. Federal Bureau of Prisons proposed the "Limited Communication for Terrorist Inmates," which would impose the strictest limitations on prisoner First Amendment rights in history by providing prison wardens with unilateral decision-making power to label a prisoner as having "an identifiable link to terrorist-related activity."[29] After this determination, a prisoner's capacity to communicate with the outside world would be all but eliminated. She would be allowed communication only with immediate family, and those communications would be limited to one six-page letter a week, one fifteen-minute phone call a month, and a single one-hour visit a month.

After the outcry over this proposed regulation and its ultimate defeat, the Bureau of Prisons (BOP) quietly proceeded to open two specialized prisons. Located in Marion, Illinois, and Terre Haute, Indiana, the BOP termed these new prisons "communication management units" (CMUs). Prisoners' communications in these new prisons would be completely monitored by virtue of their spatial containment in these specialized prisons. In a candid description summarizing the establishment of these CMUs, prison officials reasoned, "By concentrating resources in this fashion, it will greatly enhance the agency's capabilities for language translation, content analysis and intelligence sharing."[30]

The majority of the prisoners held in these CMUs are Muslim, and many are political prisoners or have a history of challenging civil rights violations in the federal prison system.[31] CMU prisoners reflect the widened range of activities and associations captured under the legal definition of terrorism endorsed by the USA PATRIOT Act. Daniel McGowan, for example, is an environmental activist held at Marion who is serving a seven-year sentence reflecting "terrorism enhancements" established by the Patriot Act. Interestingly, McGowan likened the political effect and process of the CMU to the Lexington High Security Unit (Kentucky) that opened in 1986 to house women political prisoners. International protest over gross human rights abuses in Lexington prison, and its complete lack of any reasonable "security" function, led to its court-ordered shutdown two years later.[32]

The CMU demonstrates an authoritarianism that the public has consistently endorsed since the wars on crime and terror began. These have granted officials virtually unchecked powers to make unilateral decisions about individual fates sacrificed in the name of the collective. It is not difficult to find critiques of this particular denigration of individual liberties in both liberal and radical defenses of democracy. The CMU also demonstrates the dominant response the state has consistently fallen back on in the face of these defenses of democracy. This is a response the state has mastered over the course of the last forty years through the rollback of any pretenses of rehabilitative criminal justice.[33] The history of the CMU embodies the dialectical relation between panoptic discipline (the proposed regulation) and administered life (the CMU) that is now well theorized by "new penology" scholarship.[34]

Along these lines, the tendency might be to explain the CMU as an exceptional form of punishment. Yet, if we situate the kinds of legal violations we might imagine as unique to the CMU within a general structure of debate in First Amendment prisoner-rights jurisprudence, such violations appear much more mundane and basic than the specialized technologies and rules of the CMU suggest. That is, the specific administrative protocols of the CMU resurface a fundamental legal issue: Can and should the law protect expression, one of the most essential boundaries defining the human, against the various innovations of modern punishment? So while the CMU understandably elicits feelings of alarm because of its resemblance to an Orwellian dystopia, these feelings are predictable, almost scripted. What remains beyond these expected feelings is a more fundamental difficulty—if not impossibility—of confronting the democratic amalgamation of penal and civic lifeworlds that exceed the formal, physical boundary of the prison fence that presumptively divides the sentenced from the free.[35]

One of the ways in which we might stage this confrontation is by tracing the centrality of the prisoner's letter—itself a paper trail leading back to incarcerated life, a scrutinized object of various other forms of paper trails, and a thing around which maneuvers of symbolic power are structured. In this way, the letter has become a universal substrate of the lifeworld of punishment, and by virtue of its universality can only be known by shoring up the letter's various limits.

So we might opt to move beyond the two-dimensional prison fence that largely remains untroubled as the dominant image of punishment today, and toward the "supernatural" dimension of law where the specters of the civilly dead appear as real things passing through various carceral borders, as ghosts are wont to do. In *The Law Is a White Dog*, Dayan conjures the thing that emerges under the pressures of civil death:

> The convict, though actually a living being, is not only dead but buried by the law. The body is there, but restrained in prison. The external physical conditions are clear. The internal spiritual state is not. The physical person (solely body and appetite) has no personhood (the social and civic components of personal identity). What kind of spectral form remains? . . . What is more pressing, more spectacular than the realm of the flesh-and-bones ghost, the palpable specter watching over its own perpetual degradation?[36]

"[By] the law," prisoners' physical bodies are buried in cages, but what remains of their spirits? Where do they go? My sense is that they are buried, in prison yes, but also, *in* the law. Here, law's writing takes on the architectural sense explored by Claudia Brodsky's *In the Place of Language*. Law becomes not an instrument of civil death, or the official speech act that calls civil death into existence, but a special kind of physical graveyard where the spirits of his civilly dead are put to rest through the material activity of writing and reading. Another way to understand this idea of law is through Robert Cover's argument, that "Legal interpretation takes place in a field of pain and death," to be based not in a theory of law as the state's communicative language but in a theory of law's territoriality.[37] Every writing and reading of law is a materialization of burial and demarcation. We might say, following Brodsky, that to legalize civil death is to engrave sentenced spirits in law, to spectralize words by displacing bodies.[38] And in prisoner First Amendment rights jurisprudence, the engraved word "letter" disperses the apparitional personhood of the prisoner across the written text of law.

Reading Prisoner First Amendment Rights

In 2005, California's governor Arnold Schwarzenegger renamed the California Department of Corrections as the California Department of Corrections and Rehabilitation. The illusory promise contained in the renaming, against the backdrop of all the inefficiencies and failures that the specially appointed review board found, comes off with a certain kind of earnestness.[39] Schwarzenegger was running a state that had perfected the biopolitical project of population management through imprisonment, while at the same time retaining the seemingly paradoxical commitment of punishment to the individual.[40] By that time, California had conjoined population management and individual redemption through an open secret of the state, celebrating personal justice over any other kind we might seek.[41]

So, while rehabilitative punishment as an effective policy might have been abandoned decades earlier, it emerged in the CDC's renaming as an "imaginary penality" par excellence.[42] The renaming is a paradigmatic instance of a state acting "as if": as if the curtailment of prisoner's First Amendment rights can in fact reform their souls; as if calculating and controlling the various risks attending the shades of liberty administered by the criminal justice system can in fact increase national security; as if our actuarial interests can in fact rely on policy justifications to translate, analyze, and share intelligence better. In this administrative imaginary, human self-expression is not so much a type of raw material through which populations are rendered and managed, but becomes almost unnecessary to the legal definition of human personhood. Because of this near obsolescence, the right of self-expression protected by the First Amendment slips easily down to a privilege in constitutional law.

More insidious still is that much of the civil rights gains and aspirations of the women's and black liberation movements have been refracted by this imaginary penality into what feminist criminologist Meda Chesney-Lind has called "vengeful equity."[43] Women in prison experience all kinds of harsh punishments, not because they are afforded less legal protection than men are, but because they are subject to equal punishment to men. Mandatory arrest laws for police responding to domestic violence calls have skyrocketed women's rates of incarceration and given fodder to the argument that women are as violent as men are. It is a sad state of legal affairs that appears throughout the feminist criminological literature. Equality as a democratic principle has been formalized as a matter of legal recognition of certain populations and moralized as a matter of individual experiences of structural inequality. The type of equality shaped by the imaginary penality of rehabilitative punishment has proliferated state violence against minority communities at the same time that it convolutes our critiques of the state's failures to protect women and communities of color from violence.

The prisoner of this imaginary is a strange culmination of a caring and pitiless state. She embodies the law's continued dependence on the absent presence of the slave. She is the aporia between truth and language that the term "communication" has never been able to resolve. She is the placeholder for the soul—the thoughts, desires, and interior life of the human—which in its infinite need for rehabilitation becomes, as Foucault put it, "the prison of the body."[44]

The law experiments on this soul through the language it develops to test the limits and vicissitudes of civil death. Analyzing civil death through Eighth Amendment law, Dayan makes the devastating observation that "[if] you happen to be a prisoner, without any status explicitly recognized in law, you possess rights only insofar as you have lost your skin or your mind."[45] She is speaking here of the Eighth Amendment's prohibition against the infliction of "cruel and unusual punishment" in the enforcement of criminal law, and how this prohibition has actually created a perversely legitimated system of torture for those 2 million or so prisoners living in cages across the United States. By requiring either intentionally inflicted bodily harm or mental insanity as the only forms of constitutionally relevant evidence to apply Eighth Amendment protections, prisoners suffer from all sorts of tortures falling just short of these evidentiary thresholds. These include any number of strange correctional policies that structure the everyday life of the average prisoner: from strip searches to highly specified contraband lists, from administrative segregation to the "earned time" work wage, and from group therapy sessions to mail regulations.

In law, the prisoner is a convoluted form of human to whom only the barest of rights are attached at precisely the moment when she has lost or been stripped of her desire to exist. While Eighth Amendment law generally deals with cases of extreme bodily harm and mental anguish, cases specifically on the question of whether intimacy and expression are essential features of being human brush up against First Amendment law on a prisoner's right to correspondence and contact with the outside world. It is worth pursuing this slippery slope, from the prohibition against cruel and unusual punishment to the fundamental liberty of speech and expression, precisely because of the way that the legal issue of the limits of being human is refracted into the ordinary practice of prison censorship.

Procunier v. Martinez (1974) is the landmark Supreme Court case delineating a framework for analyzing whether a regulation on prisoner mail violates the First Amendment right to freedom of expression. Hesitating to extend federal oversight into prison administration, the justices established a rule of intermediate scrutiny, balancing the interests of prison officials to maintain order and security and the interests of prisoners and their outside correspondents in communicating. Fashioned after other cases dealing with incidental restrictions on First Amendment rights arising in pursuit of legitimate governmental interests, *Martinez* holds that restrictions on prisoner mail are constitutional if they further the legitimate interests of "security, order and rehabilitation" and they are "necessary or essential" to pursuing that interest.[46] In this particular case, the regulation did not pass this test because the regulation allowed censorship of letters that "unduly complain," "magnify grievances," and contain "disrespectful comments," "derogatory remarks," or "inflammatory political, racial, religious or other views."[47]

This better conclusion aside, *Martinez* foreshadows a disturbing future for the already strained articulation of prisoner First Amendment rights. The intermediary scrutiny described above is not to ensure, as the Court explicitly states, the protection of prisoners' rights, but rather the rights of their outside correspondents. It reasons that those on the outside no doubt have a First Amendment right to communicate with a prisoner, while leaving unanswered the question of whether the prisoner has that right. Rejecting the state's argument that prisoners do not enjoy First Amendment rights because of their legal status as prisoners, the Court ruled against the state because prisoner correspondence implicates those on the outside. The question of whether the First Amendment right to freedom of expression exists for the prisoner is neither posed nor answered explicitly.

However, it is answered rhetorically by the scare-quoted reference, "prisoners' rights."[48] During the course of its analysis, the Court offered a theory of communication that becomes part of the reasoning for why prisoner mail censorship does trigger the First Amendment.

> Communication by letter is not accomplished by the act of writing words on paper. Rather, it is effected only when the letter is read by the addressee. Both parties to the correspondence have an interest in securing that result, and censorship of the communication between them necessarily impinges on the interest of each. Whatever the status of a prisoner's claim to uncensored correspondence with an outsider, it is plain that the latter's interest is grounded in the First Amendment's guarantee of freedom of speech. And this does not depend on whether the nonprisoner correspondent is the author or intended recipient of a particular letter, for the addressee as well as the sender of direct personal correspondence derives from the First and Fourteenth Amendments a protection against unjustified governmental interference with the intended communication.

The following section will discuss this theory and the First Amendment in more detail. At this point, the main issue is how this theory of correspondence recognizes that the "result" of correspondence depends on both reading and writing, sending and receiving, and addressor and addressee. The Court concluded that to the extent that communication relies on an act by the prisoner, protecting the rights of outside correspondents means that prisoner mail cannot be restricted without some justification.

This very limited reasoning paved the way for the landmark decision in *Turner v. Safely* (1987), which applied a reduced level of judicial scrutiny to a policy limiting correspondence between prisoners at different institutions. Ruling that prisoner-to-prisoner mail involves only "prisoners' rights,"[49] it looked to precedent on prisoners' general First Amendment rights.[50] The Court then identified four factors to be taken into consideration when determining reasonably justified limitations, including: (1) whether there was a "valid, rational connection" between the regulation and the interest given for it; (2) whether there were other means for prisoners to exercise the right in question; (3) whether accommodating the right would have unduly burdened prison resources; and/or (4) whether the regulation was an "exaggerated response" to whatever governmental interest stated.[51]

Finally, in 2003, the truth of *Martinez* was announced in *Overton v. Bazzetta*.[52] The Court found, through a mundane and predictable analysis, that a policy restricting prisoner visitation was constitutional according to the *Turner* framework. It reasoned that this restriction on a prisoner's right to association was reasonable because, in part, he or she had "alternative means of associating with those prohibited from visiting."[53] Here, the specific elimination of in-person communication through prison visits is reasonable because prisoners continued to retain some other means of communicating by "letter and telephone."[54] In response to the argument that these were not meaningful alternatives because "letter writing is inadequate for illiterate inmates and for communications with young children [and] phone calls are brief and expensive,"[55] the Court meagerly concluded, "Alternatives to visitation need not be ideal, however; they need only be available."[56] And by this reasoning, the specific limit form of prisoner letter writing reveals itself again as the ground from which prisoner First Amendment rights continue to be stripped.

More interesting than the ruling, however, was Justice Thomas's concurrence where he articulated the decades-long gesture of the jurisprudence on prisoner First Amendment rights. While agreeing with the majority outcome that prohibiting noncontact visitation for certain prisoners is not a violation of the First Amendment, he reoriented the language of the Court to reflect the continuously repeated jurisprudential gesture away from any notion of "prisoners' rights." He wrote, "Rather than asking in the abstract whether a certain right *survives* incarceration, the Court should ask whether a particular prisoner's lawful sentence took away a right enjoyed by free persons."[57]

In other words, Thomas believed that the Court needed to stop asking the question of how rights are curtailed by imprisonment, and to accept that punishment, by definition, is the general revocation of rights. He wanted to specify the terms of civil death that a prison sentence assumes. Both Thomas's belief in punishment as a formal deprivation of rights, and the majority's rationale of subordinating an interest in a right to the governmental interest in rehabilitation, arrive at the at the same conclusion. More critically, however, Thomas's question reveals the truth of punishment as civil death, whereas the majority analysis clings to the possibility of nominal civil life so as not to recognize the effective implications of their barely evidenced calculations. And he does this by shifting the sarcasm of the Court's "prisoners' rights" to "prisoner 'rights.'"[58] His grammatical revision is critical because it shifts the notion of rights from something prisoners possess to something of a categorical impossibility for them.

Law's negotiation of prisoner civil rights, by deferring to prison administrators' evaluations of "effective" rehabilitation, shrouds the obscene reality of punishment that Thomas's concurrence makes transparent. According to Thomas, punishment is by historical definition a form of state-imposed vengeance. Impatient with keeping up liberal pretensions of a beneficent rehabilitation, Thomas appears to encourage vengeful rage. In turn, the liberal position appears to anticipate this always-justifying rationale of deprivation within retributive punishment, and offers the meager "universal personhood" to temper it. Yet, prisoner First Amendment rights jurisprudence reveals that this offering has not prevented the perverse results of criminal justice, but has actually inflamed them with a possibly infinite number of ways in which prison administrators can experiment with penal technologies—all in the name of rehabilitation.

My point is not to moralize about Thomas's theory of punishment. Rather, it is to recognize, as with Schwarzenegger's renaming of the CDC, a brutal truth lodged in the ruse of universal legal humanity. He accused the liberal position on the bench of metaphorizing the prisoner—to him, by law, a civilly dead entity that the liberal side of the bench misrecognizes as a member of humanity and the nation. Thomas's coldness aside, his perverse rejection of liberal faith in universal humanity acts as the "tail that wags the dog" of U.S. civil rights and the rehabilitative penal discourse that Schwarzenegger opportunistically embraced.

Overton brings us back full circle to *Martinez* and its failure to explicitly state that a sentence to prison is a sentence to civil death. Instead, Douglas's concurring opinion in *Martinez* elaborated on the human spirit:

> When the prison gates slam behind an inmate, he does not lose his human quality; his mind does not become closed to ideas; his intellect does not cease to feed on a free and open interchange of opinions; his yearning for self-respect does not end; nor is his quest for self-realization concluded. If anything, the needs for identity and self-respect are more compelling in the dehumanizing prison environment. Whether an O. Henry writing his short stories in a jail cell or a frightened young inmate writing his family, a prisoner needs a medium for self-expression. It is the role of the First Amendment and this Court to protect those precious personal rights by which we satisfy such basic yearnings of the human spirit.[59]

As seductive as this eloquent language is, it is also quite eerie when read after *Overton*, where the "medium" through which the human spirit satisfies its need for expression is effectively abolished. This leaves the human spirit that Douglas describes in a state of unfulfillment, a sort of maddening state of monologue—endless and accumulating chatter that goes nowhere. The point is that acts, thoughts, and sentiments naturally gush forth from this thing—the prisoner—but foreclosed from an actualized "human quality," they continue to well up, a kind of drowning of the prisoner. I highlight this image that *Overton* casts over *Martinez*, not as an example of the extreme state of mental duress in which the prisoner exists. Rather, I want us to see how the prisoner, written by and in the law, becomes categorically the place for a type of expression that is always excessive.

Prisoner First Amendment rights jurisprudence gives us a plentitude—an unlimited materiality—in the vanishing point inhabited by the "civilly dead," a gated point of infinite expression. Where the Eighth Amendment produces civilly dead bodies in its limitless qualifications on "cruelty," the First Amendment and all the writing and reading it leaves at the wayside of the Constitution amasses piles and piles of paper, letters, sentences, and images that mute the never-silent "spirits" left in the wake of Eighth Amendment tortures. For if the Eighth Amendment demonstrates how cruelty can forever be predicated, the First Amendment demonstrates that that predicated cruelty does not snuff out expression but raises the question of it forever. Jacques Derrida might call all this expressive debris the "surplus of evidence."[60] The *Martinez* prisoners' post-*Overton* letters, files, papers, petitions, interrogatories, depositions, and so forth naggingly remind us that the question of prisoner First Amendment rights remains unresolvable.

The Purloined Prisoner

What is this law that refuses to say what it means? Whose truth can only appear after the fact, shifted, as a supplement? *Martinez*, the earliest case and most generous as a matter of doctrine, recognized the First Amendment right of prisoners as an effect of the right of those on the outside to communicate with those on the inside. Cases since then have distinguished between directions of communication. That is, by applying the distinction *Martinez* drew between inside/outside, sender/receiver, and writer/reader to implicitly adopt a theory of correspondence requiring both points/directions/acts, subsequent cases have parsed this circuit of communication by, ironically, focusing on the prisoner. As the First Amendment rights of prisoners become more and more specified (both in terms of substance and mode), the rights of those on the outside enjoy less and less commentary by the Court.

One of the alarming aspects of this fixation on the prisoner is that the First Amendment rights of those on the outside are increasingly curtailed, as are the rights of those on the inside. Another is a creeping sense that the theory of correspondence the Court takes for granted to secure some privacy for the prisoner actually covers over a knotted reality about the legal relationship between self-expression and punishment. To explore this reality, I now turn to a case that never made it to the Supreme Court because of the straightforwardness of the legal issue.

In this case, *McNamara v. Moody* (1979), the Fifth Circuit Court of Appeals ruled that censoring a letter considered to be "in poor taste" was a violation of a prisoner's First Amendment right. The court here was simply following the ruling made a few years earlier in *Martinez:* that prison administration could not censor letters because of content that fell short of planning illegal activities (such as an escape). The facts of the case might initially appear rather anticlimactic or superficial in comparison to the forms of deprivation presented above (the CMU, physical torture, solitary confinement, or even the increasing trend to limit other forms of contact and communication). However, the case highlights a profoundly difficult legal problem that embodies the unresolvable relationship between punishment and self-expression. The following is an excerpt taken from the opinion's description of the letter at issue in *McNamara*:

> The two-page letter dealt in large part with McNamara's [the prisoner's] discontent with the prison mail censorship system, but it also charged that the mail censoring officer, while reading mail, engaged in masturbation and "had sex" with a cat. Moody [the prison guard] found the part of the letter referring to the mail censoring officer to be "in poor taste" and returned it to McNamara with a warning that any future attempts to send similar letters would lead to disciplinary action.[61]

Let us take a step back to examine how the pettiness of the dispute actually reveals the vast lifeworld of the letter. This letter in "poor taste" was addressed to McNamara's girlfriend, but Moody felt so insulted that he filed a personal injury claim. He argued that "if insults such as this were made orally to prison guards, face to face, they would be punishable as breaches of discipline."[62] The court ultimately was not convinced by the argument, confidently responding, "These remarks were in writing and were directed to the inmate's girlfriend, not the prison staff,"[63] and went on to dismiss Moody's libel and obscenity claims and ordered him to pay nominal damages and attorney's fees to McNamara.

But by whom, in fact, was this letter written to be read? Someone thinking they were the intended recipient of the letter, or the fact that the letter had an addressee, does not settle for whom the letter was written. The court neglected this issue in two ways. First, it assumed a phonocentric notion of injurious speech. It implicitly assumed that verbal speech has an ability to injure, in contrast to written speech, which does not. This implied that the absence of the prisoner's body in the letter is the issue that tilted the decision in favor of the prisoner. Second, the court evaded the question by simply equating the addressee with the intended reader. Here the court implicitly granted a logocentric notion of the prisoner's letter. The prisoner's writing must stand in his/her absence, as well as the absence of the other to whom s/he writes. It fixes his/her speech, which must travel across the prison wall because the prisoner cannot. In rendering the prisoner and the other in a logocentric letter, words become bodies and injurious speech becomes substantive complaint.

These assumptions about the letter are remarkably maintained, despite the undisputed fact that prisoners knew when writing their letters that prison staff could, and very likely would, read them before mailing them to the addressee. Someone reading for security purposes does not fail to complete the circuit of writer-to-reader correspondence that the Court laid out in *Martinez*. This reader simply creates a new circuit. Given this, the additional reader's claim (in this case, the prison guard) should have been an occasion to revise *Martinez*'s theory so that the "reader" of a letter is always plural, and in turn, to recognize that writing and reading a letter is a pluralizing activity. (This is not to say, however, that the case should have been decided in favor of the guard.)

While there was no revision, this curious case demonstrates how *Martinez*'s theory of correspondence, to secure and censor such correspondence, is attended by a negative space of communication that the Court shied away from regulating. Perhaps the Court sensed that communication cannot be regulated. As Lacan insisted in his reading of Poe, "[W]hat the 'purloined letter,' nay, the 'letter in sufferance,' means is that a letter always arrives at its destination."[64] More profoundly, the case reveals how the First Amendment does not protect against the pluralizing letter as a fugitive movement. The purloined prisoner is there to be found in the movement between body, speech, and word by virtue of the letter's irreducible materiality as desire that remains.

McNamara's civil death, then, disseminated trace upon trace of his body in writing the letter. There is contact there, as in tasting, and even if in "poor taste." The prisoner is a slight masquerading in plain sight as complaint, dissolving the phono-logocentrism of the law, only to be sutured together again. The letter (the disputed and disputing epistle and the interweaving text it set in motion) deconstructed any possible arrival at the rights that would articulate civil death as something other than the "undecidable" limit of punishment that it is.[65] In this way, a revenant letter engraves the prisoner in the law with every reading of the law's words, as the letter purloins the prisoner from and in civil death. The prisoner's undead spirit may not be traced as a reader or a writer, but the letter's trace—a sort of "aftertaste"—is there.

Strange Life

By whom *are* prisoners' letters written to be read? How might we address this vanishing question we have just discovered in prisoner First Amendment jurisprudence? I now turn to the narrative plot of Cheryl Dunye's 2001 HBO television movie *Stranger Inside* for its deep engagement with the empirical experience of civil death confounding the law.[66] *Stranger Inside*'s protagonist is a prisoner named Treasure Lee, who is consumed by her fantasy of maternal love. In an unrelenting search for her mother, Treasure stabs another girl while

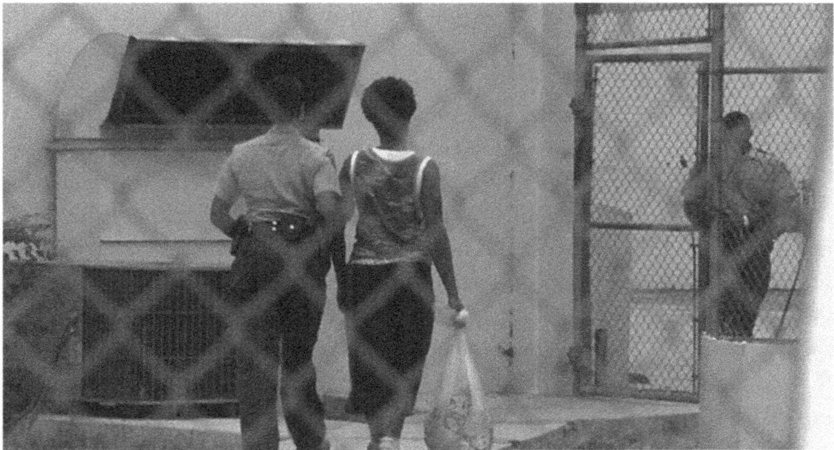

Figure 4.1. Still from *Stranger Inside*, from Shadow's perspective looking out.

at a juvenile detention center so that she will be moved to the maximum-security prison where she believes her estranged mother is housed.

From the outset, the film's reality is a lifeworld of punishment that circles around an epistolary photograph. Experience is of the prison, and the search for Treasure's truth takes place in this differentially bounded space. Memories do not render some place or time outside of it, to which there is the possibility of some return. There is no "society" separable from punishment; Treasure embodies the pressures of this social reality.

In the film's visual grammar, walls do not demarcate the division between freedom and incarceration, as is typical of the conventional camera perspective of looking into the prison from outside of it. *Stranger Inside* contains instead a diversity of shots that traverse the prison's various enclosures. Some frames show the perspective from outside the prison fence looking in, some from inside looking out, but most from within. The latter look at other women prisoners through the many walls, doors, and windows dividing the prison space. There is no visual representation of a barrier with "freedom" on the other side. The various crisscrossed images designate the law's transcendent presence from juvenile detention to super-max, cell to hole, yard to therapy, and institution to street (Figure 4.1). Indeed, the only two shots from outside the prison fence looking in are from the perspective of a prisoner in transit to another prison.

As such, Treasure's story is not one of the revolving door, or learned criminality, or her life course. It is a story of love, love for her friends, but ultimately, love for a mother. It is a mythical love. If the empirical reality of a world of the crisscrossed shot presents a dense space of prohibitions against intimacy, privacy, and self-expression between women, Treasure dives right into the darkest part of it in search of her mother. All she has to go by is a photo.

The blank spot in Treasure's memory that should be occupied by childhood images of her mother is written over by the various legal takings of Treasure's body as she is transported from one captive space to another. The blankness seems to fade as Treasure looks from one state of captivity into another for a mother. It is as if she is a lost child—not necessarily a being defined by an absence of natal history, but perhaps a being of lack *in* natal history. At the end of the film, this blankness unassumingly announces itself when she discovers that the woman in her photo, Brownie, who she thought was her mother, was in fact the woman who murdered her mother. We discover that Treasure is neither lost, nor orphaned, but is absolutely alone. The film closes with an inglorious scene in a minimum-security prison where Treasure ends up, leaving a trail of unsolvable crimes behind her. It points to a strange life haunted by a kind of antiresolution that ends Treasure's own previously unrelenting hauntedness by her mother's image. Between the knowledge of her mother's murder and her surrender to a state of aloneness, Treasure seems at a loss, but she does not appear to mourn.

What I have just recounted is *Stranger Inside*'s narrative, which is not unfamiliar.[67] However, the film is relevant in its theoretical contribution to a new way of thinking about punishment. What does the letter—Treasure's photo—have to say? Obviously, by the end of the narrative, the photo becomes a symbol of the real. Because Treasure now knows what the image of the photo refers to, its meaning no longer sustains her desire. Its contents are of no significance now. But its materiality, the developed piece of photographic paper, is how Treasure's natal alienation takes place. Clutched in her hand, stowed away, cast away, or dissolved to dust over time wherever it is, the photo brings into existence the inaccessibility of any filial origins for the prisoner and, at the same time, remains that which persists after Treasure's search for personal history has come to a close. Following Johnson in her reading of Lacan's reading of Poe, Treasure affirms that "the letter's destination is not its literal addressee, nor even whoever possesses it, but whoever is possessed by it."[68]

We do not know who took this picture or how it came into Treasure's possession, but throughout the film Treasure is never without it. The photo goes where Treasure is made to go, as if she and it are the same body. Perhaps they are not the same body, but they are, self-evidently, of the same absent mother.[69] Both are the mother's reproduction. And here is the theoretical innovation: Treasure and the photo, the prisoner and the photo, are equivalent. Treasure insists that her body is evidence of some other woman's existence and the photo

Figure 4.2. Still from *Stranger Inside*, Shadow's photo, Treasure's memory of Shadow.

insists that the thing it absents by capturing it is evidence of some truth. This point displaces the stakes involved in answering the law's vanishing question of prisoner First Amendment rights: By whom, in fact, are prisoners' letters written to be read? *Stranger Inside* finds that this is, at a certain level, an impossible question. It is impossible because it does not matter who reads the letter, just as it does not matter for whom the photo was taken. The civilly dead person's spirit survives not by individual will (writing letters, stories, press statements, complaints, and so forth), just as the photo's truth survives not by social or historical context.[70] That spirit survives in the letters of the law through which the letter of the law is written and read.

This is a dismal, but not dispiriting, conclusion. For it challenges us to have to read what we have been reading all along differently, while also challenging us to find ways to read everything we thought could not be read. The final crisscrossed shot in *Stranger Inside* is of Shadow, Treasure's girl gang "G" sister of both the inside and not-so-inside worlds, taking a picture of Treasure. Still in prison, Shadow captures Treasure looking in from the other side of the prison fence as she is escorted to a minimum-security prison (Figure 4.2).

The photo captures a line of feminine desire represented by both Treasure's and Shadow's noncorresponding looks, or what film theorist Vicky Lebeau might call the "indeterminacy of the sister's desire."[71] Their good-bye is not an exchange of words. It is literally a photo. Their intimacy is not contained in the photo, but is the photo in totality. Their bond is forged in a form that marks Treasure's lack of access to social fantasy, to intimacy, to personal history. But in this dispossession, Treasure descends upon a knowledge of the letter, what perhaps Beth Richie means by "reading women's own words."[72] And with Treasure, so might we fall, too.

REFERENCE MATTER

Notes

Introduction

1. My mobilization of Derridean deconstruction and Lacanian psychoanalysis in this book is indebted to Andrea Hurst's detailed and illuminating reading of these two philosophers in her volume *Derrida vis-à-vis Lacan: Interweaving Deconstruction and Psychoanalysis* (2008). Her chapter "The Death Drive and the Im-Possibility of Psychoanalysis" (146–82) was particularly important for conceptualizing the key ideas I discuss in this Introduction.

2. These are Vicky Lebeau's words summarizing Frantz Fanon's theoretical intervention into Lacanian psychoanalytic theory, where he prioritizes "the pressure of the real world on unconscious fantasy itself." "Psycho-politics: Frantz Fanon's *Black Skin, White Masks*," 114.

3. Teresa Brennan, *History after Lacan*, 4–7.

4. See, generally, Wendy Brown, *States of Injury: Power and Freedom in Late Modernity* (1995) and *Politics out of History* (2001).

5. Works on and in this tradition are too numerous to recount here, and are engaged and referenced through this book. The paradigmatic text is of course Cedric Robinson's *Black Marxism: The Making of the Black Radical Tradition*.

6. Against what they call "policy scholarship," Jeanne Schroeder and David Gray Carlson's "Psychoanalysis as the Jurisprudence of Freedom" offers a compelling polemical argument for doctrinal and theoretical approaches to law, which are both more speculative and more practical. Ultimately, however, my reading of racial jurisprudence in this book is a jurisprudence of freedom beyond (their jurisprudence of) freedom.

7. M. NourbeSe Philip, *Zong!*, 200 (quoting the criminal code of Canada).

8. The oceanic scene of slavery curated between Philip's and Williams's words in and against the law is that other place, that is no place because there are no words, and as such "semantic mayhem" (ibid., 193) and "weird combinations" (Patricia J. Williams, *The Alchemy of Race and Rights*, 14) overflow the page.

9. Pierre Schlag's *The Enchantment of Reason* is a particularly entertaining polemic against legal reason.

10. Sigmund Freud, *Interpretation of Dreams*, 535–50. This division between consciousness and the unconscious and censorship of the unconscious is the mechanism that he calls "regression."

11. Ibid., 545.

12. Ibid., 544.

13. Thomas Hobbes, "Introduction," in *Leviathan*, 9–12. See also Carl Schmitt, *The Leviathan in the State Theory of Thomas Hobbes: Meaning and Failure of a Political Symbol.*

14. Jacques Derrida, "Freud and the Scene of Writing," 88–89.

15. Williams, *The Alchemy of Race and Rights*, 163. Wilderson also draws a metaphor between kindling and slavery, pointing to the fact of an always remaindered desire, the "nigger in the woodpile," as he puts it. Frank B. Wilderson, *Red, White & Black: Cinema and the Structure of U.S. Antagonisms*, 85.

16. Williams, *The Alchemy of Race and Rights*, 164.

17. 347 U.S. 483 (1954). All references to "*Brown*" are to this case, unless otherwise indicated.

18. *Plessy v. Ferguson*, 163 U.S. 537 (1896) and *Parents Involved in Community Schools v. Seattle School District No. 1*, 551 U.S. 701 (2007).

19. *Brown v. Board of Education*, 349 U.S. 294 (1955).

20. *Parents Involved*, 748.

21. The conclusions of Clark and Clark's doll tests were incorporated into Kenneth Clark et al., "The Effects of Segregation and the Consequences of Desegregation—A Social Science Statement" and attached to the 1952 Appellants' Brief for the trial of *Brown v. Board of Education* (1954). See E. Martin, Jr., *Brown v. Board of Education: A Brief History with Documents*, 142–50. The statement was republished in the *Journal of Negro Education* (1953).

22. See, generally, Richard Kluger, *Simple Justice: The History of Brown v. Board of Education and Black America's Struggle for Equality*; and Mark V. Tushnet, *Making Civil Rights Law: Thurgood Marshall and the Supreme Court, 1936–1961*. See also Mary L. Dudziak, *Cold War Civil Rights: Race and the Image of American Democracy.*

23. See, generally, Daryl M. Scott, *Contempt and Pity: Social Policy and the Image of the Damaged Black Psyche, 1880–1996*; and Harold Cruse, *Plural but Equal: A Critical Study of Blacks and Minorities and America's Plural Society.*

24. See, for example, Linda Hamilton Krieger, "The Content of Our Categories"; Claude Steele, "A Threat in the Air: How Stereotypes Shape Intellectual Identity and Performance"; and Jerry Kang, "Trojan Horses of Race." But see also Charles Lawrence III, "The Id, the Ego, and Equal Protection: Reckoning with Unconscious Racism," and "Unconscious Racism Revisited: Reflections on the Impact and Origins of the Id, the Ego, and Equal Protection." Lawrence is the first legal scholar to argue that unconscious racism should be legally actionable, but whose idea of unconscious racism, as he discusses in the latter article, includes but exceeds the cognitive scientific notion of implicit bias.

25. See Sigmund Freud, "Childhood Memories and Screen Memories," in *The Psychopathology of Everyday Life*, 62–73.

26. Anthony P. Farley, "Perfecting Slavery," 229. Farley has also explored the psychical work of race and law in "Law as Trauma & Repetition."

27. Joan W. Scott, "Fantasy Echo: History and the Construction of Identity," 287–93.

28. Williams, *The Alchemy of Race and Rights*, 175. This lack is broached by Williams with a passage from Joy Kogawa's *Obasan* (1981):

> There is a silence that cannot speak.
> There is a silence that will not speak.
> Beneath the grass the speaking dreams and beneath the dreams is a sensate sea. The speech that frees comes forth from that amniotic deep. To attend its voice, I can hear it say, is to embrace its absence. But I fail the task. The word is stone. (175)

29. The definitional boundary marking the field of critical race theory is fraught and contested. One could approach this problem in the same way I approach racial jurisprudence. However, when I generally refer to critical race theory throughout the book, these formative volumes—Kimberlé W. Crenshaw et al., eds., *Critical Race Theory: The Key Writings That Formed the Movement*; Adrien K. Wing, ed., *Critical Race Feminism: A Reader*, and *Global Critical Race Feminism: An International Reader*; and Francisco Valdes et al., eds., *Crossroads, Directions, and a New Critical Race Theory*—provide an adequate representation of the field's range and limits.

30. Wilderson, *Red, White & Black*, 23.

31. See, generally, Immanuel Kant, *Critique of Practical Reason*. I note here that my reference to the categorical imperative is by way of it critical incorporation into psychoanalysis by Jacques Lacan in *The Ethics of Psychoanalysis*, 108–10; and "Kant avec Sade" in *Écrits*, 645–68. For a reading of Lacan's discussion of a possible ethics of the Real contained in and by Kant's moral law, see Alenka Zupančič, "The Subject of the Law," 63–73. What is raised as a compelling line of thought for understanding race and law, which I cannot take up here and only briefly mention, is the affective priority of "anguish" in the conceptual development of "objective feeling" that characterizes the operation of the Lacanian Real (66–67).

32. As Deleuze might think of it, the lawyer's work reflects not a sadist madness for possession, but a masochist madness for the "sign" of contract. Gilles Deleuze and Leopold Sacher-Masoch, *Masochism: Coldness and Cruelty*, 15–23. But see also Colette Soler's discussion of masochism in *What Lacan Said about Women*, 69–85. There she specifically reminds us that "Lacan notes that 'the social instance of woman' remains 'transcendent to the order of the contract'" (79). Approaching the contract from this vantage suggests that we must read it not as a sign of submission to Kantian or Sadean duty, but the mark of a preference for "the jouissance of being to that of having, the absolute to the countable" (85).

33. Wilderson, *Red, White & Black*, 23.

34. Angela Y. Davis, "Opening Defense Statement Presented by Angela Y. Davis," 331.

35. Ibid., 334.

36. Angela Y. Davis, "Unfinished Lecture on Liberation—II," 54.

37. Ibid.

38. Nahum D. Chandler, "Of Horizon," 31.

39. This argument is indebted to Nahum Chandler's reading of the Du Boisian "historial" example of "The Afro-American" as "a non-simple form, the supposed unity of which cannot be submitted to the idea or to the concept, but must rather be understood to acquire such organization only as a problematization of existence" (4). See Chandler, generally, "Of Horizon: An Introduction to 'The Afro-American' by W.E.B. Du Bois—circa 1894." The idea of "historiality" can be found throughout Chandler's writing, but is detailed in footnote 1, where he writes: "The theoretical concern is to propose the interest of a step toward something just beyond a historicism in the strict sense. I pro-

pose it to promote a rethinking [. . .] of the problematic names under the heading of concept of history as something otherwise than the events of time (whatever is such), however we might adduce meaning for such. Instead, perhaps the matter here concerns the movement in which the very possibility of event [. . .] is opened precisely in and as problem" (31). Chandler's emphasis on historiality echoes Heidegger's development of the concept of "being-in-the-world" that broaches everydayness (chapter four, "Temporality and Everydayness," sections 67–71) and historicity (chapter five, "Temporality and Historicity," sections 72–77). See Martin Heidegger, *Being and Time*, 319–83. We cannot overstate the significance of Chandler's reading of Du Bois, which gives other contemporary philosophical work potential purpose in a certain black resonance of, for example, Badiou's notion of the "supernumerary" as "the abnormal multiple, on the edge of the void"; see Alain Badiou, *Being and Event*, 178–83. See also Peter Hallward, *Think Again: Alain Badiou and the Future of Philosophy*.

40. Veena Das, *Life and Words*, 168.

41. Hortense J. Spillers, "Mama's Baby, Papa's Maybe: An American Grammar Book," 74.

42. Derrick A. Bell, "Racism Is Here to Stay: Now What?" 89–90.

43. Jared Sexton and Steve Martinot, "The Avant-Garde of White Supremacy," 197–217.

44. David Marriott, "Inventions of Existence: Sylvia Wynter, Frantz Fanon, Sociogeny, and 'the Damned,'" 45 (quoting Fanon). This leap is an essential ethical act that is captured by Marriott's conception of "Fanon's future imperfect" (84), wherein "to leap is to escape and yet remain, to continue to relate to the 'historical' and yet never abandon the possibility of an open-ended traveling where reaching towards the universal is to reach for oneself as other, not as the performance of some mask of illusion, but as a process of endless creation, infinitely expressed, and likewise perpetually self-engendering" (ibid., 53–54). Notably, Derrick A. Bell's *Faces at the Bottom of the Well*, offers a parallel reading of the same passage of Fanon revisited by Marriott. In his 1992 "Preface," Bell identifies the "struggle for racial justice" with telling "the truth about racism without causing disabling despair" (ix), which he supports with an affirmation of Fanon's concept of the "real *leap*" (x). From this, we should refer to the pessimism of Bell's theory of the permanence of racism as a "pessimism+."

45. Williams, *The Alchemy of Race and Rights*, 7.

46. Hortense Spillers, "'All the Things You Could Be by Now, If Sigmund Freud's Wife Was Your Mother': Psychoanalysis and Race," 379. Joan Copjec further highlights the urgency of Spillers's reformulation here, but in the inverse, when she argues, "The only time something can be hidden in plain sight . . . is when its invisibility is a psychical condition and not merely a physical one." Joan Copjec, *Read My Desire: Lacan against the Historicists*, 141–42.

47. This is the argument I hear in Spillers's "'All the Things You Could Be by Now," where she formulates the problem in this way:

> We are confronted, then, by divergent temporal frames, or beats, that pose the problem of adequacy—how to reclaim an abandoned site of inquiry in the critical discourse when the very question that it articulates is carried along as a part of the methodological structure, as a feature of the paradigm that is itself under suspicion,

while the question itself foregrounds a thematic that cannot be approached in any other way. (406)

The very question instantiates "a *structure* in this instance," and thus a "small integrity of the now that accumulates the tense of the presents as proofs of the past, and as experience that would warrant, might earn, the future" (396).

48. For a much more detailed critique of this intellectual trend, see, generally, Christopher Tomlins, "What Is Left of the Law and Society Paradigm after Critique? Revisiting Gordon's 'Critical Legal Histories'"; and Christopher Tomlins and John Comaroff, "'Law As . . .': Theory and Practice in Legal History."

49. These phrases come from Spillers's conceptualization of "flesh" in "Mama's Baby, Papa's Maybe," 206.

50. Drucilla Cornell, *The Philosophy of the Limit.*

51. Gayatri C. Spivak, "Constitutions and Culture Studies," 135.

52. For a critique of law's conflicted relationship with science, see Bruno Latour, "Scientific Objects and Legal Objectivity." See also Mary Poovey, *A History of the Modern Fact: Problems of Knowledge in the Sciences of Wealth and Society.*

53. Gayatri C. Spivak, "Feminism and Deconstruction, Again: Negotiating with Unacknowledged Masculinism," 213–14.

54. Ibid., 213.

55. *Fisher v. University of Texas at Austin*, 570 U.S. __ (2013).

56. 539 U.S. 306 (2003). *Grutter* was at the time the authoritative affirmative action ruling, which held that an admissions policy designed to create a "critical mass" of under-represented minorities in furtherance of its educational purpose to maintain diversity in the student body passed strict scrutiny and thus, did not violate the Equal Protection Clause of the Fourteenth Amendment.

57. *Fisher*, 13.

58. Two other controversial cases decided during this term reveal the primacy of standing doctrine in current constitutional adjudications of inequality issues, even if this is not formally raised in *Fisher*. These are the same-sex marriage cases, *U.S. v. Windsor*, 570 U.S. __ (2013), ruling that the federal Defense of Marriage Act violates the Due Process and Equal Protection clauses, and *Hollingsworth v. Perry*, 570 U.S. __ (2013), ruling that the Ninth Circuit Court of Appeals did not have jurisdiction to hear a challenge to the validity of Proposition 8. Both significantly turn on interpretations of Article III, Section 2, of the U.S. Constitution, which limits the jurisdiction of federal judicial review to "cases or controversies," and is the source from which standing doctrine issues.

Windsor reveals the liberal capacity of the Supreme Court to interpret standing doctrine when it is confronted by a "procedural dilemma" that obstructs a proper pleading of standing, by granting "prudential" standing (majority opinion, 11–12). In this case, the procedural difficulties of pleading standing were "cured" when the Supreme Court recognized the potential of a "case or controversy" to arise from DOMA's definition of marriage, at the same time that Scalia's scathing dissent argued that there was not a genuine "controversy" because the plaintiff's individual injury had become moot by virtue of the lower court's decisions in her favor (dissenting opinion, 1–11). In *Hollingsworth* the Supreme Court refused to expand claims to standing. There it refused to recognize the formal private citizen groups behind Proposition 8 as "agents" of the state of California because of a lack of fiduciary relation, and thus ruled that they did not have standing to defend Proposition 8's constitutionality in federal courts. However, even in withholding standing, it did gesture to a widened capacity for a state to claim standing through various constituency groups. In both these cases, LGBT inequality issues are able to expand the terrain of standing on both sides of the marriage debate, but do not necessarily reach the limit of standing doctrine that obliquely erupts in *Fisher*. While this limit is written across racial jurisprudence, it was famously crystallized in *Schlesinger v. Reservists Committee to Stop the War*, 418 U.S. 208 (1974). There the Court shrugged its shoulders, stating, "The assumption that if respondents have no standing to sue, no one would have standing, is not a reason to find standing" (227). And though he did not intend to, Scalia plainly restates this general, but no less brutal, truth of racial jurisprudence, when in his *Windsor* dissent he explains, "And that is why, as our opinions have said, some questions of law will never be presented to this Court, because there will never be anyone with standing to bring a lawsuit" (4).

59. *Fisher*, 14.

60. Ibid., 15.

61. Ibid., 14 (Thomas, quoting Paul Finkelman, quoting proslavery senator John C. Calhoun's famous 1837 speech, "The Positive Good of Slavery," in his critical study *Defending Slavery*).

62. 342 U.S. 350.

63. 347 U.S. 497.

64. *Fisher*, 15.

65. Here we are reminded again of the particular urgency of revisiting Harlan's reference to a "new constitutional right," which I discuss in Chapter 1.

66. W. E. Burghardt Du Bois. "Does the Negro Need Separate Schools?" 335.

67. Ibid., 333.

68. Ibid., 334.

69. Ibid., 335.

70. Ibid., 334.

71. The other controversial Supreme Court ruling during this term, *Shelby County v. Holder*, 570 U.S. __ (2013), reveals that this dead end is apparent beyond the issue of racial inequality in education. In this case, the Supreme Court ruled unconstitutional a provision of Section 4 of the Voting Rights Act of 1965 that dictated a "coverage formula" for those states and subdivisions that would need to seek preclearance from federal authorities before changing their voting policies. The majority and dissenting opinions essentially disagree over the significance of empirical evidence showing relative parity of black and white voter registration and increasing successes of minority political candidates. The majority believes that this evidence proves that the preclearance provision has outlived its utility, and that "history did not end in 1965" (4), to use Roberts's inane observation; and the dissent believes that this evidence proves a past and future utility of the provision, as part of "the most consequential, efficacious, and amply justified exercises of federal legislative power in our Nation's history" (Ginsburg, 3). Both validate the necessity of equal black participation in formal politics, but neither can entertain the question of an autonomous black politics.

72. Du Bois, "Does the Negro Need Separate Schools?" 328.

73. Williams, *The Alchemy of Race and Rights,* 165.

74. In this way, I believe Williams is the strongest response to and extension of a general problem in modern legal thought and practice that Costas Douzinas and Lynda Nead identify in their illuminating volume, *Law and the Image: The Authority of Art and the Aesthetics of Law* (1999). There they rightly observe that

> throughout history law has been the performative language par excellence, a language whose success is measured by its consequences, its ability to act on the world. A language that carries the rudiments of order and transmits the commands of the law must act on the emotions and persuade the intellect; it can only be a beautiful language and, despite protestations to the contrary, legal practice and education consciously or unconsciously have always understood this. The link between performance of law and love for the text is pervasive in practice. But the greatest impediment to its full recognition has been what we may call the resistance of genre, the belief in the Platonic injunction against poetry and rhetoric and in the Kantian separation between the normative and the aesthetic. (10)

We can restate the general problem identified here to the specific concerns of this book. That is, we have yet to fully grapple with the law as a performative language on its own terms because the fantasy of colorblindness refortifies the "resistance of genre." Law is reduced to example in J. L. Austin's speech act theory, while the performative of law must be theorized across modern law's constitution in the difference between speech and writing, reason and rhetoric, natural and positive law, and so forth. See, generally, Jacques Derrida, "Signature Event Context."

75. Williams, *The Alchemy of Race and Rights,* 201.

76. Alice Lagaay, "Between Sound and Silence: Voice in the History of Psychoanalysis," 58.

77. Mladen Dolar, *A Voice and Nothing More,* 23–32.

78. "Ani*mater*iality" is Fred Moten's aesthetic concept of the irreducible general value of that unprecedented commodity, the slave, and her relationality given in "impassioned response to passionate utterance—[that is] painfully and hiddenly disclosed always and everywhere in the tracks of black performance and black discourse on performance." Fred Moten, *In the Break: The Aesthetics of the Black Radical Tradition,* 18.

79. Jacques Derrida, "Force of Law: The 'Mystical Foundation of Authority,'" 967.

80. Ibid., 949.

81. Ibid., 945. In the introductory framing, he makes a certain embellishment, or qualification, about the relation between law and deconstruction, where he signifies, at least in my mind, the deconstruction he is talking about. This is "the *practice* of a deconstruction that, fundamentally, always leads to questions of *droit*" (ibid., my emphasis).

82. Ibid., 1007.

83. Jürgen Habermas, *Between Facts and Norms: Contributions to a Discourse Theory of Law and Democracy.*

84. Derrida, "Force of Law," 971.

85. This play with quotation marks is consistent with one of the questions Derrida poses of deconstruction (and justice), "Why does deconstruction have the reputation, justified or not, of treating things obliquely, indirectly, with 'quotation marks,' and of always asking whether things arrive at the indicated address?" (ibid., 945–47).

86. Fred Moten, "Knowledge of Freedom," 284. However, I think it fair to say that Derrida would avow this refusal or incapacity in "Force of Law," where he discusses a resonance between the "performative structure of speech acts and acts in general as acts of justice or law" (969), or what he theorizes as "decision" throughout the article. He notes, "A constative can be *juste* (right), in the sense of *justesse*, never in the sense of justice. But as a performative cannot be just, in the sense of justice, except by founding itself on conventions and so on other anterior performatives, buried or not, it always maintains within itself some irruptive violence, it no longer responds to the demands of theoretical rationality" (969). What I am trying to get at, then, is precisely how Derrida's performative of "justice" "no longer responds to the demands of theoretical rationality." He goes on, as if to warn us and himself about what is missed if we reduce "Force of Law" to a theory of law or a theory of deconstruction:

> Since every constative utterance itself relies, at least implicitly, on a performative structure ("I tell you that, I speak to you, I address myself to you to tell you that this is true, that things are like this, I promise you or renew my promise to you to make a sentence and to sign what I say when I say that, tell you, or try to tell you the truth," and so forth), the dimension of *justesse* or truth of the theoretical-constative utterance (in all domains, particularly in the domain of the theory of law) always thus presupposes the dimension of justice [what I have been referencing as "justice"] of the performative utterances, that is to say their essential precipitation, which never proceeds without a certain dissymmetry and some quality of violence (969).

For a most excellent discussion of "Force of Law," see J. Hillis Miller, "Who or What Decides, for Derrida: A Catastrophic Theory of Decision," 9–27.

87. Moten, "Knowledge of Freedom," 285.

88. Ibid., 286.

89. Ibid., 285–86.

90. Ibid., 286.

91. I do not have the space to fully expand on the foreclosed scene of slavery that at various points intrudes upon Derrida's "Force of Law," and his numerous references to examples of law and violence that rhetorically ride a certain American exceptionality in the history of modern law. Relatedly, I wish to note the national scope of my critique of legal universalism throughout this book. However, to the extent that American jurisprudence enjoys a certain privileged transnational translation into other domestic and international legal regimes (even if as negative example), I believe that my argument about the foundational structure of the fantasy of colorblindness is relevant outside of the United States. At stake is how the global reach of the fantasy of colorblindness requires us to reconceptualize the status of the nation-state in public international law, and more specifically within that jurisprudence, the assumption of formal or effective difference between national civil rights and international human rights.

92. Fred Moten, "Case of Blackness," 199.

93. Williams, *The Alchemy of Race and Rights*, 175–76.

94. Ibid., 172. In arriving at this "disappearance" immanent to law that is written across the whole of her text, Williams was grappling with the 1987 Tawana Brawley case,

in which a missing black teenage girl was found brutalized in a vacant lot. Williams recounts Brawley "in a dazed state, not responding to noise, cold or ammonia; there was urine-soaked cotton stuffed in her nose and ears; her hair had been chopped off; there were cigarette burns over a third of her body; 'KKK' and 'Nigger' had been inscribed on her torso; her body was smeared with dog feces" (169). This image of Brawley's body immediately came to stand in for "some unspeakable crime" that national politics and media discourse, promising to solve and vindicate, extended and further obscured.

95. In "A Day in the Life of Civil Rights," Hortense Spiller's 1978 short story about a New York City hospital nurse, Betty Trammel, we find something like this desire in the undying contemplation of the chance that "perhaps there is enough time left to restructure a private myth from the tattered fragments of loss and disappointment" (27).

Chapter 1

1. Hannah Arendt, *The Origins of Totalitarianism*, 290.

2. Jacques Derrida, "The Law of Genre," 57.

3. *Fisher*, 570 U.S. __ (2013), 10.

4. *Plessy v. Ferguson*, 163 U.S. 537 (1896); *Civil Rights Cases of 1883*, 109 U.S. 3 (1883); and *Dred Scott v. Sandford*, 60 U.S. 393 (1857).

5. *Grutter*, 539 U.S. 206 (2003).

6. Ibid., 333–34 (citing Brief for 3M et al. as *Amici Curiae*, Brief for General Motors Corp. as *Amicus Curiae* 3–4; and quoting Brief for Julius W. Becton, Jr. et al. as *Amici Curiae* 27).

7. *Bakke*, 438 U.S. 265 (1978).

8. Ibid., 292 (my emphasis).

9. Ibid., 293 (quoting a prior decision, *McDonald v. Santa Fe Trail Transportation Co.*, 427 U.S. 273 (1976)).

10. Ibid., 292.

11. Hortense Spillers, "Changing the Letter: The Yokes, the Jokes of Discourse, or, Mrs. Stowe, Mr. Reed," 179.

12. Ibid.

13. Saidiya V. Hartman, "The Time of Slavery," 766.

14. Alexis de Tocqueville, *Democracy in America*, 63.

15. Ibid., 412.

16. Ibid., 431.

17. Toni Morrison, "On the Backs of Blacks," 98.

18. *Plessy*, 559. For the standard critique of Harlan's famous dictum, see, generally, Neil Gotanda, "A Critique of 'Our Constitution Is Color-Blind.'"

19. Cheryl I. Harris, "The Story of *Plessy v. Ferguson*: The Death and Resurrection of Racial Formalism," 218 (my emphasis).

20. Ibid. In another version of this chapter from *Constitutional Law Stories*, Harris outlines the doctrinal intersections between state sovereignty, federal commerce power, and the law of common carriers that produce *Plessy* and its after-images, and describes this as the "shadow of Plessy." Cheryl I. Harris, "In the Shadow of Plessy," 872–85.

21. *Plessy*, 559.

22. Ibid., 561.

23. For a history of how Chinese exclusion was an extension of antiblack migration policies, see Najia Aarim-Heriot, *Chinese Immigrants, African Americans, and Racial Anxiety in the United States, 1848–82*.

24. *Plessy*, 555.

25. In this way, the colorblind citizen in U.S. racial jurisprudence is not unlike the liberal subject of justice who enters into democracy with a "veil of ignorance." See, generally, John Rawls, *A Theory of Justice*. For a critique of Rawls, see, generally, Charles Mills, *The Racial Contract.*

26. Ian Haney-López offers the important argument that whiteness today, in contrast to the era of the racial prerequisite cases he examines, is able to variously include people of color. See his revised edition of *White by Law: The Legal Construction of Race.*

27. Of particular interest is the Supreme Court case *Gong Lum v. Rice*, 275 U.S. 78 (1927). For an extended discussion of this case, see Sora Y. Han, "The Politics of Race in Asian American Jurisprudence."

28. Harlan provides a succinct summary of the historical relation between the Reconstruction Amendments and the Civil Rights bills: "They [the majority] admit, as I have said, that the Thirteenth Amendment established freedom; that there are burdens and disabilities, the necessary incidents of slavery, which constitute its substance and visible form; that Congress, by the act of 1866, passed in view of the Thirteenth Amendment, before the Fourteenth was adopted, undertook to remove certain burdens and disabilities, the necessary incidents of slavery, to secure to all citizens of every race and color, and without regard to previous servitude, those fundamental rights which are the essence of civil freedom, namely, the same right to make and enfore [*sic*] contracts, to sue, be parties, give evidence, and to inherit, purchase, lease, sell and convey property as is enjoyed by white citizens" (*Civil Rights Cases of 1883*, 35–36).

29. Ibid., 37–43.

30. Ibid., 40.

31. Ibid., 36 (italics in original).

32. Ibid., 50. At the same time, it is no small irony that Harlan relies on *Prigg v. Pennsylvania* (1842) as precedent for this principle of federalism, and, in fact, opens his dissent with a general discussion of how the Supreme Court cannot not validate the constitutionally authorized civil rights of the freedmen when it had, prior to the Civil War, validated the constitutionally authorized property rights of the master. I discuss this important case in Chapter 3, "Racial Profiling."

33. *Civil Rights Cases of 1883*, 50 (my emphasis).

34. Robert M. Cover, "Violence and the Word," 1604.

35. *Civil Rights Cases of 1883*, 10.

36. Ibid., 11–12.

37. Ibid., 17.

38. Ibid., 21.

39. Ibid., 24.

40. Ibid., 23.

41. Ibid., 22.

42. Ibid.

43. Ibid., 24.

44. Ibid., 25.

45. Joan Copjec argues that this envy is a structural feeling of political liberalism. Noting that envy is the feeling of wanting something another is perceived to have, envy as an expression of lack cannot be satisfied with any one thing identified at the outset because of the difference between what one wants and what one perceives the other to have (*Imagine There's No Woman: Ethics and Sublimation*, 158–59).

46. *Civil Rights Cases of 1883*, 22.

47. *The Civil Rights Cases of 1883* have been revitalized in recent years, beginning with the Rehnquist Court and continuing on with the Roberts Court. See, for example, *United States v. Morrison* (2000) and *Shelby County v. Holder* (2013). For an extended discussion of this recent doctrinal revival, see my chapter, "Equal Protection's Dead End, or the Slave's Undying Claim" in *New Controversies in Equal Protection* (forthcoming, June 2015, from Ashgate Publishing Ltd.).

48. Colin Dayan carefully discusses the fatal paradox of the gift of freedom for the slave in her chapter "A Legal Ethnography." She asks, "Release [of a slave from slavery] through manumission, then, was not simply a gift but an act of creation. Since the slave had no capacity to become free and could never gain it, emancipation meant something new. What was that something? Or, to put it differently, how do you bequeath freedom to enslaved persons who might not be capable of receiving it? And what kind of freedom would individual manumission promise?" (*The Law Is a White Dog: How Legal Rituals Make and Unmake Persons*, 146).

49. Avital Ronell, "The Testamentary Whimper."

50. *Scott*, 403.

51. Because Scott had already exhausted legal avenues at the state court level, Taney's conclusion that the federal courts did not have jurisdiction over Scott's case effectively meant that Scott would be unable to secure legal recognition of his free status through a civil suit.

52. Christopher L. Eisgruber, "The Story of *Dred Scott*: Originalism's Forgotten Past."

53. *Scott*, 422.

54. Ibid.

55. Ibid., 403–4.

56. To underscore this point, Taney contrasts the position of the black to the position of the Native, who he claims has the capacity to become an American citizen because she has a tradition of political organization (ibid., 419). This imagined distinction between the capacities of Native peoples and African-descendant slaves based on an evaluation of First World and African cultures is repeated in modern Enlightenment thought on America. Tocqueville also makes this distinction, which leads him to conclude that the future of Native peoples in the democratic experiment is not subject to the "imagined inequality" that prohibits a democratic future inclusive of blacks (*Democracy in America*, 389–411).

57. *Scott*, 407 (my emphasis).

58. This point ties in with my larger critique of Wendy Brown's argument that rights-based political movements are motivated by *ressentiment* (*States of Injury*, 24–29). While this might be true of late-twentieth-century rights-based movements that would make a minstrel show of the centuries-long black civil rights struggle to generalize the slave's knowledge of freedom, the accepted critique of *ressentiment* negates the differ-

ence between a natural law of freedom premised on the humanity of the legal claimant, and what Fred Moten has called the slave's "freedom drive" premised on the "objection" of the claim (*In the Break*, 7).

Chapter 2

1. Derrida, "Force of Law," 963.

2. *Metro Broadcasting, Inc. v. FCC*, 497 U.S. 547 (1990).

3. 515 U.S. 200 (1995) 237 (quoting *Fullilove v. Klutznick*, 448 U.S. 448 (1980), 519). Adam Winkler, in his article "Fatal in Theory and Strict in Fact: An Empirical Analysis of Strict Scrutiny in the Federal Courts," provides a useful index of applications of strict scrutiny from 1990 to 2003. He argues that strict scrutiny does not always lead the courts to overrule race-based laws. In fact, Fourteenth Amendment equal protection cases involving "suspect class discrimination" had a 27 percent chance of surviving strict scrutiny analysis. Based on this empirical evidence, Winkler argues that Gerald Gunther's characterization of strict scrutiny in "Forward: In Search of Evolving Doctrine on a Changing Court: A Model for a Newer Equal Protection," is untrue. But to the extent that Winkler's empirical claims speak only partially to Gunther's more general truth claim—at once historical, political, and doctrinal—Winkler's argument leaves much room for other methodological approaches to studying the fatal-ness of the doctrine in post–civil rights constitutional law.

4. Ruth Wilson Gilmore, "Race and Globalization," 261.

5. To my mind, Anthony P. Farley is engaged in a similar project of reading the law as a symptomatic space. See, for example, his application of Frantz Fanon to American racial jurisprudence in "The Poetics of Colorlined Space."

6. *Korematsu v. U.S.* 323 U.S. 214 (1944) (all references to "*Korematsu*" are to this case, unless otherwise indicated).

7. Civilian Exclusion Order No. 34 was issued by the Commanding General of the Western Defense Command under authority of Executive Order No. 9066 and the Act of March 21, 1942. It directed the exclusion from prescribed West Coast military areas of all persons of Japanese ancestry after May 9, 1942. Other orders, also pursuant to Executive Order No. 9066, provided for their mandatory reporting to assembly centers, and their detention in assembly centers and interment camps. For further details on how internment was enacted through a series of executive orders and municipal criminal codes, see Roberts's dissent, *Korematsu*, 225–29. Given this network of both military and criminal laws, Roberts observes:

> In the dilemma that he [Fred Korematsu] dare not remain in his home, or voluntarily leave the area, without incurring criminal penalties, and that the only way he could avoid punishment was to go to an Assembly Center and submit himself to military imprisonment, the petitioner did nothing. (230)

8. *Korematsu v. United States*, 584 F. Supp. 1406, 1420 (1984).

9. Clarence Thomas, in his dissenting opinion in *Grutter v. Bollinger*, 539 U.S. 306, 351 (2003), notes that the Court first articulated strict scrutiny as a standard of reviewing racial discrimination in *Korematsu*. Interestingly, he uses this historical fact as a way to negate the compelling governmental interest of diversity at issue in affirmative action cases by contrasting it to the one at issue in *Korematsu*—namely, national security

during a time of war. Other key civil rights cases using and citing *Korematsu* as authority on strict scrutiny include *Bush v. Vera*, 116 S. Ct. 1941 (1996); *Adarand Constructors, Inc. v. Pena*, 515 U.S. 200 (1995); *City of Richmond v. J. A. Croson Co.*, 488 U.S. 469 (1989); *University of California Regents v. Bakke*, 438 U.S. 265 (1978); *Loving v. Virginia*, 388 U.S. 1 (1967); and *Bolling v. Sharpe*, 347 U.S. 497 (1954).

10. *Korematsu*, 216.
11. *Grutter*, 325.
12. *Korematsu*, 220.
13. *Grutter*, 326.
14. *Korematsu*, 216.
15. Ibid., 223.
16. Ibid., 216.
17. See, for example, how *Korematsu* is used in William Cohen's and Jonathan D. Varat's casebook, *Constitutional Law: Cases and Materials* (1997), in contrast to how it is used in the casebook of Dycus, Berney, Banks, and Raven-Hansen, *National Security Law* (2002).
18. Jed Rubenfeld, "Affirmative Action," 450. In his convincing critique of the justificatory ruse of strict scrutiny analysis, Rubenfeld goes on to make the striking observation that "[s]trict scrutiny of race classifications may be the first instance in our jurisprudence of a constitutional doctrine unconstitutional under itself" (ibid.).
19. The terms of debate surrounding *Korematsu* are, interestingly enough, reproduced in the common refrain heard since 9/11 about balancing "security" and "civil liberties" in waging the War on Terror. See, for example, Tania Cruz, "Judicial Scrutiny of National Security: Executive Restrictions of Civil Liberties When 'Fears and Prejudices are Aroused'"; and Samuel Issacharoff and Richard H. Pildes, "Between Civil Libertarianism and Executive Unilateralism: An Institutional Process Approach to Rights during Wartime." However, this purported tension has been noted and critiqued prior to 9/11. See Eric K. Yamamoto, "Korematsu Revisited—Correcting the Injustice of Extraordinary Government Excess and Lax Judicial Review: Time for a Better Accommodation of National Security Concerns and Civil Liberties." For a critique of how the Japanese internment cases have undergone a "noncontextual resurrection" in the War on Terror enemy combatant cases, see Jerry Kang, "Watching the Watchers: Enemy Combatants in the Internment's Shadow," 278–80.
20. *Korematsu*, 235.
21. Ibid., 242 (my emphasis).
22. Ibid., 240 (Murphy, dissenting).
23. Rubenfeld is worth quoting again on this point:

> [If] racial classifications do in fact fall squarely within the language and spirit of the Equal Protection Clause, they should be held unconstitutional *even if they are narrowly tailored to further a compelling state interest*. There is something deeply wrong with the cost-benefit picture of strict scrutiny. Economizing equal protection is unacceptable. . . . Offsetting state benefits cannot 'justify' a law violating an individual's equal protection rights. That is what it means to have an equal protection right; the right is not subject to any ordinary cost-benefit calculus. Treating an ethnic group as a menial class may serve any number of compelling

state interests. Most peoples since the dawn of time have thought as much. Racial subjugation might even, conceivably, produce the greatest happiness for the greatest number. But the Fourteenth Amendment blocks every state action directed to this end, whatever interests it might serve. (440–41, my emphasis)

24. Gotanda first articulated this notion of racial foreignness in critical race theory, and this concept generally informs recent critiques of the racial politics of immigration law and detention. See, generally, Neil Gotanda, "'Other Non-Whites' in American Legal History: A Review of 'Justice at War'"; and "The Story of *Korematsu*: The Japanese-American Cases."

25. The state of exception to which Japanese Americans were subjected occurred against a quotidian and far more complex state of exception structuring a Jim Crow society. The legal archive of Jim Crow America contains the simultaneous violations of civil rights by federal executive, legislative, and judicial enactments and omissions; state and municipal segregation laws empowered by the constitutionally derived "police powers"; and northern state and municipal laws unwilling to intervene on a private law of black segregation. That Japanese Americans and other racial minorities also found themselves caught in the wide net of this structure of antiblack racial segregation is unexceptional as a matter of history. According to historians Greg Robinson and Toni Robinson, cases predating *Korematsu* document how Japanese American plaintiffs argued for their right to live and work without discrimination. These cases, along with *Korematsu* and the hundreds, if not thousands, of antidiscrimination cases argued on behalf of African American plaintiffs, together comprise the legal grounds upon which *Brown v. Board of Education* was decided in 1954 under a strict scrutiny framework. Robinson and Robinson, "*Korematsu* and Beyond: Japanese Americans and the Origins of Strict Scrutiny."

This historical point is crucial to remark the persistence of this domestic racial scene in our current moment that crudely crops this complex legal history by assuming that wars on terror displace antiblack racism. Still, my interest in *Korematsu* as the origin of the doctrine of strict scrutiny is less historical, and more literal. Relatedly, then, I hope my reading of *Korematsu* as a judicial opinion on judicial review of state racisms is not be assimilated into a politics of "trauma envy," richly elaborated by Mowitt in his article of the same name. There he persuasively calls into question a dominant notion of trauma and its discourse of *ressentiment* mobilized by contemporary Leftist cultural critique because it is "expressly designed to displace another" (John Mowitt, "Trauma Envy," 292). Sharing Mowitt's concern, albeit with a different set of intellectual debates in mind, I offer my reading of *Korematsu* as a potential way out of "the movement of a certain analytical misogyny," as Mowitt strikingly puts it, that guides critical identity studies, including their various iterations in legal studies.

26. *Korematsu*, 219–20.

27. Ibid., 223.

28. Ibid.

29. Ibid., 224. This is a curious compensatory statement, again indicating a motivation other than the one outlined in the rationality of his legal opinion. In fact, Eugene Gressman, a law clerk to Murphy in 1944, in his article "*Korematsu*: A Mélange of Military Imperatives," argues that racism was undeniably present in the opinion. For a legal history of how the government used or neglected various sources of information for

evidentiary purposes in the World War II Japanese internment cases, see, generally, Peter H. Irons, *Justice at War: The Story of the Japanese American Internment Cases*; see also Murphy's arguments related to the lack of evidence to impute disloyalty on all Japanese Americans. *Korematsu*, 235–40.

30. Ibid., 233.

31. Derrida, "Force of Law," 993.

32. *Korematsu*, 233 (Murphy, dissenting).

33. See, generally, Shoshana Felman and Dori Laub, *Testimony: Crises of Witnessing in Literature, Psychoanalysis, and History*; and Lisa Yoneyama, *Hiroshima Traces: Time, Space, and the Dialectics of Memory*.

34. I am thinking here, of course, of Wendy Brown and Chantal Mouffe and their various critical approaches to understanding democracy, rights, and difference.

35. Robert M. Cover, "Violence and the Word," 1602. Cover further argues that "Legal interpretation is either played out on the field of pain and death or it is something less (or more) than law." My reading of strict judicial review of the racial discrimination claim would revise Cover's division between legal realism and politics by arguing that legal interpretation is *both* dealings in pain and death, *and* something less and more than law.

36. Jacques Derrida, *Memoirs of the Blind: The Self-Portrait and Other Ruins*, 13.

37. Ibid.

38. Ibid., 15. We can also note at this point the similar topography of the cave with the vase, both of which appear in Lacan's Seminar VII, *The Ethics of Psychoanalysis*. Raising the example of the vase in her own discussion of the Lacanian reading of *Antigone*, Alenka Zupančič reminds us, "A vase can be considered 'as an object made to represent the existence of the emptiness at the center of the real that is called the Thing, this emptiness as represented in the representation presents itself as a *nihil*, as nothing'" ("Ethics and Tragedy in Lacan," 185, quoting Lacan).

39. I am indebted to Roshanak Kheshti for our ongoing conversations about sound. For this particular point about a relation of racial/sexual subjection that takes place in the material structure of sound, see Kheshti's discussion of the concept of *signifiance* in "Inversion, Signifiance and the Loss of the Self in Sound," 68–77.

40. See George Steiner's study, *Antigones*.

41. Jacques Lacan, *The Ethics of Psychoanalysis, 1959–1960: The Seminar of Jacques Lacan, Book VII*, 278.

42. Ibid., 263.

43. Ibid., 248.

44. Ibid., 262–63.

45. Ibid., 264–265.

46. Ibid., 247.

47. Ibid.

48. Joan Copjec, "The Tomb of Perseverance," 30.

49. Ibid.

50. Ibid. (quoting Lacan).

51. Ibid., 31 (quoting Lacan).

52. Lacan, *The Ethics of Psychoanalysis, 1959–1960*, 247.

53. *Grutter*, 326 (quoting *Adarand*).

54. Lacan, *The Ethics of Psychoanalysis, 1959–1960*, 281.

55. Ibid., 281–83. Beyond the formal distinctions between *ius divinum*, *ius humanum*, and mythology in classical times, and how those distinctions bear on our contemporary understanding of law and sovereign power, it seems here that those distinctions also bear on our understanding of law and criminality. That issue is beyond the scope of this chapter.

56. Ibid., 280.

57. Copjec, "The Tomb of Perseverance," 33 (referencing Nietzsche).

58. Ibid., 34.

59. Ibid.

60. *Fisher*, 13.

61. Zupančič, "Ethics and Tragedy in Lacan," 185.

62. Joan Copjec, "Vampires, Breast-Feeding, and Anxiety," 122.

63. Joan Copjec, quoting Gilles Deleuze, is discussing specifically the filmic technique of the close-up, which shifts the function of the face from one of individuating a person to deindividuating a person by lifting her from represented space and suspending her in a negative condition of possibility for enunciation. She calls this "a depredication of the subject," which I find useful for understanding the function of the abyss in legal discourse. "The Tomb of Perseverance," 76.

64. Jacques Derrida and Marie-Françoise Plissart, *Right of Inspection*, xxxvi. The implication of this right to look into the abyss is the central issue of Chapter 3, which finds that if such a right to look exists, as those in visual studies have recently focused on, it would be an assertion against the force of legal interpretation that issues from the racial profile as the fugitive figure of constitutional law's gaze.

65. See generally, Bell, *Faces at the Bottom of the Well*. I take Bell's insistence here on the radical spirit of the Civil Rights Movement as an affirmation of Copjec's argument about the political importance of understanding depredication.

Chapter 3

1. John Locke, *An Essay Concerning Human Understanding*, 480.

2. Spillers, "Changing the Letter," 179.

3. Ibid.

4. 388 U.S. 1 (1967).

5. 539 U.S. 558 (2003).

6. William N. Eskridge, Jr., "Destabilizing Due Process and Evolutive Equal Protection," 1194. For particularly illuminating critical discussions of the cultural politics of marriage equality, see Angela P. Harris, "Loving before and after the Law"; and R. A. Lenhardt, "Beyond Analogy: *Perez v. Sharp*, Antimiscegenation Law and the Fight for Same-Sex Marriage." Other commentary on the intersection of race and sex in *Loving* are represented in the *Fordham Law Review* symposium issue, "Forty Years of Loving: Confronting Issues of Race, Sexuality, and the Family in the Twenty-first Century" (2008). However, the queer cultural studies approaches in this issue, and their various forms of legal misreadings and nonreadings, are precisely what I hope to push back against in this chapter through my critique of *Lawrence* and legal interpretation more generally.

7. *Loving*, 9.

8. Ibid., 11.
9. Ibid., 12.
10. Ibid.
11. 478 U.S. 186 (1986).
12. This has not been without a thorough and convincing critique of the homonormativity of mainstream LGBT politics. See, for example, Craig Willse and Dean Spade, "Freedom in a Regulatory State?: *Lawrence*, Marriage and Biopolitics" 309–29; and Katherine M. Franke, "The Politics of Same-Sex Marriage Politics," 236–48.
13. Dale Carpenter, "The Unknown Past of *Lawrence v. Texas*," 1509 (quoting from the Probable Cause Affadavit filed by Officer Joseph Quinn, one of the arresting officers). However, Carpenter in his subsequent book-length investigation, *Flagrant Conduct: The Story of* Lawrence v. Texas, notes that "[p]recisely what he [Eubanks] said to the sheriff's office is unknown" (62). Specifically, it is unknown whether Eubanks referred to Garner as "a black male" or a "nigger," and this slippage is evidenced in Carpenter's two versions of the history of *Lawrence*.
14. These facts I recount are from Carpenter, "The Unknown Past of *Lawrence v. Texas*," 1508–19. See also Carpenter, *Flagrant Conduct*, 59–74.
15. For a discussion of these various modes of racial profiling, see, generally, Bernard E. Harcourt, "Rethinking Racial Profiling: A Critique of the Economics, Civil Liberties, and Constitutional Literature, and of Criminal Profiling More Generally."
16. They go on, "It should be looked upon, however, as an acquired imaginary set rather than as an image: as a stereotype through which, as it were, the subject views the other person. Feelings and behaviour, for example, are just as likely to be concrete expressions of the imago as are mental images." Jean Laplanche and J.-B. Pontalis, *The Language of Psycho-Analysis*, 84.
17. Aporia here, and in the rest of this chapter, is used to reference the deconstructed logocentric relationship between writing and speech, and law and violence, elaborated by Jacques Derrida's 1972 essay "Signature Event Context."
18. As a matter of litigation, it is certainly understandable that the defendants' attorneys did not raise the issue of racial profiling under Fourteenth Amendment Equal Protection and Due Process doctrines. There is a good deal of evidence suggesting that they would not have won on this point, as officially declared wars on crime and drugs have continually eroded the sanctity of home and personal sovereignty under the broader interests of public morality, safety, and effective law enforcement. The Court could have just as likely ruled against including gays and lesbians within sexual privacy, as for equal enforcement of the antisodomy statute irrespective of sexual orientation, or for a wider notion of probable cause that could include racist statements. Indeed, this would be in line with the entrenched political priorities of tough-on-crime and formal equality policies we see in racial jurisprudence. Still, as a matter of discursive struggle, questioning equal protection and probable cause would have expanded the possibilities of registering the racial dynamics of the case in the historical and legal record.
19. Perhaps O'Connor's opinion does a little better by analyzing antisodomy law under an equal protection framework, but again, the language of the statute determines her analysis. *Lawrence*, 579–85.
20. Lewis R. Gordon, *Bad Faith and Antiblack Racism*. I should also note that I am not interested in a comparative analysis of the extent to which the current Court is

willing to affirm gay rights over minority rights, or vice versa. The meager language of racial equality I examined in Chapter 1, including that of *Grutter v. Bollinger*, 539 U.S. 306 (2003), the affirmative action case announced during the same term as *Lawrence*, mirrors the meager language of sexual freedom in *Lawrence*. The more important issue is instead to draw our attention to the play of doctrine, precedence, and construction of facts in constitutional interpretation, and the way that this play is put into play in the first instance by an imago of blackness.

21. *Lawrence*, 562–63.

22. See *Terry v. Ohio*, 392 U.S. 1 (1968) and *Whren v. United States*, 517 U.S. 806 (1996). But see the recent "stop-and-frisk" decision from the U.S. District Court of the Southern District of New York, *Floyd et al. v. City of New York et al.*, No. 08-cv-1034 (SAS), 2013 WL 4046209 (S.D.N.Y. Aug. 12, 2013), which ruled that the NYPD's use of racial profiling and "stop-and-frisk" violated both the Fourth Amendment right to be free from unreasonable searches and the Fourteenth Amendment right to equal protection. For a complete procedural history of this case, see its coverage by the Center for Constitutional Rights as plaintiff cocounsel, www.ccrjustice.org/ourcases/current-cases/floyd-et-al (accessed June 12, 2014).

23. Kendall Thomas, "Beyond the Privacy Principle."

24. Ibid., 1459.

25. *Powell v. State*, 270 Ga. 327 (1998).

26. Ibid., 332.

27. *State of Georgia v. Anthony San Juan Powell*, Crim. No. 96-B-3448–6 (Gwinnett Superior Ct. Aug. 8, 1997), 230–40.

28. *Powell*, 327.

29. I am indebted to Lynne Huffer's work on *Lawrence* for this point. See "Queer Victory, Feminist Defeat? Sodomy and Rape in *Lawrence v. Texas*."

30. *Lawrence*'s majority opinion characterizes the sex act in this way: "The present case does not involve minors. It does not involve persons who might be injured or coerced or who are situated in relationships where consent might not easily be refused. It does not involve public conduct or prostitution. It does not involve whether the government must give formal recognition to any relationship that homosexual persons seek to enter. The case does involve two adults who, with full and mutual consent from each other, engaged in sexual practices common to a homosexual lifestyle." *Lawrence*, 578. The dissenting opinion described the sex act as "homosexual sodomy" no less than sixteen times, while the majority opinion used the term only twice (and once preceded by the additional adjective "consensual").

31. See, for example, Kristin Bumiller, "Rape as a Legal Symbol: An Essay on Sexual Violence and Racism"; Kimberlé W. Crenshaw, "Race, Gender, and Sexual Harassment"; and Saidiya V. Hartman, "Seduction and the Ruses of Power."

32. I see this reading as an extension of Cornell's deconstruction, in *The Philosophy of the Limit*.

33. *Prigg v. Pennsylvania*, 41 U.S. 539 (1842), 550.

34. Sanford Levinson, "Slavery in the Canon of Constitutional Law," 97.

35. Paul Finkelman, *An Imperfect Union: Slavery, Federalism, and Comity*.

36. This Act, in part, states: "The Congress shall have power to dispose of and make all needful rules and regulations respecting the territory or other property belonging to

the United States; and nothing in this Constitution shall be so construed as to prejudice any claims of the United States, or of any particular state." U.S. Constitution, Article IV, Section 3.

37. President Millard Fillmore then enacted the Fugitive Slave Law of 1850, the harshest fugitive slave measure the United States had ever seen. This law struck down abolitionist efforts, like the Pennsylvania law at issue in *Prigg*, across the several states. See Horton and Horton, "Federal Assault: African Americans and the Impact of the Fugitive Slave Law of 1850." For a legal history of this lasting federal structure of criminal rendition, see Christopher Lasch, "Rendition Resistance."

38. *Prigg*, 622. Here, Story references the "necessary and proper" clause of the Constitution, which grants Congress the power to "make all laws which shall be necessary and proper for carrying into execution the foregoing powers, and all other powers vested by this Constitution in the government of the United States, or in any department or officer thereof." U.S. Constitution, Article I, Section 8, Clause 18.

39. For a thorough critique of Story's faulty reasoning, see Barbara Holden-Smith, "Lords of Lash, Loom, and Law: Justice Story, Slavery and *Prigg v. Pennsylvania*," 1128–34. See also Douglass, "The Constitution of the United States: Is It Pro-Slavery or Anti-Slavery?"

40. This repetition effects a formal transcendence of doctrinal boundaries, and might be the unique quality of slave law. The study of slave law is too expansive to recount adequately here. However, several key studies for purposes of this chapter include Robert M. Cover, *Justice Accused: Antislavery and the Judicial Process*; Don E. Fehrenbacher, *The Dred Scott Case: Its Significance in American Law and Politics*; Paul Finkelman, *Law, the Constitution, and Slavery*; Paul Finkelman, *Slavery and the Law*; Walter Johnson, *River of Dark Dreams: Slavery and Empire in the Cotton Kingdom*; Dylan C. Penningroth, *The Claims of Kinfolk*; Mark V. Tushnet, *The American Law of Slavery, 1810–1860: Considerations of Humanity and Interest*; Alan Watson, *Slave Law in the Americas*; and Edlie L. Wong, *Neither Fugitive nor Free: Atlantic Slavery, Freedom Suits, and the Legal Culture of Travel.*

41. Yifat Hachamovitch, "In Emulation of the Clouds: An Essay on the Obscure Object of Judgment," 56.

42. *Prigg*, 612.

43. "The modern mind is so thoroughly attuned to the calculative sciences that it is difficult to accept that the body is made present for the subject by means of an image. Even if this is accepted, it is difficult to take the further step of admitting that the status of the body is thereby modified, that in its translation by representation the body loses its status as a biological object and becomes something fictional. In other words, the body is not the body. Its construction has been transposed into the domain of the image; the body which we inhabit is indissociable from the grip of the image." Pierre Legendre, Peter Goodrich, and Alain Pottage, "Introduction to the Theory of the Image: Narcissus and the Other in the Mirror," 211.

44. Tim Murphy, "As If: *camera juridica*," 92.

45. For a more complete history of the evolution of fugitive slave law, see Christopher L. Eisgruber, "Justice Story, Slavery, and the Natural Law Foundations of American Constitutionalism."

46. U.S. Constitution, Article IV, Section 2, Clause 3, the Fugitive Slave Clause, was superseded in 1865 by the Thirteenth Amendment, which reads, "Neither slavery nor

involuntary servitude, except as a punishment for crime whereof the party shall have been duly convicted, shall exist within the United States, or any place subject to their jurisdiction."

47. Other relevant slavery provisions of the original Constitution repeat such silences, referring to slaves as "three-fifths of all other Persons" (Article I, Section 2, Clause 3) or as "persons" whom the states shall think it proper to import (Article I, Section 9, Clause 1).

48. Barbara Johnson, "Apostrophe, Animation, and Abortion," 29–30.

49. *Prigg*, 611, my emphasis. But see Holden-Smith, "Lords of Lash, Loom, and Law," 1129–30, where she argues that the "historical fact" upon which Story relies to arrive at the intent behind the sweeping reach of the Fugitive Slave Clause is severely overstated, or even patently untrue.

50. Michael Foley, *Silence of Constitutions: Gaps, "Abeyances," and Political Temperament in the Maintenance of Government*, 81. See also Marianne Constable, *Just Silences: The Limits and Possibilities of Modern Law.*

51. Toni Morrison, *Playing in the Dark: Whiteness and the Literary Imagination*, 5.

52. Ibid., 5–6.

53. Ibid., 5.

54. Sexual privacy is not the only fundamental right haunted by the racial profile. A fundamental right protecting against state-based physical coercion, also derived from the substantive due process clause of the Fourteenth Amendment, is haunted by the history of lynching by the case, *Brown v. Mississippi*, 297 U.S. 278 (1936). The deputy officer in this case testified that he had whipped one of the defendants before obtaining his confession, "but not too much for a Negro."

55. Addressing this issue in part, Anthony Farley has argued that the legal discovery and enforcement of the African slave as commodity is survived today through the availability of blackness for consumption and pleasure through a field of vision. Anthony P. Farley, "The Poetics of Colorlined Space."

56. Hortense J. Spillers, "Who Cuts the Border? Some Readings on America," 326 (emphasis in original).

57. The issue of a transformative interpretation derives from Derrida's idea of justice as that which "remains, is yet, to come, *à venir*, it has an, it is *à-venir*." The transformative force of justice can only be precipitated by "this overflowing of the performative, because of this always excessive haste of interpretation getting ahead of itself." Derrida, "Force of Law," 969. I thank David Marriott for his timely reminder on this point.

58. Cheryl I. Harris, "Whiteness as Property," 1711.

59. Ibid.

60. Ibid.

61. Ibid., 1720.

62. Ibid., 1721.

63. Ibid., 1720.

64. Ibid., 1725.

65. Ibid., 1729.

66. This is Fanon's main object in *Black Skin, White Masks*. Not insignificantly, a Fanonian psychoanalysis of racist culture would complicate the recent turn to cognitive psychology by scholars and courts to address issues of "unconscious racism," and is but

one of the implications of bringing Fanon fully to bear on the intellectual project of critical race theory.

67. Harris, "Whiteness as Property," 1721.

68. Ibid., 1736.

69. Ibid., 1743.

70. Lacan, *Écrits*, 262. For more on symbolic death, see also Slavoj Žižek, "You Only Die Twice," in *The Sublime Object of Ideology*, 145–67.

71. Harris, "Whiteness as Property," 1748 (quoting Tourgée).

72. *Plessy v. Ferguson*, 163 U.S. 537 (1896), 459.

73. Ibid. (my emphasis).

74. Harris, "Whiteness as Property," 1777–91. She states early in her article that the "purported benefits of Black heritage" (1712)—a projected and not real property interest in blackness—becomes the basis for an attack on affirmative action, and also an "inability to see the property interest in whiteness" (1715).

75. There is a striking similarity between *Prigg* and *Plessy* in this sense. A similar racial profile outlined by the unwritten slave of the Constitution, between Clauses 1 and 3 in Article IV, Section 2, is also outlined by the unwritten freedmen between the Thirteenth and Fourteenth Amendments at issue in *Plessy*. Subsequent legal interpretations of the two Amendments have been determined by principles of formal equality and equal treatment. See, generally, Cheryl I. Harris, "Equal Treatment and the Reproduction of Inequality."

76. Robert M. Cover, "The Supreme Court 1982 Term—Foreword: Nomos and Narrative," 15. Thanks to Fred Moten, who illuminated the richness of this concept.

77. Williams, *The Alchemy of Race and Rights*, 133–45.

78. Ibid., 37.

79. Ibid., 142 (quoting evasive answers given by various public officials and law enforcement personnel to questions posed by television reporter Gil Noble).

80. Williams asks specifically, Why "the animus . . . inspired such fear and impatient contempt in a police officer that the presence of six other well-armed men could not allay his need to kill a sick old lady fighting off hallucinations with a knife"? Ibid., 144.

81. Ibid., 139, 140, 141, 141, and 142.

82. Ibid., 139.

83. Sexton and Martinot, "The Avant-Garde of White Supremacy."

84. Williams, *The Alchemy of Race and Rights*, 143.

85. And here I'm gesturing toward the Lacanian Real with which Williams's writing grapples. Žižek writes that "the Real designates a substantial hard kernel that precedes and resists symbolization and, simultaneously, it designates the left-over, which is posited or 'produced' by symbolization itself." *Tarrying with the Negative*, 36. Žižek's reading, of course, is engaged with Freud's observation that "[t]here is at least one spot in every dream at which it is unplumbable—a navel, as it were, that is its point of contact with the unknown." Sigmund Freud, *The Interpretation of Dreams*, 135. Lacan continually revisits and revises Freud's notion of the navel as that which is both in and in excess of the symbolic order through topological concepts such as the knot, the quilting point, and so on. For a feminist reading of the navel, see Shoshana Felman, "Competing Pregnancies: The Dream from which Psychoanalysis Proceeds (Freud, *The Interpretation of Dreams*)."

86. Williams, *The Alchemy of Race and Rights*, 139.

87. This particular sentence is my answer to Fred Moten's question to me on a panel we shared at the "Violence and the Law" symposium organized by David Lloyd at the University of Southern California on September 23–25, 2010. There he asked why Eubanks called the cops on himself. I heard this as a version of the general question Moten poses in his article "Knowledge of Freedom" about Kant's argument in *Critique of Judgment* that "understanding must 'severely clip the wings' of imagination" (269, quoting Winfried Menninghaus, *In Praise of Nonsense: Kant and Bluebeard*, quoting Kant). At stake in descending into the depths of "the revelation of this ambivalence in Kant" (270) is a knowledge that takes flight in the "lawless freedom" of imagination that categorical understanding attempts to regulate and transcend. This is all to say, Moten's question is how I came to read Williams anew.

88. Williams, *The Alchemy of Race and Rights*, 139.

89. Jacques Derrida, *Given Time: Counterfeit Money*.

Chapter 4

1. Dayan, "Legal Slaves and Civil Bodies," 4.

2. Peter Goodrich, "The Iconography of Nothing: Blank Spaces and the Representation of Law in Edward VI and the Pope," 97.

3. Ibid., 109.

4. Davis and Dent, "Prison as a Border," 1236.

5. Caleb Smith, *The Prison and the American Imagination*, 23.

6. See, generally, Assata Shakur, "Women in Prison: How We Are"; Cassandra Shaylor, "'It's Like Living in a Black Hole': Women of Color and Solitary Confinement in the Prison Industrial Complex"; and Julia Sudbury "Maroon Abolitionists: Black Gender-oppressed Activists in the Anti-Prison Movement in the US and Canada."

7. Shaylor, "It's Like Living in a Black Hole."

8. Anthony P. Farley, "Perfecting Slavery," 222.

9. Jacques Lacan, "The Instance of the Letter in the Unconscious, or Reason since Freud," 139.

10. Heidegger, *Being and Time*, 33–35.

11. "Declaration to the People of America," in *Attica Prison Uprising 101: A Short Primer*, ed. Mariame Kaba, 21–22.

12. Ibid., 23. See, generally, Joy James, *The New Abolitionists: (Neo)Slave Narratives and Contemporary Prison Writings*.

13. Mary A. Favret, *Romantic Correspondence: Women, Politics, and the Fiction of Letters*, 10.

14. Angela Y. Davis, Bettina Aptheker, et al., *If They Come in the Morning: Voices of Resistance*, 19.

15. Cornelia Vismann, *Files: Law and Media Technology*, 6.

16. Ibid., 13.

17. Ibid.

18. Ibid., 11.

19. Barbara Johnson, "The Frame of Reference: Poe, Lacan, and Derrida," 230 (quoting Derrida and modifying translation of his "The Purveyor of Truth").

20. Ibid.

21. Ibid., 244–45.

22. Ibid., 228. Johnson is playing here on Derrida's development of the notion of the frame, not as "the borderline between the inside and outside, but precisely what subverts the applicability of the inside/outside polarity to the act of interpretation" (231), and his "framing" of the "'average reading' of Lacan's text" (227).

23. Fred Moten, "Blackness and Nothingness (Mysticism in the Flesh)," 741–42. The question of a mass scene of writing reaches for that possibility of what Moten calls "an aesthetic sociology or a social poetics of nothingness" that glimmers in his inhabitation of "[Frank] Wilderson's and [Nathaniel] Mackey's gestures toward 'fantasy in the hold'" (750, quoting Wilderson).

24. By using double negatives, I am trying to describe prisoners' being as between absence and presence. Positive descriptions (that is, communicating, corresponding, trying, writing, calling, wanting) cannot capture a degree of impossibility those activities face under such conditions of duress and censorship.

25. As a point of clarification, I am not interested in pursuing a Durkheimian notion of punishment as communication. Rather, I am interested in how the law's decisions negotiating the relationship between criminal justice administration and expression (what *the law* oftentimes calls "communication") offer a place to forge a language adequate to thinking about the negative space of communication. And so if some of the phrases and terms used throughout seem unnecessarily complicated, evocative more than definitional, or even tortuous, it is because they are trying to get at this negative space (and because I am not a poet).

26. Paul W. Kahn, "The Question of Sovereignty," 265.

27. The localization of the fantasy of colorblindness can be tracked across a casebook I coauthored with David Oppenheimer and Sheila Foster, *Comparative Equality and Anti-Discrimination Law: Cases, Codes, Constitutions, and Commentary*.

28. Kahn, "The Question of Sovereignty," 265. He goes on further:

> For Americans, the rule of law bears the weight of political identity; it shapes the meaning of individual participation in the collective enterprise of the state. In and through participation in law, the American citizen realizes the political truth of his or her identity. This linkage of law and positive sovereignty produces the confusing appearance of a United States that seems to oppose international law in the name of law itself. Thus, a country that regards itself fundamentally committed to the rule of law often appears lawless in its attitude toward the international order." (265)

29. U.S. Department of Justice, "Limited Communication for Terrorist Inmates," 16523.

30. Dan Eggan, "Facility Holding Terrorism Inmates Limits Communication" in *The Washington Post*, February 25, 2007, A07.

31. For more information on the CMU, see the Center for Constitutional Rights' webpage on the recent case, *Aref v. Holder* (2010), challenging policies and conditions at the two prisons in Illinois and Indiana. Available at www.ccrjustice.org/cmu (last accessed June 13, 2014).

32. See the documentary film, *Through the Wire* (dir. Nina Rosenblum), on the history of the Lexington High Security Unit.

33. Francis A. Allen, *The Decline of the Rehabilitative Ideal: Penal Policy and Social Purpose*.

34. Malcolm M. Feeley and Jonathan Simon, "The New Penology: Notes on the Emerging Strategy of Corrections and its Implications."

35. The term "lifeworld" was first discussed by phenomenologist Edmund Husserl (1936) in *The Crisis of European Sciences and Transcendental Phenomenology* (trans. Carr D., 1970) and denotes all the things experienced collectively in a world. I cannot present a proper intellectual history of this idea in the space of this chapter. Nonetheless, I introduce phenomenological thought as a way to open up the field of punishment and society scholarship to approaches developed in various disciplines to the study of material cultures. Even within sociology, this phenomenological concept has had a significant impact, for example, through Pierre Bourdieu's notion of the habitus in *Outline of a Theory of Practice* (1977).

36. Colin Dayan, *The Law Is a White Dog: How Legal Rituals Make and Unmake Persons*, 57.

37. Cover, "Violence and the Word," 1601.

38. Claudia Brodsky, *In the Place of Language: Literature and the Architecture of the Referent*, 135–43, explores the rich, polysemic history of the English word "grave," which includes meanings such as place of burial, to dig, weightiness, to carve, death, physical gravity, earnestness, a pen, and more.

39. For a state self-assessment of the prison system in California, see, generally, George Deukmejian et al., *Reforming Corrections: Report of the Corrections Independent Review Panel* (2004). Based in part on this review, the renaming was announced in Schwarzenegger's *Governor's Reorganization Plan 2: Reforming California's Youth and Adult Correctional System*, 9.

40. I use "biopolitical" here as an adjective, not a theoretical concept. I am consciously avoiding an Agambian rubric because it does not account for the racial core of American constitutional law. See, generally, Jared Sexton, "People-of-Color-Blindness: Notes on the Afterlife of Slavery."

41. See, generally, Ruth W. Gilmore, *Golden Gulag: Prisons, Surplus, Crisis, and Opposition in Globalizing California*; and Jonathan Simon, *Governing through Crime: How the War on Crime Transformed American Democracy and Created a Culture of Fear.*

42. Pat Carlen, ed., *Imaginary Penalties.*

43. Meda Chesney-Lind, "Patriarchy, Crime, and Justice."

44. Michel Foucault, *Discipline and Punish: The Birth of the Prison*, 30.

45. Dayan, "Legal Slaves and Civil Bodies," 27.

46. *Procunier v. Martinez*, 416 U.S. 396 (1974), 413–14.

47. Ibid., 215.

48. Ibid., 408, 409.

49. *Turner v. Safely* (1987) 482 U.S. 78, 87. During this same term, the Supreme Court also handed down another First Amendment prisoner rights case, *O'Lone v. Shabazz* (1987) 482 U.S. 342, in which it affirmed the constitutionality of a prison policy restricting Muslim prisoners housed in the prison's maximum security unit from attending Jumu'ah, a religious congregational service held in a separate facility known as "the Farm" (344–45). This case involves the First Amendment Free Exercise right, which implies a right to accommodation or exemption for religious individuals subject to otherwise valid law. Generally, when an infringement on this Free Exercise right occurs in the "free world," the Court will apply a relatively strict standard of review and require a showing

from the state of a compelling interest. However, *Shabazz* lowers this standard of review, requiring only a demonstration of "reasonableness," because of a general judicial trend to defer to the professional expertise of prison administration. See, generally, Sharon Dolovich, "Forms of Deference in Prison Law." While *Shabazz* mirrors the lower standard of judicial review applied to infringements on prisoner First Amendment rights more generally taken up *Turner*, I limit my focus in this chapter to cases involving prisoner First Amendment right to freedom of expression for the specific form of letter writing that emerges as a limit.

50. *Turner*, 86–89. The precedents examined include *Pell v. Procunier*, 417 U.S. 817 (1974); *Jones v. North Carolina Prisoners' Union*, 433 U.S. 119 (1977); and *Bell v. Wolfish*, 441 U.S. 520 (1979). Regulations on prisoner face-to-face media interviews, union organizing materials, and access to hard cover books, respectively, were found not to violate the First Amendment.

51. *Turner*, 89–91.

52. *Overton v. Bazzetta*, 539 U.S. 126 (2003).

53. Ibid., 135.

54. Ibid.

55. Ibid.

56. Ibid.

57. Ibid., 139. In a concurring opinion to *Beard v. Banks*, 548 U.S. 521 (2006), Thomas reiterates this point regarding a case prohibiting magazines, photos, and certain newspapers in a long-term segregation unit.

58. *Overton*, 139.

59. *Martinez*, 428.

60. Jacques Derrida, "The Purveyor of Truth," 176–85.

61. *McNamara v. Moody*, 606 F.2d 621 (1979), 622–23.

62. Ibid., 624.

63. Ibid.

64. Jacques Lacan, "Seminar on the 'Purloined Letter,'" 53.

65. Derrida, "Force of Law," 24–26.

66. See, generally, Maria St. John and Cheryl Dunye, "Making Home/Making 'Stranger': An Interview with Cheryl Dunye."

67. This reading of the film is possible because of Saidiya Hartman's *Lose Your Mother: A Journey along the Atlantic Slave Route.*

68. Johnson, "The Frame of Reference," 248.

69. How to pose the question of "self-evidence" is, arguably, at the heart of phenomenology. See Martin Heidegger, "The Phenomenological Method of Investigation," 278–87.

70. Roland Barthes, *Camera Lucida: Reflections on Photography.*

71. Vicky Lebeau, *Lost Angels: Psychoanalysis and Cinema*, 154.

72. Beth E. Richie, "Feminist Ethnographies of Women in Prison," 450.

Bibliography

Aarim-Heriot, Najia. *Chinese Immigrants, African Americans, and Racial Anxiety in the United States, 1848–82*. Urbana: University of Illinois Press, 2003.

Allen, Francis A. *The Decline of the Rehabilitative Ideal: Penal Policy and Social Purpose*. New Haven: Yale University Press, 1981.

Arendt, Hannah. *The Origins of Totalitarianism*. New York: Harcourt, Brace and World, 1976.

Badiou, Alain. *Being and Event*. London: Continuum, 2005.

Barthes, Roland. *Camera Lucida: Reflections on Photography*. New York: Hill and Wang, 1981.

Bell, Derrick A. "Racism Is Here to Stay: Now What?" *Howard Law Journal* 35.1 (1991): 79–93.

Bell, Derrick A. *Faces at the Bottom of the Well: The Permanence of Racism*. New York: Basic Books, 1992.

Bourdieu, Pierre. *Outline of a Theory of Practice*. Cambridge: Cambridge University Press, 1977.

Brennan, Teresa. *History after Lacan*. London: Routledge, 1993.

Brodsky, Claudia. *In the Place of Language: Literature and the Architecture of the Referent*. New York: Fordham University Press, 2009.

Brown, Wendy. *States of Injury: Power and Freedom in Late Modernity*. Princeton: Princeton University Press, 1995.

Brown, Wendy. *Politics out of History*. Princeton: Princeton University Press, 2001.

Bumiller, Kristin. "Rape as a Legal Symbol: An Essay on Sexual Violence and Racism." *University of Miami Law Review* 42.1 (1987): 75–91.

Carlen, Pat, ed. *Imaginary Penalties*. Portland, OR: Willan Publishing, 2008.

Carpenter, Dale. "The Unknown Past of *Lawrence v. Texas*." *Michigan Law Review* 102.7 (2004): 1464–1527.

Carpenter, Dale. *Flagrant Conduct: The Story of* Lawrence v. Texas. New York: W. W. Norton and Company, 2013.

Chandler, Nahum D. "Of Horizon: An Introduction to 'The Afro-American' by WEB Du Bois—circa 1894." *Journal of Transnational American Studies* 2.1 (2010): 1–41.

Chesney-Lind, Meda. "Patriarchy, Crime, and Justice." *Feminist Criminology* 1.1 (2006): 6–26.

Clark, Kenneth, et al. "The Effects of Segregation and the Consequences of Desegregation—A Social Science Statement." *Journal of Negro Education* 22.1 (1953): 68–76.

Clark, Kenneth, et al. "The Effects of Segregation and the Consequences of Desegregation—A Social Science Statement." In *Brown v. Board of Education: A Brief History with Documents*, edited by Waldo E. Martin, 142–50. Boston: Bedford/St. Martin's, 1998.

Cohen, William, and Jonathan D. Varat. *Constitutional Law: Cases and Materials*. New York: Foundation Press, 1997.

Constable, Marianne. *Just Silences: The Limits and Possibilities of Modern Law*. Princeton: Princeton University Press, 2005.

Copjec, Joan. "The *Unvermögender* Other." In *Read My Desire: Lacan against the Historicists*, 141–62. Cambridge, MA: MIT Press, 1994.

Copjec, Joan. "Vampires, Breast-Feeding, and Anxiety." In *Read My Desire: Lacan against the Historicists*, 117–39. Cambridge, MA: MIT Press, 1994.

Copjec, Joan. *Imagine There's No Woman: Ethics and Sublimation*. Cambridge, MA: MIT Press, 2002.

Copjec, Joan. "The Tomb of Perseverance." In *Imagine There's No Woman: Ethics and Sublimation*, 12–47. Cambridge, MA: MIT Press, 2002.

Cornell, Drucilla. *The Philosophy of the Limit*. New York: Routledge, 1992.

Cover, Robert M. *Justice Accused: Antislavery and the Judicial Process*. New Haven: Yale University Press, 1975.

Cover, Robert M. "The Supreme Court 1982 Term—Foreword: Nomos and Narrative." *Harvard Law Review* 97.1 (1983): 4–68.

Cover, Robert M. "Violence and the Word." *Yale Law Journal* 95.8 (1986): 1601–29.

Crenshaw, Kimberlé W. "Race, Gender, and Sexual Harassment." *Southern California Law Review* 65.3 (1992): 1467–76.

Crenshaw, Kimberlé W., Neil Gotanda, Gary Peller, and Kendall Thomas, eds. *Critical Race Theory: The Key Writings That Formed the Movement*. New York: New Press, 1995.

Cruse, Harold. *Plural but Equal: A Critical Study of Blacks and Minorities and America's Plural Society*. New York: William Morrow, 1987.

Cruz, Tania. "Judicial Scrutiny of National Security: Executive Restrictions of Civil Liberties When 'Fears and Prejudices Are Aroused.'" *Seattle Journal for Social Justice* 2.1 (2003): 128–97.

Das, Veena. *Life and Words: Violence and the Descent into the Ordinary*. Berkeley: University of California Press, 2007.

Davis, Angela Y. "Opening Defense Statement Presented by Angela Y. Davis in Santa Clara County Superior Court, March 29, 1972." In *The Angela Y. Davis Reader*, edited by Joy James, 329–46. Malden, MA: Blackwell, 1998.

Davis, Angela Y. "Racialized Punishment and Prison Abolition." In *The Angela Y. Davis Reader*, edited by Joy James, 96–107. Malden, MA: Blackwell, 1998.

Davis, Angela Y. "Unfinished Lecture on Liberation—II." In *The Angela Y. Davis Reader*, edited by Joy James, 53–60. Malden, MA: Blackwell, 1998.

Davis, Angela Y., Bettina Aptheker, and other members of the National United Committee to Free Angela Davis and All Political Prisoners. *If They Come in the Morning: Voices of Resistance*. New York: The Third Press, 1971.

Davis, Angela Y., and Gina Dent. "Prison as a Border: A Conversation on Gender, Globalization, and Punishment." *Signs: Journal of Women in Culture and Society* 26.4 (Summer 2001): 1235–41.

Dayan, Colin. *The Law Is a White Dog: How Legal Rituals Make and Unmake Persons*. Princeton: Princeton University Press, 2011.

Dayan, Colin. "Legal Slaves and Civil Bodies." *Nepantla: Views from South* 2.1 (2001): 3–39.

Dayan, Colin. "A Legal Ethnography." In *The Law Is a White Dog: How Legal Rituals Make and Unmake Persons*, 138–76. Princeton: Princeton University Press, 2011.

de Tocqueville, Alexis. *Democracy in America*. Translated by Henry Reeve. New York: Bantam Books, 2000.

Deleuze, Gilles, and Leopold Sacher-Masoch. *Masochism: Coldness and Cruelty*. New York: Zone Books, 1991.

Derrida, Jacques. "Freud and the Scene of Writing." *Yale French Studies* 48 (1972): 74–117.

Derrida, Jacques. "The Law of Genre." Translated by Avital Ronell. *Critical Inquiry* 7.1 (1980): 55–81.

Derrida, Jacques. "The Purveyor of Truth." Translated by Alan Bass. In *The Purloined Poe: Lacan, Derrida, and Psychoanalytic Reading*, edited by John P. Muller and William J. Richardson, 173–212. Baltimore, MD: Johns Hopkins University Press, 1988.

Derrida, Jacques. "Signature Event Context." In *Limited Inc.*, 1–23. Evanston, IL: Northwestern University Press, 1988.

Derrida, Jacques. "Force of Law: The 'Mystical Foundation of Authority.'" Translated by Mary Quaintance. *Cardozo Law Review* 11:5–6 (1990): 919–1046.

Derrida, Jacques. *Given Time: Counterfeit Money*. Translated by Peggy Kamuf. Chicago: University of Chicago Press, 1992.

Derrida, Jacques. *Memoirs of the Blind: The Self-Portrait and Other Ruins*. Chicago: University of Chicago Press, 1993.

Derrida, Jacques, and Marie-Françoise Plissart. *Right of Inspection*. New York: Monacelli Press, 1998.

Deukmejian, George, et al. *Reforming Corrections: Report of the Corrections Independent Review Panel*. Sacramento, CA: Corrections Independent Review Panel, 2004.

Dolar, Mladen. *A Voice and Nothing More*. Cambridge, MA: MIT Press, 2006.

Dolovich, Sharon. "Forms of Deference in Prison Law." *Federal Sentencing Reporter* 24.4 (2012): 245–59.

Douglass, Frederick. "The Constitution of the United States: Is It Pro-Slavery or Anti-Slavery?" In *Frederick Douglass: Selected Speeches and Writings*, edited by Philip Foner and Yuval Taylor, 379–89. Chicago: Chicago Review Press, 1999.

Douzinas, Costas, and Lynda Nead, eds. *Law and the Image: The Authority of Art and the Aesthetics of Law*. Chicago: University of Chicago Press, 1999.

Du Bois, W. E. Burghardt. "Does the Negro Need Separate Schools?" *Journal of Negro Education* 4.3 (1935): 328–35.

Dudziak, Mary L. *Cold War Civil Rights: Race and the Image of American Democracy*. Princeton: Princeton University Press, 2000.

Dycus, Stephen, A. L. Berney, W. C. Banks, and P. Raven-Hansen. *National Security Law*. Third Edition. New York: Aspen Publishers, 2002.

Eggen, Dan. "Facility Holding Terrorism Inmates Limits Communication." *Washington Post*, February 25, 2007, A07.

Eisgruber, Christopher L. "Justice Story, Slavery, and the Natural Law Foundations of American Constitutionalism." *University of Chicago Law Review* (1988): 273–327.

Eisgruber, Christopher L. "The Story of *Dred Scott*: Originalism's Forgotten Past." In *Constitutional Law Stories*, edited by Michael C. Dorf, 151–80. New York: Foundation Press, 2004.

Eskridge, William N., Jr., "Destabilizing Due Process and Evolutive Equal Protection." *UCLA Law Review* 47.5 (2000): 1183–1219.

Fanon, Frantz. *Black Skin, White Masks*. Translated by Charles Lam Markmann. New York: Grove Press, 1967.

Farley, Anthony P. "The Poetics of Colorlined Space." In *Crossroads, Directions, and a New Critical Race Theory*, edited by Francisco Valdes, Jerome M. Culp, and Angela P. Harris, 97–158. Philadelphia: Temple University Press, 2002.

Farley, Anthony P. "Perfecting Slavery." *Loyola University Chicago Law Journal* 36.1 (2004): 225–56.

Farley, Anthony P. "Law as Trauma & Repetition." *NYU Review of Law and Social Change* 31.3 (2007): 613–26.

Favret, Mary A. *Romantic Correspondence: Women, Politics, and the Fiction of Letters*. Cambridge: Cambridge University Press, 1993.

Feeley, Malcolm M., and Jonathan Simon. "The New Penology: Notes on the Emerging Strategy of Corrections and Its Implications." *Criminology* 30.4 (1992): 449–74.

Fehrenbacher, Don E. *The Dred Scott Case: Its Significance in American Law and Politics*. New York: Oxford University Press, 1978.

Felman, Shoshana. "Competing Pregnancies: The Dream from which Psychoanalysis Proceeds (Freud, *The Interpretation of Dreams*)." In *What Does a Woman Want?: Reading and Sexual Difference*, 68–120. Baltimore, MD: Johns Hopkins University Press, 1993.

Felman, Shoshana, and Dori Laub. *Testimony: Crises of Witnessing in Literature, Psychoanalysis, and History*. New York: Routledge, 1991.

Finkelman, Paul. *An Imperfect Union: Slavery, Federalism, and Comity*. Chapel Hill: University of North Carolina Press, 1981.

Finkelman, Paul ed. *Law, the Constitution, and Slavery*. New York: Garland, 1989.

Finkelman, Paul, ed. *Slavery and the Law*. Madison, WI: Madison House, 1996.

Foley, Michael. *The Silence of Constitutions: Gaps, "Abeyances," and Political Temperament in the Maintenance of Government*. London: Routledge, 1989.

Foucault, Michel. *Discipline and Punish: The Birth of the Prison*. New York: Vintage Books, 1995.

Franke, Katherine M. "The Politics of Same-Sex Marriage Politics." *Columbia Journal of Gender & Law* 15 (2006): 236–48.

Freud, Sigmund. "Childhood Memories and Screen Memories (1901)." In *The Psychopathology of Everyday Life*, 62–73. New York: W. W. Norton, 1971.

Freud, Sigmund. *The Interpretation of Dreams*. Translated and edited by James Strachey. New York: Basic Books, 2010.

Gilmore, Ruth Wilson. "Race and Globalization." In *Geographies of Global Change: Remapping the World*, edited by R. J. Johnston, Peter J. Taylor, and Michael Watts, 261–74. Malden, MA: Blackwell, 2002.

Gilmore, Ruth W. *Golden Gulag: Prisons, Surplus, Crisis, and Opposition in Globalizing California*. Berkeley: University of California Press, 2007.

Goodrich, Peter. "The Iconography of Nothing: Blank Spaces and the Representation of Law in Edward VI and the Pope." In *Law and the Image: The Authority of Art and the Aesthetics of Law*, edited by Costas Douzinas and Lynda Nead, 89–114. Chicago: University of Chicago Press, 1999.

Gordon, Avery F. "Globalism and the Prison Industrial Complex: An Interview with Angela Davis." *Race & Class* 40.2–3 (1999): 145–57.

Gordon, Lewis R. *Bad Faith and Antiblack Racism*. Atlantic Highlands, NJ: Humanities Press, 1995.

Gotanda, Neil. "'Other Non-whites' in American Legal History: A Review of 'Justice at War.'" *Columbia Law Review* 85.5 (1985): 1186–92.

Gotanda, Neil. "A Critique of 'Our Constitution Is Color-Blind.'" *Stanford Law Review* 44.1 (1991): 1–68.

Gotanda, Neil. "The Story of *Korematsu*: The Japanese-American Cases." In *Constitutional Law Stories*, edited by Michael C. Dorf, 249–96. New York: Foundation Press, 2004.

Gressman, Eugene. "*Korematsu*: A Mélange of Military Imperatives." *Law and Contemporary Problems* 68.2 (2005): 15–27.

Gunther, Gerald. "Forward: In Search of Evolving Doctrine on a Changing Court: A Model for a Newer Equal Protection." *Harvard Law Review* 86.1 (1972): 1–48.

Habermas, Jürgen. *Between Facts and Norms: Contributions to a Discourse Theory of Law and Democracy*. Cambridge, MA: MIT Press, 1996.

Hachamovitch, Yifat. "In Emulation of the Clouds: An Essay on the Obscure Object of Judgment." In *Politics, Postmodernity and Critical Legal Studies Movement*, edited by Costas Douzinas, Peter Goodrich, and Yifat Hachamovitch, 33–67. London: Routledge, 1994.

Hallward, Peter. *Think Again: Alain Badiou and the Future of Philosophy*. London: Continuum, 2004.

Han, Sora Y. "The Politics of Race in Asian American Jurisprudence." *Asian Pacific American Law Journal* 11 (2006): 1–40.

Han, Sora Y. "Equal Protection's Dead End, or the Slave's Undying Claim." In *Controversies in Equal Protection in America*, edited by Anne R. Oakes. Surrey: Ashgate Publishing, forthcoming, June 2015.

Haney-López, Ian. *White by Law: The Legal Construction of Race*. Revised Edition. New York: New York University Press, 2006.

Harcourt, Bernard E. "Rethinking Racial Profiling: A Critique of the Economics, Civil Liberties, and Constitutional Literature, and of Criminal Profiling More Generally." *University of Chicago Law Review* 71.4 (2004): 1275–1381.

Harney, Stefano, and Fred Moten. *The Undercommons: Fugitive Planning & Black Study*. New York: Minor Compositions, 2013.

Harris, Angela P. "Loving before and after the Law." *Fordham Law Review* 76 (2008): 2821–47.

Harris, Cheryl I. "Whiteness as Property." *Harvard Law Review* 106.8 (1993): 1707–91.

Harris, Cheryl I. "Equal Treatment and the Reproduction of Inequality." *Fordham Law Review* 69.5 (2001): 1753–83.

Harris, Cheryl I. "The Story of *Plessy v. Ferguson*: The Death and Resurrection of Racial Formalism." In *Constitutional Law Stories*, edited by Michael C. Dorf, 181–222. New York: Foundation Press, 2004.

Harris, Cheryl I. "In the Shadow of Plessy." *University of Pennsylvania Journal of Constitutional Law* 7.3 (2005): 867–901.

Hartman, Saidiya V. "Seduction and the Ruses of Power." *Callaloo* 19.2 (1996): 537–60.

Hartman, Saidiya V. "The Time of Slavery." *South Atlantic Quarterly* 101.4 (2002): 757–77.

Hartman, Saidiya V. *Lose Your Mother: A Journey along the Atlantic Slave Route*. New York: Farrar, Straus and Giroux, 2007.

Heidegger, Martin. *The Essence of Truth: On Plato's Parable of the Cave and the Theaetetus*. New York: Continuum, 2002.

Heidegger, Martin. "The Phenomenological Method of Investigation." In *The Phenomenology Reader*, edited by Dermot Moran and Timothy Mooney, 278–86. New York: Routledge, 2002.

Heidegger, Martin. *Being and Time*. Translated by Joan Stambaugh. Albany: State University of New York Press, 2010.

Hobbes, Thomas. *Leviathan*. Edited by Richard Tuck. Cambridge: Cambridge University Press, 1996.

Holden-Smith, Barbara. "Lords of Lash, Loom, and Law: Justice Story, Slavery and *Prigg v. Pennsylvania*." *Cornell Law Review* 78.6 (1993): 1086–1151.

Horton, James Oliver, and Lois E. Horton. "Federal Assault: African Americans and the Impact of the Fugitive Slave Law of 1850." *Chicago-Kent Law Review* 68 (1992): 1179–97.

Huffer, Lynne. "Queer Victory, Feminist Defeat? Sodomy and Rape in *Lawrence v. Texas*." In *Feminist and Queer Legal Theory: Intimate Encounters, Uncomfortable Conversations,* edited by Martha Fineman, Jack E. Jackson, and Adam P. Romero, 411–32. Surrey: Ashgate, 2009.

Hurst, Andrea. *Derrida vis-à-vis Lacan: Interweaving Deconstruction and Psychoanalysis*. New York: Fordham University Press, 2008.

Husserl, Edmund. *The Crisis of European Sciences and Transcendental Phenomenology: An Introduction to Phenomenological Philosophy*. Evanston, IL: Northwestern University Press, 1970.

Irons, Peter H. *Justice at War: The Story of the Japanese American Internment Cases*. Berkeley: University of California Press, 1993.

Issacharoff, Samuel, and Richard H. Pildes. "Between Civil Libertarianism and Executive Unilateralism: An Institutional Process Approach to Rights during Wartime." *Theoretical Inquiries in Law* 5 (2004): 1–46.

James, Joy. *The Angela Y. Davis Reader*. Malden, MA: Blackwell, 1998.

James, Joy. *The New Abolitionists: (Neo)Slave Narratives and Contemporary Prison Writings*. Albany: State University of New York Press, 2005.

Johnson, Barbara. "Apostrophe, Animation, and Abortion." *diacritics* 16.1 (1986): 29–47.

Johnson, Barbara. "The Frame of Reference: Poe, Lacan, and Derrida." In *The Purloined Poe: Lacan, Derrida & Psychoanalytic Reading*, edited by John P. Muller and William J. Richardson, 213–51. Baltimore, MD: Johns Hopkins University Press, 1988.

Johnson, Walter. *River of Dark Dreams: Slavery and Empire in the Cotton Kingdom*. Cambridge, MA: Harvard University Press, 2013.

Kaba, Mariame. *Attica Prison Uprising 101: A Short Primer.* Chicago: Project NIA. 2011.

Kahn, Paul W. "The Question of Sovereignty." *Stanford Journal of International Law* 40.2 (2004): 259–82.

Kang, Jerry. "Trojan Horses of Race." *Harvard Law Review* 118.5 (2005): 1489–1593.

Kang, Jerry. "Watching the Watchers: Enemy Combatants in the Internment's Shadow." *Law and Contemporary Problems* 68 (2005): 255–83.

Kant, Immanuel. *Critique of Practical Reason*. Translated by James C. Meredith. New York: Oxford University Press, 2007.

Kheshti, Roshanak. "Inversion, Signifiance and the Loss of the Self in Sound." *Parallax* 14.2 (2008): 68–77.

Kluger, Richard. *Simple Justice: The History of Brown V. Board of Education and Black America's Struggle for Equality*. New York: Knopf, 1976.

Kogawa, Joy. *Obasan*. Boston: D. R. Godine, 1981.

Krieger, L. Hamilton, "The Content of Our Categories: A Cognitive Bias Approach to Discrimination and Equal Employment Opportunity." *Stanford Law Review* 47.6 (1995): 1161–1248.

Lacan, Jacques. "Seminar on the 'Purloined Letter.'" In *The Purloined Poe: Lacan, Derrida & Psychoanalytic Reading*, edited by John P. Muller and William J. Richardson, 28–54. Baltimore, MD: Johns Hopkins University Press, 1988.

Lacan, Jacques. *The Ethics of Psychoanalysis, 1959–1960: The Seminar of Jacques Lacan, Book VII*. Edited by Jacques-Alain Miller. New York: W. W. Norton and Company, 1997.

Lacan, Jacques. *Écrits*. Translated by Bruce Fink. New York: W. W. Norton and Company, 2006.

Lacan, Jacques. "The Instance of the Letter in the Unconscious, or Reason since Freud." In *Écrits*, translated by Bruce Fink, 412–41. New York: W. W. Norton, 2006.

Lacan, Jacques. "Kant with Sade." In *Écrits*, translated by Bruce Fink, 645–68. New York: W. W. Norton, 2006.

Lagaay, Alice. "Between Sound and Silence: Voice in the History of Psychoanalysis." *e-pisteme* 1.1 (2008): 53–62.

Laplanche, Jean, and J.-B. Pontalis. *The Language of Psycho-Analysis*. New York: Norton, 1974.

Lasch, Christopher. "Rendition Resistance." *North Carolina Law Review* 92.1 (2013): 149–235.

Latour, Bruno. "Scientific Objects and Legal Objectivity." In *Law, Anthropology and the Constitution of the Social*, edited by A. Pottage and M. Mondy, 73–113. Cambridge: Cambridge University Press, 2004.

Lawrence III, Charles R. "The Id, the Ego, and Equal Protection: Reckoning with Unconscious Racism." *Stanford Law Review* 39.2 (1987): 317–88.

Lawrence III, Charles R. "Unconscious Racism Revisited: Reflections on the Impact and Origins of the Id, the Ego, and Equal Protection." *Connecticut Law Review* 40.4 (2007): 931–78.

Lebeau, Vicky. *Lost Angels: Psychoanalysis and Cinema*. London: Routledge, 1995.

Lebeau, Vicky. "Psycho-politics: Frantz Fanon's *Black Skins, White Masks*." In *Psycho-politics and Cultural Desires*, edited by Jan Campbell and Janet Harbord, 107–17. London: Routledge, 1998.

Legendre, Pierre, Peter Goodrich, and Alain Pottage. "Introduction to the Theory of the Image: Narcissus and the Other in the Mirror." *Law and Critique* 8.1 (1997): 3–35.

Lenhardt, R. A. "Beyond Analogy: *Perez v. Sharp*, Antimiscegenation Law and the Fight for Same-Sex Marriage." *California Law Review* 96.4 (2008): 839–900.

Lenhardt, R. A., Elizabeth B. Cooper, Sheila R. Foster, and Sonia K. Katyal. "Forty Years of Loving: Confronting Issues of Race, Sexuality, and the Family in the Twenty-First Century." *Fordham Law Review* 76 (2008): 2669–2905.

Levinson, Sanford. "Slavery in the Canon of Constitutional Law." *Chicago-Kent Law Review* 68 (1992): 1087–1111.

Locke, John. *An Essay Concerning Human Understanding*. Edited by Peter H. Nidditch. Oxford: Clarendon Press, 1975.

Marriott, David. "Inventions of Existence: Sylvia Wynter, Frantz Fanon, Sociogeny, and 'the Damned.'" *CR: The New Centennial Review* 11.3 (2011): 45–89.

Martin, Waldo E., ed. *Brown v. Board of Education: A Brief History with Documents*. Boston: Bedford/St. Martin's, 1998.

Menninghaus, Winfried. *In Praise of Nonsense: Kant and Bluebeard*. Stanford: Stanford University Press, 1999.

Miller, J. Hillis. "Who or What Decides, for Derrida: A Catastrophic Theory of Decision." In *For Derrida*, 9–27. New York: Fordham University Press, 2009.

Mills, Charles. *The Racial Contract*. Ithaca, NY: Cornell University Press, 1997.

Morrison, Toni. *Playing in the Dark: Whiteness and the Literary Imagination*. Cambridge, MA: Harvard University Press, 1992.

Morrison, Toni. "On the Backs of Blacks." In *Arguing Immigration: The Debate over the Changing Face of America*, edited by Nicolaus Mills, 97–100. New York: Touchstone, 1994.

Moten, Fred. *In the Break: The Aesthetics of the Black Radical Tradition*. Minneapolis: University of Minnesota Press, 2003.

Moten, Fred. "Knowledge of Freedom." *CR: The New Centennial Review* 4.2 (2005): 269–310.

Moten, Fred. "The Case of Blackness." *Criticism* 50.2 (2009): 177–218.

Moten, Fred. "Blackness and Nothingness (Mysticism in the Flesh)." *South Atlantic Quarterly* 112.4 (2013): 737–80.

Mowitt, John. "Trauma Envy." *Cultural Critique* 46 (2000): 272–97.

Murphy, Tim. "As If: *camera juridica*." In *Politics, Postmodernity and Critical Legal Studies Movement*, edited by Costas Douzinas, Peter Goodrich, and Yifat Hachamovitch, 68–106. London: Routledge, 1994.

Oppenheimer, David B., Sheila R. Foster, and Sora Y. Han. *Comparative Equality and Anti-Discrimination Law: Cases, Codes, Constitutions, and Commentary*. New York: Foundation Press Thomson/West, 2012.

Penningroth, Dylan C. *The Claims of Kinfolk*. Chapel Hill: University of North Carolina Press, 2003.

Philip, M. NourbeSe. *Zong!* Middletown, CT: Wesleyan University Press, 2008.

Poovey, Mary. *A History of the Modern Fact: Problems of Knowledge in the Sciences of Wealth and Society*. Chicago: University of Chicago Press, 1998.

Rawls, John. *A Theory of Justice*. Cambridge, MA: Belknap Press of Harvard University Press, 1971.

Richie, Beth E. "Feminist Ethnographies of Women in Prison." *Feminist Studies* 30.2 (2004): 438–50.

Robinson, Cedric J. *Black Marxism: The Making of the Black Radical Tradition*. Chapel Hill: University of North Carolina Press, 2000.

Robinson, Greg, and Toni Robinson. "Korematsu and Beyond: Japanese Americans and the Origins of Strict Scrutiny." *Law and Contemporary Problems* 68.2 (2005): 29–55.

Ronell, Avital. "The Testamentary Whimper." *South Atlantic Quarterly* 103 (2004): 489–99.

Rubenfeld, Jed. "Affirmative Action." *Yale Law Journal* 107.2 (1997): 427–72.

Schlag, Pierre. *The Enchantment of Reason*. Durham, NC: Duke University Press, 1998.

Schmitt, Carl. *The Leviathan in the State Theory of Thomas Hobbes: Meaning and Failure of a Political Symbol*. Translated by G. Schwab and W. Hilfstein. Chicago: University of Chicago Press, 2008.

Schroeder, Jeanne, and David Carlson. "Psychoanalysis as the Jurisprudence of Freedom." *Cardozo Legal Studies Research Paper* 200 (2007). Available at http://ssrn.com/abstract=1011175.

Schwartz, Bernard. *Main Currents in American Legal Thought*. Durham, NC: Carolina Academic Press, 1993.

Schwarzenegger, Arnold. *Governor's Reorganization Plan 2: Reforming California's Youth and Adult Correctional System*. Sacramento, CA: Office of the Governor, 2005.

Scott, Daryl M. *Contempt and Pity: Social Policy and the Image of the Damaged Black Psyche, 1880–1996*. Chapel Hill: University of North Carolina Press, 1997.

Scott, Joan W. "Fantasy Echo: History and the Construction of Identity." *Critical Inquiry* 27.2 (2001): 284–304.

Sexton, Jared. "People-of-Color-Blindness: Notes on the Afterlife of Slavery." *Social Text* 28.103 (2010): 31–56.

Sexton, Jared, and Steve Martinot. "The Avant-Garde of White Supremacy." In *Warfare in the American Homeland: Policing and Prison in a Penal Democracy*, edited by Joy James, 197–217. Durham, NC: Duke University Press, 2007.

Shakur, Assata. "Women in Prison: How We Are," *Black Scholar* 12.6 (1981): 50–57.

Shaylor, Cassandra. "'It's Like Living in a Black Hole': Women of Color and Solitary Confinement in the Prison Industrial Complex." *New England Journal on Criminal and Civil Confinement* 24.2 (1998): 385–416.

Simon, Jonathan. *Governing through Crime: How the War on Crime Transformed American Democracy and Created a Culture of Fear*. Oxford: Oxford University Press, 2007.

Smith, Caleb. *The Prison and the American Imagination*. New Haven: Yale University Press, 2009.

Soler, Colette. *What Lacan Said about Women: A Psychoanalytic Study*. New York: Other Press, 2006.

Spillers, Hortense. "A Day in the Life of Civil Rights." *Black Scholar* 9.8/9 (1978): 20–27.

Spillers, Hortense. "Mama's Baby, Papa's Maybe: An American Grammar Book." *diacritics* 17.2 (1987): 65–81.

Spillers, Hortense. "'All the Things You Could Be by Now, if Sigmund Freud's Wife Was Your Mother': Psychoanalysis and Race." In *Black, White, and in Color: Essays on American Literature and Culture*, 376–427. Chicago: University of Chicago Press, 2003.

Spillers, Hortense. "Changing the Letter: The Yokes, the Jokes of Discourse, or, Mrs. Stowe, Mr. Reed." In *Black, White, and in Color: Essays on American Literature and Culture*, 176–202. Chicago: University of Chicago Press, 2003.

Spillers, Hortense. "Who Cuts the Border? Some Readings on America." In *Black, White, and in Color: Essays on American Literature and Culture*, 319–35. Chicago: University of Chicago Press, 2003.

Spivak, Gayatri C. "Constitutions and Culture Studies." In *Legal Studies as Cultural Studies: A Reader in (post)Modern Critical Theory*, edited by Jerry D. Leonard, 155–74. Albany: State University of New York Press, 1995.

Spivak, Gayatri C. "Feminism and Deconstruction, Again: Negotiating with Unacknowledged Masculinism." In *Between Feminism and Psychoanalysis*, edited by Teresa Brennan, 206–23. New York: Routledge, 1989.

Spivak, Gayatri C. *A Critique of Postcolonial Reason: Toward a History of the Vanishing Present*. Cambridge, MA: Harvard University Press, 1999.

St. John, Maria, and Cheryl Dunye. "Making Home/Making 'Stranger': An Interview with Cheryl Dunye." *Feminist Studies* 30.2 (2004): 325–38.

Steele, Claude M. "A Threat in the Air: How Stereotypes Shape Intellectual Identity and Performance." *American Psychologist* 52.6 (1997): 613–29.

Steiner, George. *Antigones*. Oxford: Clarendon Press, 1984.

Sudbury, Julia. "Maroon Abolitionists: Black Gender-oppressed Activists in the Anti-Prison Movement in the US and Canada." *Meridians: Feminism, Race, Transnationalism* 9.1 (2008): 1–29.

Thomas, Kendall. "Beyond the Privacy Principle." *Columbia Law Review* 92.6 (1992): 1431–1516.

Tomlins, Christopher. "What Is Left of the Law and Society Paradigm after Critique? Revisiting Gordon's 'Critical Legal Histories.'" *Law and Social Inquiry* 37.1 (2012): 156–66.

Tomlins, Christopher, and John Comaroff. "'Law as . . .': Theory and Practice in Legal History." *UC Irvine Law Review* 1.3 (2011): 1039–79.

Tushnet, Mark V. *The American Law of Slavery, 1810–1860: Considerations of Humanity and Interest*. Princeton: Princeton University Press, 1981.

Tushnet, Mark V. *Making Civil Rights Law: Thurgood Marshall and the Supreme Court, 1936–1961*. New York: Oxford University Press, 1994.

Umoja, Akinyele O. *We Will Shoot Back: Armed Resistance in the Mississippi Freedom Movement*. New York: New York University Press, 2013.

U.S. Department of Justice, Bureau of Prisons. "Limited Communication for Terrorist Inmates." 28 CFR Part 540, BOP Docket No. 1135-P. *Federal Register*. 71.63 (2006): 16523–525.

Valdes, Francisco, Jerome M. Culp, and Angela P. Harris, eds. *Crossroads, Directions, and a New Critical Race Theory*. Philadelphia: Temple University Press, 2002.

Vismann, Cornelia. *Files: Law and Media Technology*. Stanford: Stanford University Press, 2008.

Watson, Alan. *Slave Law in the Americas*. Athens: University of Georgia Press, 1989.

Wilderson III, Frank B. *Red, White & Black: Cinema and the Structure of U.S. Antagonisms*. Durham, NC: Duke University Press, 2010.

Williams, Patricia J. *The Alchemy of Race and Rights*. Cambridge, MA: Harvard University Press, 1991.

Willse, Craig, and Dean Spade. "Freedom in a Regulatory State?: *Lawrence*, Marriage and Biopolitics." *Widener Law Review* 11 (2004): 309–29.

Wing, Adrien K., ed. *Global Critical Race Feminism: An International Reader*. New York: New York University Press, 2000.

Wing, Adrien K., ed. *Critical Race Feminism: A Reader*. New York: New York University Press, 2003.

Winkler, Adam. "Fatal in Theory and Strict in Fact: An Empirical Analysis of Strict Scrutiny in the Federal Courts." *Vanderbilt Law Review* 59.3 (2006): 793–871.

Wong, Edlie L. *Neither Fugitive nor Free: Atlantic Slavery, Freedom Suits, and the Legal Culture of Travel*. New York: New York University Press, 2009.

Yamamoto, Eric K. "Korematsu Revisited—Correcting the Injustice of Extraordinary Government Excess and Lax Judicial Review: Time for a Better Accommodation of National Security Concerns and Civil Liberties." *Santa Clara Law Review* 26 (1986): 1–62.

Yoneyama, Lisa. *Hiroshima Traces: Time, Space, and the Dialectics of Memory*. Berkeley: University of California Press, 1999.

Žižek, Slavoj. *Tarrying with the Negative: Kant, Hegel, and the Critique of Ideology*. Durham, NC: Duke University Press, 1993.

Žižek, Slavoj. "You Only Die Twice." In *The Sublime Object of Ideology*, 145–67. London: Verso, 2008.

Zupančič, Alenka. "The Subject of the Law." In *Cogito and the Unconscious*, edited by Slavoj Žižek, 41–73. Durham, NC: Duke University Press, 1998.

Zupančič, Alenka. "Ethics and Tragedy in Lacan." In *The Cambridge Companion to Lacan*, edited by Jean Michel Rabaté, 173–90. Cambridge: Cambridge University Press, 2003.

Cases

Adarand Constructors, Inc. v. Pena, 515 U.S. 200 (1995)

Arizona v. U.S., 132 S.Ct. 2492 (2012)

Beard v. Banks, 548 U.S. 521 (2006)

Bell v. Wolfish, 441 U.S. 520 (1979)

Bolling v. Sharpe, 347 U.S. 497 (1954)

Bowers v. Hardwick, 478 U.S. 186 (1986)

Briggs v. Elliott, 342 U.S. 350 (1952)

Brown v. Board of Education, 347 U.S. 483 (1954)

Brown v. City of Oneonta, 221 F. 3d 329 (1999)

Brown v. Mississippi, 297 U.S. 278 (1936)

Brown v. Plata, 131 S.Ct. 1910 (2011)

Bush v. Vera, 517 U.S. 952 (1996)

Civil Rights Cases of 1883, 109 U.S. 3 (1883)

Dred Scott v. Sandford, 60 U.S. 393 (1857)

Fisher v. University of Texas at Austin, 570 U.S. __ (2013)

Floyd v. City of New York, No. 08-cv-1034 (SAS), 2013 WL 4046209, (S.D.N.Y. August 12, 2013)

Fullilove v. Klutznick, 448 U.S. 448 (1980)

Gong Lum v. Rice, 275 U.S. 78 (1927)

Grutter v. Bollinger, 539 U.S. 306 (2003)

Hollingsworth v. Perry, 570 U.S. __ (2013).

Jones v. North Carolina Prisoners' Labor Union, Inc., 433 U.S. 119 (1977)

Korematsu v. United States, 323 U.S. 214 (1944)

Korematsu v. United States, 584 F. Supp. 1406 (N.D. Cal. 1984)

Lawrence v. Texas, 539 U.S. 558 (2003)
Loving v. Virginia, 388 U.S. 1 (1967)
Metro Broadcasting, Inc. v. FCC, 497 U.S. 547 (1990)
McDonald v. Santa Fe Trail Transp. Co., 427 U.S. 273 (1976)
McNamara v. Moody, 606 F.2d 621 (5th Cir. 1979)
O'Lone v. Estate of Shabazz, 482 U.S. 342 (1987)
Overton v. Bazzetta, 539 U.S. 126 (2003)
Parents Involved in Community Schools v. Seattle School District No. 1, 551 U.S. 701 (2007)
Pell v. Procunier, 417 U.S. 817 (1974)
Pigford v. Glickman, 185 F.R.D. 82 (1999)
Plessy v. Ferguson, 163 U.S. 537 (1896)
Prigg v. Pennsylvania, 41 U.S. 539 (1842)
Procunier v. Martinez, 416 U.S. 396, 94 S. Ct. 1800, 40 L. Ed. 2d 224 (1974)
Richmond v. J.A. Croson Co., 488 U.S. 469 (1989).
Rogers v. American Airlines, 527 F. Supp. 229 (1981)
Schlesinger v. Reservists Committee to Stop the War, 418 U.S. 208 (1974)
Shelby County, Ala. v. Holder, 570 U.S. __ (2013)
Terry v. Ohio, 392 U.S. 1 (1968)
Turner v. Safely, 482 U.S. 8485 (1987).
U.S. v. Windsor, 570 U.S. __ (2013).
United States v. Morrison, 529 U.S. 598 (2000).
University of California Regents v. Bakke, 438 U.S. 265 (1978).
Whren v. United States, 517 U.S. 806, 116 S. Ct. 1769, 135 L. Ed. 2d 89 (1996).
Yick Wo v. Hopkins, 118 U.S. 356 (1886)

Films

Dunye, Cheryl, et al., *Stranger Inside*. DVD. Dir. Cheryl Dunye. New York: HBO Home Video, 2010.

Rosenblum, Nina, et al., *Through the Wire*. Videocassette. Dir. Nina Rosenblum. New York: Cinema Guild, 1990.

Index

THE CULTURAL LIVES OF LAW

Austin Sarat, Editor

The Cultural Lives of Law series brings insights and approaches from cultural studies to law and tries to secure for law a place in cultural analysis. Books in the series focus on the production, interpretation, consumption, and circulation of legal meanings. They take up the challenges posed as boundaries collapse between as well as within cultures, and as the circulation of legal meanings becomes more fluid. They also attend to the ways law's power in cultural production is renewed and resisted.

Our Word Is Our Bond: How Legal Speech Acts
Marianne Constable
2014

The Street Politics of Abortion: Speech, Violence, and America's Culture Wars
Joshua C. Wilson
2013

Better Left Unsaid: Victorian Novels, Hays Code Films, and the Benefits of Censorship
Nora Gilbert
2013

Zooland: The Institution of Captivity
Irus Braverman
2012

After Secular Law
Edited by Winnifred Fallers Sullivan, Robert A. Yelle, and Mateo Taussig-Rubbo
2011

All Judges Are Political—Except When They Are Not: Acceptable Hypocrisies and the Rule of Law
Keith J. Bybee
2010

Riding the Black Ram: Law, Literature, and Gender
Susan Sage Heinzelman
2010

Tort, Custom, and Karma: Globalization and Legal Consciousness in Thailand
David M. Engel and Jaruwan S. Engel
2010

Law in Crisis: The Ecstatic Subject of Natural Disaster
Ruth A. Miller
2009

The Affective Life of Law: Legal Modernism and the Literary Imagination
Ravit Reichman
2009

Fault Lines: Tort Law as Cultural Practice
Edited by David M. Engel and Michael McCann
2008

Lex Populi: The Jurisprudence of Popular Culture
William P. MacNeil
2007

The Cultural Lives of Capital Punishment: Comparative Perspectives
Edited by Austin Sarat and Christian Boulanger
2005

The authorized representative in the EU for product safety and compliance is:
Mare Nostrum Group
B.V Doelen 72
4831 GR Breda
The Netherlands

www.ingramcontent.com/pod-product-compliance
Lightning Source LLC
Chambersburg PA
CBHW030847270326
41928CB00007B/1255

* 9 7 8 1 5 0 3 6 0 2 7 9 3 *